IN SEARCH OF SPANISH TREASURE

IN SEARCH OF
SPANISH TREASURE

A Diver's Story

Sydney Wignall

David & Charles

Newton Abbot   London   North Pomfret (Vt)

British Library Cataloguing in Publication Data

Wignall, Sydney
  In search of Spanish treasure.
  1. Shipwrecks
  2. Underwater archaeology
  I. Title
  910.4'53   G525

  ISBN 0-7153-8244-6

Photoset by Typesetters (Birmingham) Ltd,
and printed in Great Britain
by Butler & Tanner, London and Frome
for David & Charles (Publishers) Limited
Brunel House Newton Abbot Devon

Published in the United States of America
by David & Charles Inc
North Pomfret Vermont 05053 USA

Contents

Foreword
and Acknowledgements

When I first became involved in underwater archaeology, in 1962, I was motivated by a deep and abiding interest in maritime history. Having climbed and mapped in unknown country in the high Himalaya on the border of Nepal and Tibet, I had satisfied my curiosity as to what lay on the other side of the hill. I therefore regarded a quest to ascertain what lay on the other side of the reef as a natural extension into vertical exploration. My ambition to locate and archaeologically excavate shipwrecks of antiquity became so obsessive, I withdrew from all other activities and concerned myself with the task of involving young people in a desire for knowledge about their maritime heritage.

Over the past twenty-five years, my expeditions have involved more than 150 people of 13 nationalities: Europeans, Asians and representatives of North, Central and South America. Our success in the underwater field the reader can judge for himself. We did learn to live with one another, and to respect each other's nationality, religion and personal foibles. We also learned a great deal about the sea and its history. I have always made it a point never to risk human life or limb needlessly; consequently participants in my diving projects have logged more than 7,000 individual dives in European, mid-Atlantic and Caribbean waters, with no accidents more serious than the occasional sprained ankle and one broken finger.

We also learned that civilisation lies not in quality of living, but in the acquisition and dissemination of knowledge. The title of my book might mislead the reader into believing that my motivation was that of the profit orientated treasure hunter. It was not. Underwater treasure to me consists of bronze cannon, ship's fittings, and all the appurtenancies that supported the seamen of bygone years. Gold and silver treasure occasionally fell into our hands. It always ended up in a museum and not in private collections. I have never believed in the solo virtuoso performance in the field of exploration; on the contrary, all we have achieved has been the product of teamwork and cooperation. Those who have been instrumental in promoting my plans are too numerous to list in full; I must therefore give well-earned credit to only a few.

My introduction to underwater archaeology came from my old friend Squadron Leader 'Mike' Edmonds, RAF (ret). Support in the early years of my Spanish Armada period was furnished by Joseph Casey, Eric Reynolds and Desmond Branigan; followed by Dr Peter N. Davies and Peter Start, MA, MSc. Special mention in the Armada context must be made of Colin Martin, who was expedition surveyor and later expedition leader, and Commander John Grattan, OBE, RN (ret), who trained my team of divers in Ireland to a high degree of professionalism. Credit for untangling the legal problems concerning wreck protection through the High Court of Admiralty in Dublin goes to my lawyer, John P. King. I must also express appreciation for the written encouragement I received from the late Mr Erskine Childers, President of the Irish Republic, and Admiral Pietro Nieto Antunez, former Minister of Marine, Madrid.

My expedition to search for Grenville's *Revenge* in the Azores could never have taken place if it had not been for the generosity of Sir Alexander Glen and Mr Costas Lemos. I am also indebted to Professor Jose Teixera of the Naval Academy in Lisbon and Dr Manoel Baptista de Lima, director of the Azores regional museums, for help in obtaining the required archaeological permits. A special 'thank you' must be in order for Jorge Albuquerque of the Portuguese amateur diving organisation, CPAS, who ironed out many of my problems and recruited CPAS amateur divers for me.

For the climax of my underwater archaeological career — the expedition to Porto Bello, Panama, to search for a Columbus wreck and Drake in his lead coffin — I am indebted to the following for their advice and support: Dr Reina Torres de Arauz, director of the Panama museums; Dean Edwin C. Webster; Frank Robinson and Dr Harold E. Edgerton. Special mention must be made of the work of Anne and Don Carter whose assistance in tracking down the elusive sixteenth-century reprisal pirate, William Parker (the man who knew where Drake's coffin lay), was invaluable. Credit for staff work in the UK goes to Dr D. Cecil Jones, while finance was provided at considerable personal sacrifice by Dennis Hamber and his brothers. I am also grateful to the Hamber brothers for free charter of their beautiful schooner *Jylland*, and for their almost superhuman effort in building our expedition village at Porto Bello.

For support during the *Bonhomme Richard* period, I am grateful to Charles Matthews, president of National Ocean Industries Association; Clive Cussler; Rear Admiral David Cooney USN; Lieutenant Commander (Dr) and Mrs Eric Berryman, USN (res); Marty Klein; Wayne Gronquist; Derek Goodwin; Patricia Hamilton; Tony Jarman; Valerie and Townsend Burden III; Jane and Gerard Moore and Tom Darragh, and the staff of the Decca Survey Company Ltd.

In accordance with the maxim 'excavation should not proceed unless the means of conservation are available', I have for many years put a high priority on laboratory conservation of artifacts, and must therefore place on record my appreciation of the efforts of Dr Dee Anne Storey of the Texas Archaeological Research Laboratory, University of Texas at Austin; Dr Donny L. Hamilton, late of that laboratory but now of the research laboratory of the Institute of Nautical Archaeology, College Station, Texas; and Keith Priestman, Keeper of Conservation, Merseyside Museums, for providing basic tuition in laboratory conservation for a member of my Panama expedition.

All my foreign-going expeditions in the underwater field have enjoyed the approval of the Council for Nautical Archaeology of London, to whom I am most grateful.

A well-deserved tribute for their on-going programme of involving the amateur diver in underwater archaeology in the Principality of Wales goes to Dr D. Cecil Jones of the University College of North Wales, Bangor; Robert Kennedy, Curator of the County Museums, Haverfordwest; and Dr Peter N. Davies of the University of Liverpool. Of all my supporters, if asked to single out any one for an accolade of merit, I would without reservation draw attention to Joseph Casey of St Helens, who has supplied not only a fortune in equipment plus occasional much needed finance, but also unceasing loyalty.

Last, but far from least, are the individual divers who provided not only diving and technical skills, but also enthusiasm, and the collective sense of purpose without which even the best equipped and organised project must surely fail. It is to the latter, as a form of testimonial, that I dedicate this book.

Chapter 1

Tibet, Gold Bullion and a Roman Shipwreck

The 16th of December 1955 proved to be a watershed in my life for, seated on top of a 19,500ft pass in the Nepal Himalaya, frostbitten, exhausted, suffering from both malnutrition and dysentery, I made the decision that if I survived the journey which lay ahead of me, I would give up mountaineering forever and choose a safer sport, such as badminton, tennis, or even aqualung diving.

My winter predicament at high altitude had come about because, during the first Welsh Himalayan expedition, which I had been privileged to lead, expedition surveyor John Harrop, Nepalese liaison officer Damodar Narayan Suwal and I had been surprised at a camp in the Jung Jung Khola by a detachment of armed Chinese communist infantry from the nearby Tibetan provincial centre of Taklakot, where we were taken for interrogation. Now nearly two months later, we had been released due to the intervention of Prime Minister Nehru's government, the two months in prison on a diet of one meal a day of yak intestines fried in mustard oil having reduced us to shadows of our former selves. Attempts to make us sign confessions that we were imperialist spies working for the CIA had been without avail. We did not sign, fearing that if we did we would be sentenced to a long term of imprisonment in China proper. At that time I had not even heard of the CIA and in point of fact thought that my Chinese interrogators were referring to an American trade union!

My defence against 'brain washing' or 'thought reform' had been poetry. Since the Chinese did not believe us when we told the truth, I persuaded them that I had inside information on a huge Anglo-American Himalayan conspiracy, which had had its climax in 1953 when the English climbed Mount Everest, and Hillary and Tensing had transported down the mountain, from the summit, uranium ore in their oxygen cylinders.

My reward from my interrogators for that confession was the

returning to me of a paperback book *A Century of Poetry: from Pope to Keats*. I tore the book in half down the centre, and threw one half through the window of Harrop's cell as I was returning from a session of 'thought reform'. I learned Byron by rote and repeated 'the isles of Greece, the isles of Greece, where burning Sappho loved and sung' to my interrogators. Harrop regaled them with the second half of Coleridge's 'Rhyme of the Ancient Mariner' — I had the first half.

On our release from south-west Tibet, the Chinese had refused to return our high altitude rations, which they had held in store, and also my anti-dysentery drugs which they had confiscated because I had refused to sign a confession, and we were now faced with a 200 mile march back across the Himalaya in winter, on a few pounds of native flour as our only diet. On that fateful day in December, sitting freezing on top of the Urai Lekh pass, we were undoubtedly the highest men in the world, our position being 4,000ft higher than the summit of Mont Blanc. Nobody but a madman would venture to such a height in winter.

The rest of the journey back was arduous and harrowing and we only got through by the skin of our teeth. Looking back from the foothills of the Himalaya on the Indian border, I renewed my resolution that I had climbed my last mountain. At our base camp in Nepal, I had read a book entitled *Under the Red Sea* by Hans Hass, and been enchanted by Hass's description of the relatively unexplored regions of our continental shelves. I decided that aqualung exploration, with an emphasis on history beneath the sea, would be for me. Harrop, after listening to my plans, offered the comment, 'Sounds too dangerous for me'. When I last heard from him, he was lecturing on soil science at a university in Indonesia.

Back in the UK again, I wrote the book of my adventures *Prisoner in Red Tibet*, and purchased a second-hand aqualung (Self-Contained Underwater Breathing Apparatus: SCUBA) and dry suit with mask and fins, for £25, walked into the sea in Colwyn Bay and very nearly drowned myself. Such was my crude beginning in an activity which was to take me on many expeditions, and involve me in maritime history through the location, survey and physical excavation of more than a dozen ancient shipwrecks, over the next twenty-five years.

My formative years in scuba diving were orthodox for that period. To my somewhat primitive diving apparatus, I added a speargun with the intention of combining a thirst for adventure with the means to provide the odd fish for the table. I shot one fish only and, completely revolted by the sight of the poor, wriggling, mortally wounded creature, promptly gave the speargun away to the first diver I met on the beach as I left the water. The young man promptly shot himself before I had gone ten paces, and we hauled him off to hospital in Caernarvon with the spear protruding from his leg. I decided that ancient shipwrecks could be more interesting than spear-fishing, and over the next two years located several of the nineteenth-century barques and schooners which lie around the shores of north Wales.

In the spring of 1958, accompanied by my diving colleague Eric Reynolds, I dived on the site of the *Royal Charter* wreck, close to Moelfre on the east coast of the island of Anglesey. We were aware that a great deal of treasure in the form of gold bars and gold coin had been raised from the wreck by official salvors in 1859–60. We certainly did not expect to find gold; we did, however, hope to swim amongst the broken remains of a very interesting shipwreck, for the story of the disaster of the *Royal Charter* is one of tragedy, great loss of life and deeds of personal heroism. So famous was the incident that the storm which resulted in her sinking was thereafter referred to as the 'Royal Charter gale'.

In October 1859, the *Royal Charter,* a clipper ship of 719 tons pro-pelled by both sail and steam, came in sight of Anglesey on her homeward voyage to Liverpool from the Australian gold fields. Carrying 371 passengers and 112 crew, her hold contained a registered cargo of no less than £322,440 in gold bullion, coin and gold dust. Quite possibly as much again was carried, unregistered, in the baggage and on the persons of many of the passengers, who had dug and panned their treasure from Australia's inhospitable outback.

As she sailed past the north-east coast of Anglesey on the last leg of her journey, with the wind from the west, she made good speed in a freshening gale. Suddenly the wind reversed its direction and the *Royal Charter*'s master found his vessel on a lee shore, with insufficient power in his solitary steam engine to combat the force of the storm. Slowly the *Royal Charter* was driven back, her head still to wind, towards the rocky east coast of the island. Sails were torn to shreds as the crew tried to reef them in; both bower anchors were shot, but they failed to check the stricken vessel's progress towards destruc-tion. Finally, in the blackening gloom of the night, the roar of waves breaking on nearby rocks could be heard above the screech and howl of the gale.

The *Royal Charter* struck almost broadside on, and immediately broke her back, the two halves bumping and grinding on the rocks beneath her keel. Distress signals were fired as the terror-stricken passengers stared at the jagged coastline only fifty yards away. In that storm there would be little point in launching the lifeboats, for they would be smashed to matchwood amongst the sharp fangs of rock which broke through the boiling foam. As the ship ground her inexorable path to destruction, she came within twenty-five yards of the rocky beach, while waves swept her decks taking crew and passengers to their doom, and a crowd gathered on the beach, attracted by the ship's emergency rockets.

An effort was made on board to get a man ashore with a light line, which could be used to pull ashore a heavy rope cable, along which passengers could be passed. A Maltese seaman, Joseph Rogers, made three valiant attempts before he at last succeeded in handing the end of that fragile lifeline to those on the beach. But only a handful of people made the journey to safety along the rope. By dawn's light, the two halves of the broken ship could be seen, lying low in the water, with great white rollers crashing over her deck. No survivors were to be seen. More than 400 people had lost their lives, the majority of them killed as the force of the waves drove their struggling weakened bodies against the rocks. Many of the corpses were without arms or legs.

The ghouls soon got to work, and several of the local people set about stripping rings, watches and other valuables off the dead. Charles Dickens, who visited the site and reported the disaster for *The Times* of London, wrote:

> So tremendous had the force of the sea been when it broke up the ship, that it had beaten one great ingot of gold deep into a strong and heavy piece of solid ironwork; in which also, several loose sovereigns that the ingot had swept in before it, had been found as firmly embedded as though the iron had been liquid when they had been forced there.

Hard-hat divers, working for the official salvors, brought up more than £300,000 worth of gold bullion and coin. The gold dust on the official manifest had vanished, lost in the sea when the leather and canvas bags in which it was contained were rendered apart amongst the broken ironwork of the wreck. The registered treasure had been easy for the salvors to find, for the shipping agent's plan of the ship showed exactly where the bullion bars and boxes of gold coin had been stacked. But there is no record of any attempt to search for the private treasure. The salvors probably did not know that a vast quantity of gold lay locked in the baggage and travelling trunks of the drowned passengers, even though several of the gold miners had died because they tried to swim ashore wearing money belts filled with gold coin or gold dust. Their wealth was now presumably scattered over a wide area.

The site of the wreck is easy to find, for a granite obelisk, describing the loss of the *Royal Charter*, stands on the cliff top overlooking the place where she struck and broke up. Both Reynolds and I were surprised how close the wreck lay to the shore. Within a few yards of our point of entry into the water, we were swimming amongst broken iron ribs and frames, and buckled iron plates, embedded in sand. With curiosity we examined and discarded the odd porthole, stanchion and deck fitting, and it was then that I chanced on a large yellow ingot protruding from the sand, jammed between an iron frame and a huge piece of torn, jagged iron plate. It seemed to be a copper bar, and I struggled to free my wreck souvenir. Reynolds joined me and we struggled away at the metal ingot until we eventually ran out of air. Reynolds was first to surface, leaving me struggling alone. In the end, in desperation, I drew my diving knife and, using its saw edge, sawed into the ingot. The metal was soft and yellow. At that moment I realised that I had found a gold bullion bar.

Completely out of air, I surfaced and told Reynolds the news. In 1958 we had no access to a compressed-air supply for our scuba cylinders on the north Wales coast; the nearest charging point was the British Oxygen Company in Cheshire, about a hundred miles away by road. Three days later we were back, anxious to dive into the sea and recover our prize. We were to be disappointed — a gale was raging in all its fury. A few days later, when the storm had abated, we returned to the site and swam to the spot where a fortune in salvor's reward awaited us. To our horror, the whole configuration of the wreck appeared to have changed. Where we had seen ribs and plates, there rose a mound of sand; where we had seen sandy areas, we were now confronted by previously hidden twisted ironwork. The wreck of the *Royal Charter* had taken the treasure of 1859 back into her bosom.

When friends laughed at my story, accusing me of inventing the incident, I decided to mention it no more. Some months later, when cleaning my diving gear, I noticed golden specks on the saw edge of my diving knife. I had them assayed by a friendly jeweller who advised me that it was in fact 23-carat gold. My approximate measurements, based on the hypothesis that two-thirds of the ingot were buried beneath the sand jammed in the ship's ironwork, suggested that my ingot weighed about 70lb — at that time worth about £14,000. At the time of writing this book, the ingot still presumably lies on the wreck of the *Royal Charter*, in about 15ft of water, no more than 20yd from the rocks at the water's edge. The 1981 price of gold would put the value of the ingot at not less than £300,000.

We never went back. Treasure-hunting was not my thing, and I went into underwater photography while reading maritime history. Roman wine amphorae or Spanish bronze cannon were more to my liking, not gold or silver, although over the years I was to find more than a modicum of Spanish treasure. By 1961 I had become somewhat disenchanted with nineteenth-century shipwrecks in cold northern waters. I wanted sunshine and warmer seas, and my wife Jean was complaining about the endless hours she spent sitting in a car, reading or listening to the radio, while Reynolds and I dived in a nearby cove. The island of Malta appeared to offer a suitable compromise with its low rainfall, lots of sun, English spoken, tea shops abounding, and underwater visibility which sometimes exceeded 100ft.

On the island, written introductions to Maltese divers from English friends resulted in many friendships, but also in many utterly boring and pointless dives with people whose only interest was to shoot as many fish as possible. The English fraternity, however, sent me along to the RAF base at Luqa airfield where I was to meet a Flight Lieutenant Mike Edmonds. I was warned that Edmonds was quite mad, but at least he was not interested in spear-fishing, only under-water archaeology, which my friends said he talked about incessantly. In a bar, after a very enjoyable first dive off St Paul's Bay, Edmonds — a tall, dark-skinned, Latin-looking fellow, seemingly dour, but possessed of a sharp mind, a quick wit and an engagingly dry humour — told me that I had been fobbed off onto him by the spear-fishing fraternity as 'this fellow Wignall, who is quite mad'. Our friendship burgeoned from that moment.

Edmonds was attempting to interest the local Royal Air Force Sub Aqua Club in underwater archaeology, without success due to that organisation's leanings towards spear-fishing. I informed him that my background was that of a former Himalayan explorer who knew some-thing about geography, cartography and photography. 'Sounds to me like you should have a crack at surveying ancient shipwrecks,' Edmonds suggested. My interest was aroused. 'How can I get onto an

16

Wine amphorae from a Roman wreck off the island of Filicudi, north of Sicily

The personnel of the opening phase of the 1968 *Santa Maria de la Rosa* expedition
Back row left to right Brian Maidment, Keith Hosking Taylor, Ken Snowball, Nick La Hive, Karl Lees, Sally Barrett, Tiger Lees, Mick Roberts
Front row left to right Colin Martin, Bryan Barrett, John Grattan, Syd Wignall, Smudge Smith

Spanish 7in diameter 'whole cannon' 50lb cast-iron shot produced in a fraudulent fashion by Spanish shot founders. A smaller diameter ball has been placed in the mould to use up unwanted shot and to speed up production

underwater archaeological expedition?' I queried. 'Just hang about,' Edmonds said, 'I may have something to interest you next year.'

The year 1962 saw me back in Malta for my fifth trip in twelve months, only this time it was at Edmonds' request. He had something planned. He had been visiting Sicily and had met the director of the museum at the island of Lipari, Dr Madeleine Cavalier. She had told Edmonds that a Romano-Greek wreck of approximately 200 BC had been accidently found by spear-fishermen in an unbelievable 130ft of water off Cape Graziano on the Aeolian island of Filicudi, which was part of the Lipari group to the north of Sicily. There were rumours of organised looting, and Dr Cavalier had given sympathetic hearing to Mike Edmonds's suggestion that he organise a 'rescue' operation to relocate the wreck and survey the cargo of wine amphorae, then excavate and salvage the ship's contents. She forwarded the proposals to Professor Bernabo Brea in Sicily, who quickly agreed. Edmonds then proceeded to put his plan into operation. The RAF Expeditions Fund gave limited financial support and a volunteer crew of divers was recruited mainly from the RAF Coastal Command base at St Mawgan in Cornwall, to which Edmonds had recently been posted.

He wanted me to join his expedition for two reasons; firstly that I had experience in surveying, albeit at high altitude, in the West Nepal Himalaya; secondly that I had just ventured into the field of 16mm underwater cine photography. There was just one fly in the ointment. The RAF, having generously agreed to fly the entire air force contingent to Sicily via Gibraltar in a Shackleton maritime reconnaissance aircraft, would have nothing to do with a civilian diver-cum-surveyor-cum-underwater novice cameraman. However, there was one loophole. The RAF would, under certain circumstances, provide a seat for an accredited press representative, which of course I was not. Luckily the matter was resolved by a friendly journalist providing me with a blank sheet of stationery which boasted the heading of one of the most prestigious of northern provincial newspapers. In a jiffy, I had typed out my own combined testimonial and press accreditation. It did the trick, and in due course nine RAF men, led by Mike Edmonds, and one 'journalist' hugging official flight pass and forged credentials, were winging their way first to Gibraltar and then to the American naval air base at Sigonella, outside Catania in Sicily.

On the quayside at Messina, we were met by the old 'capo' who owned the filthy dirty 60ft fishing boat Edmonds had chartered for the duration of the expedition. The old seadog had two boasts, namely that he was very well connected with the Mafia and that he could drink anyone under the table. It took a night and a day for the leaky old fishing vessel to transport us and our equipment to the tiny island of Filicudi, where we camped ashore under canvas, in close proximity to a local bar, bringing to mind Dr Johnson's statement when shown a painting of a pastoral scene devoid of habitation: 'The most beautiful of landscapes is oft enhanced by a comfortable inn in the foreground.'

We set off for the approximate site of the wreck, accompanied by a representative of the museum, and anchored the boat at the edge of a submerged reef. The wreck was located on the first dive and we were all amazed and exhilarated by the enormous cascade of amphorae which had spilled down the edge of the reef to lie on a sandy slope. The shallowest part of the wreck was in 130ft of water, and the deepest part in over 150ft. A strict regimen of time-keeping was observed as we worked in pairs, conscious of the dangers we were flirting with by working in such a depth without the safety factor of a recompression chamber on the surface for the treatment of 'bends'. Ten minutes was all we allowed ourselves on the sea bed, surveying the layers of wine jars by means of tape trilateration from arbitrary base lines we had established at either end of the wreck.

It has been said that surveying underwater is difficult because one is working in an alien environment. I found it simplicity itself compared to surveying at high altitude in the Himalaya where one might wait days, sitting on some freezing mountainside, praying for the clouds to clear so that one could obtain a theodolite angle on a peak of known height. As the wine amphorae were registered on a waterproof drawing-board, they were fitted into a rope sling attached to a buoyancy bag. The bag was filled with compressed air from a spare scuba cylinder, and the wine jars shot up to the surface at a fast speed, so much so that one amphora gave me a badly bruised leg as I filmed it passing me at 70ft depth. On shore, the amphorae were catalogued and sketched. There was great competition to find one with its neck-seal intact, and to possibly sample 2,000-year-old wine. It was not to be, for all the neck-seals had imploded due to the water pressure, which at the lower end of the wreck site approached 75lb per square inch.

There was only one near accident, but it brought home to me the dangers inherent in deep diving if one is far removed from a hospital. Some idiot had put the RAF air compressor, which was malfunctioning and producing a great deal of smoke, close to the air intake of my own compressor, which I had loaned to the expedition. As it happened, the air tasted no fouler than usual, and I descended to the 150ft depth to attach half a dozen amphorae to air-filled lifting bags which I despatched to the surface. My diving buddy ran out of air before I did and I stayed on to prepare two more wine jars for the next pair of divers, who were on the surface about to descend. When my air reached the prearranged level at which I should have ascended to the decompression shot-line, situated under the salvage boat, I began to feel more light-headed than usual. Nitrogen narcosis is measurable at almost any depth below 60ft; it is certainly noticeable in sloppy performance or erratic behaviour at 150ft. I felt drowsy and wanted to lie down and go to sleep, but something urged me to head for the surface.

I finned slowly upwards and, at a depth of about 80ft, could see the shimmering surface of the water above, like a sheet of quicksilver. I could also make out the two divers in their scuba gear going past me on their way down. The surface started to go round in circles like a phonograph record. I felt dizzy and decidedly nauseated, and remembered no more until I came to on the surface, being pulled towards the boat by one of the RAF team. The expedition doctor wanted me inboard for examination, but Mike Edmonds would have none of it. 'He goes down and does fifteen minutes decompression,' he shouted, 'or he will get a bend and the nearest recompression chamber is ninety miles away and he'll die before we get him there.'

Feeling sick as a dog I descended the shot-line, accompanied by two other divers, who held onto my arms as I took my mouthpiece out of my mouth and replaced it with one from the spare cylinder we kept attached to the bottom of the shot-line. At the end of the line, we had tied a galvanised iron bucket, and in it there was usually a magazine for the recompressing diver to read during his seemingly endless strap-hanging session. I had no thought for the magazine, my only thought was whether I could get through my decompression stops without throwing up, and thereby choking on my own vomit. After ten minutes I was given the signal to move up the line, for five minutes at the final shallower stop.

After the recompression, I was helped aboard the boat feeling weak and helpless, my legs like jelly. The 'doc' gave me a thorough check-over and diagnosed carbon monoxide poisoning from the faulty compressor gases entering the air intake of my working compressor, and inner ear problems due to my too rapid ascent, which had given me the strange feeling that I had all the while been spinning round in circles. The duty compressor-man received a sharp word or two from

Edmonds, and a lesson was learned by all present.

One of the greatest aids to safety in scuba diving today is the Adjustable Buoyancy Life Jacket, or ABLJ as it is called. This apparatus can be fitted either with a small high-pressure air bottle for high-speed inflation, or a direct-feed hose to one's breathing regulator. In 1962 such aids were not even contemplated, and our sole safety factor in emergency was a yachtsman's life jacket, inflated by a small CO_2 cylinder. Its main disadvantage was that at a depth of 60ft or more, the pressure of the surrounding water prevented the jacket from fully inflating. Also, if one inflated too quickly, a rapid ascent took place and one ran the risk of an air embolism, which can prove fatal. Mike Edmonds had his own answer to this — the Edmonds Patent Ascent Regulator and Decompression Brake (ARDB). To operate it one needed an ordinary old-fashioned umbrella. Prior to inflating the life jacket at depth, one opened the umbrella and raised it above one's head. The CO_2 cylinder firing-cord was pulled, the jacket inflated, and the diver sailed slowly and majestically to the surface, the umbrella acting like a parachute, only in reverse. We tried it in 40ft of water and it worked like a dream. I even included a sequence in my television film of the expedition, but the BBC edited it out — on the grounds that underwater archaeology was supposed to be a serious business.

When the RAF team's allotted leave came to an end, we demobilised the expedition. There were still several hundred wine amphorae lying in the sand, buried up to their necks. I took my umbrella and, neatly folded, it ended its days standing upright out of the neck of a wine jar in 150ft of water. Any traveller passing that way, espying the umbrella, would be mystified to learn from the printed label inside that it had been made by a Mr R. H. Dass of New Delhi. From this, some desk academic might hypothesise that the Indians were carrying out a considerable trade with Italy in the second century BC. I was simply continuing the old English tradition of sowing confusion wherever we travel.

Once more back in the UK, I rough edited my 16mm film and showed it to BBC producer David Attenborough, who gave the affirmative for BBC screening and worldwide distribution. It was screened nationwide in 1963 under the title 'Diving into History', and later won an award for technical merit at an underwater film festival in California.

Later, Edmonds advised me that he was planning to take an expedition to either Malta or Chios, and would I care to come along?

But I declined. My main historical interest had always been in the 1588 Spanish Armada and the undeclared war between England and Spain in the sixteenth century. Not only did I want to locate and excavate a Spanish Armada galleon, I had designs on a flagship. I also had long-term visions of expeditions to locate Spanish galleons at their victualling place at Terceira in the Azores, on their journey laden with treasure from Panama home to Seville. What about Porto Bello, and excavation of galleons of the great plate-fleets? There was also Nombre de Dios, 7 miles inland where, in 1572, Drake had attacked a Spanish mule train laden with silver, to make his fortune. Perhaps this site could be re-located. I was to achieve all those ambitions, and many more, but a great deal of time was to pass — thirteen years no less.

In the meantime I spent weeks researching in the archives of the Public Record Office in Chancery Lane, London, and in the library of the British Museum. This was followed by visits to archival sources in the Netherlands. My trip to the Spanish royal archives at the castle of Simancas in Spain, the old capital of Ferdinand and Isabella, I regarded almost as a pilgrimage. I gathered my information, and planned an expedition to Ireland for 1963, to locate one of the most famous and most recorded of all the 1588 Spanish Armada losses — the *Santa Maria de la Rosa*.

But before describing this, my first Armada project, the scene must be set by dealing with the famed, but in some ways much overrated, Battle of the Narrow Seas of the year 1588.

Chapter 2

The Battle
of the Narrow Seas

By the late 1580s, war clouds had been gathering for several years, as English depredations against Spanish shipping and colonies in the Americas increased in frequency. Philip of Spain smouldered with rage at the activities of Queen Elizabeth's reprisal pirates — Drake, Hawkins, Frobisher, Fenton and the Fenners — whose arrogant disdain for Spanish might and interests grew daily. But his impending Enterprise of England was proving a costly exercise. Inflation was rife in Spain, and was fired even further by Philip's disastrous war against the Protestant Dutch and their revolt in the Netherlands, supported by Elizabeth of England whose court favourite Robert Dudley, Earl of Leicester, had led an army of 4,000 men in a bid to loosen Spain's grip on the Low Countries.

Drake's successful attack on Spanish shipping at anchor in Cadiz harbour in 1587 well and truly singed the king of Spain's beard. And in February 1588, with preparations for the forthcoming invasion of England slowing down due to the age and senility of Spain's premier admiral, the Marques de Santa Cruz, the latter died, leaving the fleet without a commander. Inexplicably, and ignoring the advice of his admirals, Philip appointed a landsman, the Duke of Medina Sidonia, to command the invasion fleet. Much maligned by English historians, Medina Sidonia was in fact a highly successful administrator, with some military experience. He was shrewd, loyal to his monarch and, as he was to prove in the final day's sea fight off Gravelines, a very brave man.

The duke examined the plans for the forthcoming naval confrontation with England, conferred with his admirals and sea captains, and found that much was amiss. Casks were in short supply, thanks to Drake's Cadiz escapade of the previous year, so that meat and water stank abominably. The guns of the Armada were light in comparison with those carried by the English, and there was insufficient cast-iron shot for the minimum five days of sea battle envisaged by the admirals. A drastic reorganisation of supply was undertaken to remedy this deficiency, the duke insisting on a crash programme of shot-casting in hastily built blast furnaces, resulting in the fleet's shot allocation being increased by 80 per cent. The poor quality of that shot was later to be evidenced in battle. During these preparations, the Duke of Medina Sidonia received a letter from the king containing the following instructions and advice:

> Above all it must be borne in mind that the enemy's object will be to fight at a long distance, in consequence of his advantage in artillery; the aim of our men, on the contrary, must be to bring him to close quarters and grapple with him.

Orthodox historians accepted this inferiority of Spanish naval artillery until the twentieth century when, in 1942–3, the late Professor Michael Lewis published a series of articles purporting to establish that the Spanish fleet in 1588 possessed guns which threw a far heavier shot than those mounted in the English ships. Lewis based his hypothesis on his examination of the gun calibres of weapons carried in the two captured Spanish galleons *Nuestra Señora del Rosario* and *San Salvador*, and on the known gun strengths of the Neapolitan galleasses which sailed with the Armada, and which carried the huge 'whole cannon' that fired a 50lb shot. At no time, however, did he consult the Spanish royal archives at Simancas, with the result that when, in 1961, his collected papers were published in book form as *Armada Guns*, something of a red herring was thrown into the arena of maritime research. Lewis's hypothesis was accepted in the main by the vast majority of naval historians including myself, until Dr I. A. A. Thompson of Keele University visited the Archives General at Simancas and located the fleet artillery lists for most of the major ships of Spain's 1588 Armada. The latter's paper 'The Spanish Armada Guns', published in the *Mariner's Mirror* in 1975, threw Michael Lewis's detailed hypothesis into discredit; the Spanish Armada vessels were mainly armed with lightweight artillery, and had few 'ship smashing guns'. But if long-range gunnery duelling was to be England's answer to Spanish 'infantry warfare at sea' tactics, it had disadvantages, one being that they would seldom be able to sink an enemy ship by gunfire alone.

On 4 May 1588, the 'Invincible Armada' shook loose its sails, and departed from the River Tagus. Carrying with it the blessings of the

Pope, the largest fleet Spain had ever raised must have made a grand sight to those watching on shore, the principal flagships flying not only Spain's royal colours, but also those of the Knight of the Golden Fleece, the Knight of Alcantara, and Spain's patron saint, Iago. In the van, the place of honour, sailed the Levant squadron commanded by Martin de Bertandona, followed by Miguel Oquendo with his Guipuzcoan squadron. Then came the huge troop and land-artillery carriers — the *urcas* (hulks) commanded by Gomez de Medina. Next came the Duke of Medina Sidonia in his galleon the *San Martin*, leading the fighting galleons of the Portuguese squadron, followed close behind by the duke's principal adviser Florez de Valdez with his squadron of Castille. The rearguard was made up of the Biscayan squadron, commanded by that redoubtable old warrior, Juan Martinez de Recalde, and Florez de Valdez's cousin Pedro de Valdez with his Andalusian ships. *Pataches* and *zabras* — small, fast scout vessels used for reconnaissance ahead and to the flanks of the main Armada and commanded by Antonio Hurtado de Mendoza — were spread throughout the fleet, to enable the duke and his principal officers to communicate speedily with each other. Hugo de Moncada's oar-and-sail propelled galleys and galleasses made good headway as their hundreds of slaves toiled at the long sweeps.

Clear of the coast of Portugal, Medina Sidonia allowed his fleet relatively loose rein, the ships keeping as close as possible without the irksome responsibility of the crescent-shaped defensive configuration which was to be the order of the day once off England's shores. There has been a great deal of discussion by historians concerning the disposition of the Spanish ships, Professor Lewis hypothesising that the fleet sailed with the cargo and infantry carriers in a large block protected by wings of fighting galleons, giving the mistaken impression, when viewed from eye level, of a crescent-shaped formation. The Armada, however, certainly appeared so to the English seamen.

The Spaniards were unlucky. Storm clouds gathered, and as the wind rose in its fury, ships became detached from their squadrons, and communications between the duke and his commanders became increasingly difficult. The main priority was to place as much distance as possible between the fleet and the nearby Portuguese shore, to avoid loss of ships on the rocky coast should the wind blow towards land. When the wind abated, the duke sent his scout vessels around the fleet to shepherd back those of the flock who had scattered. It soon became apparent that some ships had suffered considerable damage to sails and rigging, while others were leaking badly due to opened seams. Medina Sidonia decided to put into the Spanish port of Corunna, to take stock and carry out essential repairs. The *nao* (large armed merchant ship) *Santa Maria de la Rosa* (945 tons), vice-flagship of the Guipuzcoan squadron, had broken her stays in the gale, unstepping her mainmast. The duke ordered that a new mast be stepped, and this major repair was completed in the relatively short time of six hours.

Also in Corunna were the agents of Elizabeth's chief spymaster and personal secretary, Sir Francis Walsingham, and they soon reported back to England that the Armada was delayed. This brief respite allowed the English time to better their preparations, but even so, aspects of Elizabeth's fleet were not to the liking of her most experienced commanders. There was a shortage of both powder and shot, Drake complaining that they had enough for only one and a half days' fight. The men were behind with their pay, the food was rotten. It sounded like Medina Sidonia's pleas to Philip of Spain but, parsimonious though she was, Elizabeth did not have the wealth of the treasure from the Americas to fall back on. England was far from being a rich kingdom. But the Duke of Medina Sidonia himself was dispirited. He foresaw the difficulties ahead and was concerned that the Duke of Parma's army for the invasion of England might not make the essential rendezvous at Dunkirk. Cautiously the duke suggested that the enterprise be called off, to the wrath of his principal commanders, the main 'fire eaters' being Pedro and Florez de Valdez, Hugo de Moncada and Miguel Oquendo. The duke reluctantly decided that the Armada would proceed. Thus, on 12 July the Armada Felicidad sailed from Corunna — 130 ships, 30,000 men and 2,431 pieces of iron and bronze ship's artillery. The die was now finally cast.

A fair wind took the Armada towards the Narrow Seas, but on 15 July another storm suddenly sprang up. The oar-propelled galleys with their low free-board were designed for the calmer Mediterranean and they shipped a great deal of water, suffering damage in the process. They fell behind and eventually limped away towards the coast of France. The *Santa Anna*, flagship of Recalde's squadron, lost contact with the main fleet and, storm damaged, headed for the French port of Havre de Grace, never to rejoin. Nevertheless, on Friday, 19 July, the Spaniards made their English landfall, whereupon Medina Sidonia hove to and anchored to allow his fleet to gather and take up their prearranged positions in the defensive crescent-shaped formation. The next day the Armada sailed parallel to the English coast, the small scout vessels sweeping ahead for intelligence of the presence of the queen of England's fleet.

Meanwhile, on shore in England signal beacons were being lit, and trained bands were put in a state of readiness. The defences of Cornwall and Devon had been placed in the hands of one of Elizabeth's bravest seamen, Sir Richard Grenville, who must have sweated and fumed at the thought that a great sea fight might soon be under way while he was engrossed in land defences.

The duke anchored again, and called another council of war. Should they proceed as ordered, to collect Parma's army at Dunkirk for the planned invasion of England's Kent coast, or should they make a long tack to port, with the wind behind them, and bottle up England's fleet in Plymouth harbour? In retrospect, an attack on Plymouth would have been most advantageous for the Spaniards. They would have greatly outnumbered the English in ships, and their disadvantage in artillery would have been greatly outweighed by their ability to fight a hand-to-hand battle using the 18,000 seasoned troops they had on board. The duke listened to the calls to fight of his squadron commanders, who were well aware of the inferior position they would be in if the king's orders to proceed were carried out to the letter. The crescent-shaped formation essential for defensive purposes and designed to protect the troop and equipment carriers would mean that, once the English were upon the seas, the Spaniards would be forced to fight a defensive battle, all the way to Dunkirk. Such loss of mobility, so vital for the prosecution of a sea battle, irked the Spanish admirals who argued that the English ships were swift and reputedly handier than those of the Spanish, and the English had more artillery. However, having taken everyone's counsel into consideration, the duke made up his own mind and would not be persuaded to any other point of view. He had his orders, and to disobey the king's express command could bring shame and dishonour on the Medina Sidonia family name. Thus a great opportunity was lost to blockade the English fleet in Plymouth Sound, and to destroy that fleet in a grappling hand-to-hand mêlée. The course of history was to remain unchanged because Spain's overall commander of the mighty Armada decided that everything must be done strictly according to the book.

By the time the Spaniards had upped anchor and continued on their slow progress up channel, the English were making their preparations. Queen Elizabeth's overall commander, Lord High Admiral Lord

Howard of Effingham, held a council of war with Drake, John Hawkins and Martin Frobisher. With the prevailing wind blowing into Plymouth Sound, it seemed impossible for their square-rigged ships to sail out to sea and give combat; but the superb seamanship and daring which epitomised the individuality of the English approach to sea warfare now came to the fore. The English ships were warped, or towed, out by cables from the ships' bows to the shore. There, hundreds of stout hands hauled the ships to the harbour mouth, after which the task was taken over by longboats and pinnaces which took the ships' bower cables and, with the dipping of oars and straining of broad Devon shoulders, edged their charges out to sea.

By nightfall the English had done the seemingly impossible; they had taken the entire fleet out of Plymouth harbour against the wind. The Spaniards, conscious of the fact that the wind was still onshore and therefore of great disadvantage to the English, were hardly concerned when, at dusk, lookouts in the fighting tops on the seaward side of the Armada cried 'Sail ho!' It could not be the English, not even 'El Draque', with all his powers of superb seamanship, could do the impossible. The morning broke fine and clear to reveal, to the consternation of the Spaniards, English squadrons offshore with the wind behind them, beating down on the Armada's southern flank.

Due to the tack on which the Armada was sailing, Bertandona's vanguard squadron was now in fact on the seaward outer edge of the Spanish crescent. It was he who took the brunt of the opening engagement in which the English galleons, under press of sail, ran out their guns and fired their broadsides into Bertandona's ships as they passed. There is no direct evidence that the English used 'line ahead' tactics for the first time in this opening phase of the Battle of the Narrow Seas. We must, however, assume that this was so, because the opposing ships did not stay 'broadside to broadside' as they were later to do during the Napoleonic Wars. The Spaniards later spoke of the speed of the English ships, their nimbleness, and their ability to put about on a reciprocal tack with an alacrity that surprised even the most experienced of the Spanish admirals.

This opening attack by the English deeply vexed the Spanish squadron commanders, who fumed at Medina Sidonia's strict adherence to his crescent-shaped battle plan which hinged entirely on defensive strategy. History was to prove that in this at least the duke took the right decision — the English found the Spanish crescent difficult to break up. The Spaniards on the other hand learned that the greatest handicap for a convoy composed of a mixture of cargo and troop carriers and fighting galleons, was that the speed of the convoy's progress was restricted to that of the slowest ships in the fleet. The Armada was presenting to the English a slow-moving, easily out-manoeuvred target.

That the Duke of Medina Sidonia had both sailing and fighting instructions discussed with and issued to his admirals is a matter of recorded history. If the English fleet possessed fighting instructions, they are no longer extant. In point of fact there is little evidence to suggest that the English went into battle with any preconceived plan of attack, other than the general rule that the Armada be harried from the windward position, and that the English ships should endeavour never to lose the eye of the wind.

The seeming impregnability of the Spanish formation was now about to be challenged. As the English squadrons passed by the stern of Bertandona's Levant squadron, firing their broadsides, they reloaded their guns at a speed which astounded the Spaniards. Putting about onto the opposite tack to deliver broadsides to Recalde's Biscayan ships, Elizabeth's galleons showed also their high turn of speed. As the bombardment increased, so Recalde dropped back, to ensure that his slowest ships were not 'cut out' by the English; and it became apparent to Medina Sidonia that Recalde's squadron was in danger of becoming completely detached from the main Spanish battle fleet. But at this early stage of the conflict, Spanish discipline and adherence to instructions paid off. The Duke of Medina Sidonia ordered his flagship, the *San Martin*, to put about and go to Recalde's rescue; and signals were exchanged which resulted in the duke being supported by two of his best fighting galleons, the *San Mateo* and the *San Felipe*. This suggests that the duke was still in command of the situation, and as skilled as the most experienced of his squadron commanders. The action ended as it began, with English broadsides fired from well beyond point-blank range, and English captains showing no desire to come to close quarters. When, shortly after midday, the gunnery exchange drew to a close, the English had suffered no damage whatsoever, and the only recorded injury to a Spanish vessel was slight damage to Recalde's flagship, but nothing to impair the Armada's continued resolute passage up channel. As Drake wrote: 'There passed some cannon shot between some of our fleet and some of them.' Hawkins wrote: 'We had some small fight with them in the afternoon.' Lord Howard of Effingham summed up English timidity quite succinctly in a letter to the queen's secretary Sir Francis Walsingham: 'We durst not venture to put in amongst them, their fleet being so strong.' On the Spanish side, Admiral Pedro de Valdez wrote: 'Our ordnance played a long while on both sides, without coming to handstroke [point-blank range]. There was little damage done, because the fight was far off.'

Having successfully fought off England's naval might, the Spaniards were now to experience a double tragedy — the loss of two important fighting ships; the English in no way contributing to their demise. The first to fall by the wayside was the *San Salvador*, vice flagship of Oquendo's squadron. A lighted gunner's linstock fell onto loose powder, and the stern of the ship was blown off, causing many casualties and making the ship unmanageable. The English ships later seized this valuable prize and took her in tow.

The other casualty was the flagship of the Andalusian squadron, bearing Admiral Don Pedro de Valdez. She, fouling her bowsprit against the stern of another vessel, snapped her forestay and her unsupported foremast became unstepped. As helpless as the shattered *San Salvador*, de Valdez's *Nuestra Señora del Rosario* lay at the mercy of the English. It is at this point that the old morality of what was believed by the Spaniards to be a gentlemanly code of conduct, came into conflict with the new morality of tactical expediency as vouchsafed by the duke's adviser Florez de Valdez. The duke wanted to take off Pedro de Valdez and his men, and take the stricken vessel in tow. Florez de Valdez would have none of it. He postulated that the ensuing delay would give the English time to re-engage a static enemy; the duke's bounden duty was to proceed up channel to that rendezvous off Dunkirk with Parma. In the council of war which followed, the other admirals were with the duke and in strong opposition to Florez de Valdez's advice — honour was at stake. But this time the duke, quite sensibly, took the advice of Florez de Valdez and left the latter's cousin to his fate, which was eventual capture by Sir Francis Drake under somewhat mysterious circumstances. Incidentally, from that moment Florez de Valdez became the most hated man in the Spanish fleet. On his return to Spain, the other admirals laid charge against him for the desertion of his cousin, and King Philip threw the loyal but unfortunate commander into prison.

The decision was made, the *Nuestra Señora del Rosario* was left wallowing in the sea and, as dusk fell, she vanished from sight far behind the Spanish rearguard, while Elizabeth's fleet drew up into squadron formation intent on continuing the battle at first light on the following morning. That evening Effingham held a council on board his flagship, the *Ark Royal,* his lordship giving Drake pride of place by ordering that he should lead the fleet during the hours of darkness. The other ships in Drake's squadron were to follow their commander's stern lantern, and Effingham's, Frobisher's and Hawkins's squadrons were to do the same. So the English fleet proceeded, and in the blackness of the night each ship's lookout kept careful watch for the stern lantern of the ship ahead. At least that was what should have happened; the account of what actually took place, and what happened to the *Nuestra Señora del Rosario,* belongs to Chapter 9. Here it need only be said that, on 22 July, the Armada was given a full twenty-hour respite, and that some of the English admirals began to express long-held grievances against Sir Francis.

On the morning of the 23rd, the wind changed direction and the Spaniards found that at last they had the eye of the wind. Frobisher, attempting to regain the wind gauge, disdaining to await reinforcements, sailed his *Triumph* right up to the Spanish rearguard. Accompanied by five other ships, he hammered at the Armada as it sailed past Portland Bill. Effingham's squadron met Medina Sidonia's galleons only briefly, drawing off when the Spaniards tried to close the range. Frobisher was now in a perilous position, for the duke unleashed Hugo de Moncada with his four oar-and-sail propelled galleasses armed with 50 guns, some of which were the formidable 'whole cannon' firing a 50lb shot. Sped on their way by 250 oarsmen in each vessel, the galleasses should have been in their element, unrestricted as they were by the vagaries of the strength and direction of the wind. But in that short action the value of the galleass against the English galleon was seen to be as nought; Frobisher's blistering broadsides sent Moncada's squadron off in headlong retreat.

Meanwhile, on the southern wing of the Armada, about fifty English galleons made their attack led by both Hawkins and Drake. Effingham again came up to the Spaniard's rear centre and gave them a few desultory long-range ineffective rounds of shot. Beset from port, starboard and centre, the Armada should by all accounts have been in dire straits and yet it was not. When the smoke of the day's action had cleared away, the Armada was still to be seen proceeding sedately up channel, its crescent-shaped formation still intact. The damage done to either side was insufficient to injure a single ship seriously, which must have come as a great disappointment to the English. For the

Spaniards, all was going according to plan.

On 24 July the wind had backed around once again giving the English the advantage of the wind gauge. The Armada was now abreast the Isle of Wight, and there was a great opportunity for the English to crowd the Spaniards onto a deadly lee shore. But the morning and afternoon passed with not even a demonstration from the English, suggesting either timidity or, more likely, an almost complete breakdown in communications. Towards evening an attack slowly developed on the Spanish rearguard resulting in the flagship of the hulks, the *Gran Grifon*, being temporarily cut off from the main body of the Spanish ships. Medina Sidonia signalled for the fleet to check its progress and for several fighting galleons to drop back and engage the English. The latter appeared to have no stomach for an eyeball to eyeball confrontation and immediately withdrew. Thursday the 25th saw a slightly more aggressive spirit on the part of the English fleet. The *San Louis* and the *Santa Anna* dropped behind the Armada, and Hawkins clapped on sail and took his squadron into the attack. Don Alonzo de Leyva in the *Rata Encoronada*, assisted by Moncada with his galleasses, met Hawkins's squadron which was not supported by the Lord High Admiral, but at this point the English again drew off. On the Spanish right wing, the *San Mateo* was attacked and driven into the ranks of her squadron, the Spaniards with great skill and seamanship avoiding the danger of collision.

Failure to break up the Spanish defensive formation effectively and bring on a general mêlée in which the English advantage in artillery could be effective, suggests that neither Effingham nor his admirals had any great grasp of fleet battle-tactics, and that his squadron commanders did just what they pleased. In contrast the Spaniards mainly conducted themselves as a well-disciplined force, with the emphasis on teamwork and not on individual acts of bravery. How odd that the English Victorian historian James Anthony Froude should describe the events of 24 July as 'a resounding strategic victory for England and a fatal setback for Spain'.

For the whole of Friday 26 July, no action ensued. The English and the Spaniards were running short of ammunition, although there has been some misunderstanding about the situation. The fact that some of the Spanish galleons were constantly in the thick of the fight would ensure that their shot-lockers were well and truly depleted by that date. But this would not apply to those vessels which had not borne the brunt of the English attacks. Professor Lewis's mention that the

Spaniards had shot off the *whole* of their 123,000 plus rounds of shot by the end of the final battle off Gravelines, is not supported by examination of the Spanish Armada shipwrecks located in recent years. I have been involved in the excavation of two such ships, the *Santa Maria de la Rosa* and the *Gran Grifon*; both contained a considerable quantity of ammunition, and in the case of the *Santa Maria de la Rosa* the forepeak of the wreck contained several tons of shot. As regards the English fleet, the fact that it made use of Spanish shot from the captured *San Salvador* and *Nuestra Señora del Rosario*, supplied to the fleet by fast despatch boats, confirms that as far as the English shot-lockers were concerned, Lord Howard of Effingham and his squadron commanders were in very dire straits. Yet we must not be misled into believing that all the English ships were out of shot for, at the final battle off Gravelines, Sir William Wynter stated that his ship *Vanguard* fired off 500 rounds of ammunition. This question of the relative armament strength of the two fleets is examined in detail in Chapter 5.

What is certain is that Medina Sidonia's only chance of replenishment of ammunition would be his rendezvous with the Duke of Parma, and that there was no need for him to seek battle; the Spaniards had succeeded in their purpose most admirably. For the English, their performance prior to the final battle off Gravelines can only be described as lacklustre, revealing as it did that such figures as Drake, Hawkins, Frobisher and the other great captains were at their best when operating in the manner to which their past sea experience had accustomed them — highly individual actions in which combined fleet tactics paid little or no part.

On the morning of the 26th, Effingham exercised his prerogative of bestowing knighthoods. Hawkins was honoured, as was Frobisher, followed by Lord Thomas Howard, Lord Sheffield, Roger Townshend and George Beeston. After the battle, Effingham was chided by the queen for his profligacy in handing out so many honours. She herself was to do the same eight years later in 1596, after Effingham, supported by the Earl of Essex, Sir Walter Raleigh and many other notable gentlemen, successfully attacked, took and plundered the Spanish port of Cadiz. It is interesting to compare the quality of the men to whom Effingham gave just rewards, with those who received honours from the queen's hand in person. Undoubtedly some merited distinction, but in the main those honoured by Elizabeth of England were hangers on and court sycophants.

Setting off for the search for the *Santa Maria de la Rosa* in Blasket Sound, Ireland

Setting up the survey of the wreck of the *Santa Maria de la Rosa*. Diver using the expedition's design for apparatus for establishing base line right angles

The half anchor, broken in twain in the middle of the shank, left in Blasket Sound by the Spanish Admiral Marcos de Aramburu of the squadron of Castille

Two pieces of pewter plate inscribed with the name 'Matute' positively identified the wreck as that of the *Santa Maria de la Rosa*. The only survivor of the wreck stated that 'Matute was the captain of the infantry of that ship'

At 5pm on Saturday 27 July, the Armada luffed up and dropped anchor in Calais Roads. The English anchored offshore at a safe distance. Medina Sidonia had sent despatch boats in advance of his coming to enquire urgently if the Duke of Parma was ready to embark his troops off Dunkirk, and was surprised and dismayed at the response. Parma was not at Dunkirk, but at Bruges, some miles inland. Furthermore, none of Parma's soldiers, cavalry, cannon and siege train was ready to sail out from the coast in the barges and lighters which had been hired or built for the purpose. Medina Sidonia's secretary Arceo reported that, in his opinion, Parma would not be ready for another two weeks.

At this point King Philip's Enterprise of England was doomed to failure. England's shores would still be inviolate due not to the queen's fleet, which had been unable to damage Spanish naval might seriously, but to the rebellious Dutch who were grinding away the mightiest and most experienced army in the world. Not even Parma's brilliance as a strategist and a general could overcome the war which Imperial Spain was destined never to win — the war in the Netherlands. Even if he had been ready to embark his troops, Parma knew they stood little chance of setting foot on board the king of Spain's mighty Armada. He did not control any deep-water ports; they were all in the hands of the Dutch. To embark his troops, he would have to sail hundreds of unarmed barges and lighters across the Flemish shoals, all of which were completely dominated by the Dutch 'Sea Beggars', commanded by Admiral Justinus of Nassau. The latter's 200 small, but very well-armed fighting ships, with their flat bottoms and lee-boards, could sail in waters so shallow no Spanish galleon dare follow them. If Parma put his army to sea in undefended barges, they would be slaughtered. Parma temporised. He had no heart for a war with England, his hands were already full, his men unpaid and in some instances mutinous.

Meanwhile the English captains held yet another council of war, and unanimously agreed that they would send in fire ships in an attempt both to set part of the Spanish fleet to the torch, and make the rest cut their anchors and scatter. It was a sound decision. The anchorage in Calais Roads had never seen such a conglomeration of great sailing ships; there was insufficient room for the Spanish vessels to swing to their anchors, and many of them had had to put down three or even four anchors — bowers at the bow of the ship and kedges at the stern.

Eight fire ships were prepared, Drake providing one, Hawkins another, until the requisite number were ready. The smallest of the infernal machines was of 90 tons burthen, the largest 200 tons. They were loaded with pitch, their guns double-shotted, with timed fuses to the cannons' touch-holes. Their crews sailed them until it was plain that they would run straight into the heart of the Spanish fleet, whereupon the English seamen jumped over the side into waiting pinnaces and longboats, and rowed themselves clear of the anticipated conflagration. Something approaching panic spread amongst the Spanish crews. There was no time to raise anchors so cables were cut, many ships leaving four anchors behind; an act which was to ensure their inevitable destruction when, on their journey back to Spain, they became embayed on Ireland's inhospitable rocky coast. In the confusion which followed, Hugo de Moncada's galleass, the *San Lorenzo*, fouled her rudder on the *San Juan de Sicilia* and, becoming unmanageable, ran aground under the ramparts of Calais Castle.

The Lord High Admiral of England had previously given instructions on how his squadron commanders would fight the battle about to ensue. He, Effingham, would lead the attack on the Spanish offshore flank and be followed by Drake, Hawkins, Frobisher, Wynter and Lord Henry Seymour. But if the Spaniards were thrown into great confusion, there was also something approaching it in the English fleet. Howard of Effingham, seeing the disabled galleass aground off Calais, ignored the orders he had issued to his fleet and the attack he himself was supposed to lead and, drawing his squadron after him, sailed to attack a vessel which was already out of the fight, and which therefore posed no threat to the English.

For this action on the morning of Monday 29 July, Lord Howard of Effingham must surely stand condemned as grossly incompetent, and unworthy to command the English fleet. After bombarding the helpless galleass, which was keeled over so that her offshore guns pointed to the sky, Howard sent in pinnaces packed with seamen and a handful of soldiers. In the musketry battle which ensued, the English suffered the largest number of casualties they were to have in the whole of the eight days' engagement! Among the Spanish casualties was Hugo de Moncada, killed by a musket ball.

Eventually the English boarded and captured the *San Lorenzo*, to be confronted by Calais officials and other distinguished French citizens who pointed out to them that they were in breach of France's neutrality. The excited victors responded by holding the French governor's spokesman and friends at sword and pistol point, after which they robbed them of their personal jewellery. Howard of

Effingham's part in the battle had now descended to a looting foray. Apart from the fifty or so Englishmen killed in the taking of the *San Lorenzo*, another twenty were drowned during their departure from the galleass's side.

What of the main body of the Spanish fleet? Lewis states, 'For this time there was a real mix up. The Spaniards were in no tactical formation at any time'; but this ignores the testimony of Sir William Wynter, who confirmed that the Spaniards quickly resumed their defensive crescent-shaped formation. Nevertheless, in the absence of Lord Howard of Effingham, Drake, who was next in line, took his squadron into the attack. He fired his bow chase-guns on approach, and his broadside when abreast of the leading offshore Spanish galleon. In this engagement, his ship suffered damage, but it was far from serious. Ubaldino, in his 'Narrative', stated that Drake's flagship, the *Revenge*, was pierced by cannon balls of all sizes. No evidence exists that Ubaldino examined any of the English galleons after the battle; we must therefore assume that he was taking his narrative direct from Drake. Sir John Hawkins's examination of the queen's ships after the battle gives the lie to alleged piercing of the sides of the *Revenge* by cannon balls of any size: 'Drake's flagship had suffered no hull damage whatsoever and her only battle damage was a mast split by great shot.' We have no further evidence as to Drake's part in the final crucial battle as it developed off Gravelines. In Chapter 9 we will look at 'Mathew Starke's Deposition', in which Martin Frobisher stated categorically that after his initial broadside at the Spaniards, Drake took no further part in the battle. Frobisher further asserted that Drake was a coward.

As the other English squadrons sailed into battle, so for the first time the fight got down to point-blank range. The English were in for the kill, and would at last do their damnedest to sink Spanish ships. The Duke of Medina Sidonia, far from being the cowardly landsman some English historians make him out to be, stayed in the thick of the fight and when, due to gun smoke, he could no longer clearly discern where the heart of the battle lay, he climbed the rigging into the fighting tops of his galleon the *San Martin*, from where he conned her deep into the centre of the battle. The final phase of the battle was fought so close that an Englishman, calling from the fighting tops for the Spaniards to surrender, was shot out of the rigging by a well-aimed musket ball.

As already mentioned, the Spanish captains were amazed at the speed and handiness of the English ships, and also at the rapidity of their rate of fire. English gunnery was evolving towards the stage where, 200 years later, it was estimated that Nelson's gun crews were so well worked up that they could load and fire their pieces three times to the French's and Spaniards' once. But historians misinterpret the statements made by the Spaniards of the Armada. The Duke of Medina Sidonia states that he was only able to reply to the English gunnery by using musketry. It has been presumed from this that the duke was unable to fight his artillery because of lack of shot. This was not the case. An understanding of how ship's artillery was loaded in the sixteenth century suggests that the duke was unable to reply with his artillery after firing his first broadside, owing to the rapid 'line ahead' attack of the English ships, one behind the other 'which prevented the Spanish gunners from loading their pieces'.

This may seem a surprising statement, but it was not until the Napoleonic era that gunners loaded their gun inboard, ran it out with its muzzle projecting from the gun-port and fired; after which the gun rebounded inboard on the recoil, to be restrained by the 'breeching rope', then swabbed and reloaded inboard ship. The use of the gun's recoil to bring it inboard for reloading was not understood in the sixteenth and seventeenth centuries. The gun would be loaded initially inboard and then run out, at which point it was lashed firmly to the ship's bulwarks. After firing, the gun was kept lashed to the side of the ship so that the hapless gunner had to crawl out through the gun-port and swab the barrel out with a flexible-rope rammer, ram home the powder, shot and wad, while either sitting astride the barrel of the gun or standing on a plank which had been inserted in a notch in the ship's side. Incredible as this may seem, it was standard practice throughout the sixteenth century, and also during the three wars fought between the English and the Dutch in the 1600s. There is a sketch in existence by the seventeenth-century Dutch artist Van der Velde the younger, executed during the third Dutch war which ended in 1674, which illustrates quite clearly the two systems in use for loading guns outboard.

As late as the Battle of the Glorious First of June of 1794, when the English *Brunswick* was hard alongside the French *Vengeur* with each ship's gun muzzles almost touching the opponent's sides, an English gunner about to ram a 32lb demi-cannon shot down the barrel of his piece looked out through the gun-port, and saw a French gunner on the deck below loading his gun outboard 'in the old fashioned way, sitting astride the barrel of his gun, looking down, as he popped the iron shot down the muzzle'. The English gunner, showing great presence of mind and an astute grasp of the desirability of economy in the use of propellent gunpowder, held his cannon ball out at arm's length and dropped it on the unsuspecting Frenchman's head, killing him outright.

Armed with this knowledge, it takes little imagination to understand the predicament in which Medina Sidonia and his outlying galleons found themselves. If the English sped past, firing broadsides as they came, then wore ship and came about for the other broadside while reloading the first broadside outboard, but with their vulnerable gunners now on the opposite side to the Spanish enemy, the duke's gunners would be forced to reload their pieces after their first broadside in the face of point-blank gunnery and musket fire from each of the English ships as it passed in line ahead. The English were firing solid shot, bar shot and, for the outboard Spanish gunners most devastating of all, grape shot. The slaughter of Spanish gunners must have been prodigious. The duke would be left with no alternative but to order his men to reply with arquebus and musket.

Thus English superior tactics prevailed. When the battle off Gravelines drew to a close after eight hours of fighting, the shattered *San Mateo* and *San Felipe*, leaking badly, their decks awash with blood, one with most of her maindeck guns dismounted, stood in to the Flemish coast to avoid foundering and were taken by the Dutch Sea Beggars. Shortly afterwards, the galleon *Maria Juan* foundered with heavy loss of life. She was the only confirmed sinking by English gunnery in eight days of sea battle.

The English, ammunition almost completely exhausted, drew off and shepherded the Spanish Armada along the Flemish coastline, where an onshore breeze threatened to perform greater execution than Queen Elizabeth's admirals could ever have hoped to achieve. To the east of the two fleets lay the dreaded Flemish shoals, and the Spaniards were boxed in between a hostile fleet and a lee shore. Soundings were frequently taken, and each successive sounding heralded the death knell for the entire Spanish fleet, as the waters became shallower and shallower. Prayers were offered to the Virgin, and many a Spanish seaman and soldier fingered his rosary beads or religious medallions and prayed fervently for God's grace. Then, just when disaster appeared to be imminent, the wind changed direction and freshened to an offshore breeze. The Armada was safe, for the time being at least.

On board the duke's flagship *San Martin*, the Spanish admirals held council. It was agreed that, if the wind changed direction and there was a possibility of reversing their course, they would do so, and take on the English again. It was not to be, the wind held fair for an uneventful journey up into the North Sea. The English followed at a safe distance; Lord Howard of Effingham in a letter to the queen's secretary Walsingham dated 7 August, admitted that he was in no condition to attack. By the time the Firth of Forth was reached, it was obvious that if Spain were ever to invade England, it would have to be in another year.

As the Armada sailed north, the need for the crescent-shaped defensive formation passed. Vessels straggled, and the duke took his vengeance on those he believed had shown something less than the valour King Philip expected from his hand-picked band of admirals and sea captains. The masters of two ships which had sped ahead of the fleet in their progress up into the North Sea were suspected of cowardice, and of being more concerned with putting as great a distance as possible between themselves and the English than standing close to badly damaged ships which needed support. Both were condemned to be hanged, their bodies to be put on display and paraded around the fleet in pinnaces. One of these unfortunates was to have been Captain Francisco de Cuellar; he, however, was saved at the last minute by the intervention of the Armada's auditor general, Martin de Aranda, in spite of the fact that five years earlier, off the coast of Brazil, he had been charged with cowardice when he took refuge behind another Spanish ship in an action with the English captain Edward Fenton.

As night fell, the ships lost contact with each other and, by the third day after the final action off Gravelines, Medina Sidonia was no longer in touch with more than a third of his fleet. Several ships were seen to turn away and head for the coast of Scotland, never to be seen again. Even greater losses were to occur on the north and west coasts of Ireland, the reason for this being readily understood if we examine sixteenth-century maps. In these the west coast is shown as a vertical north–south axis, with bays shown as shallow indentations. In point of fact, the west coast of Ireland, when viewed from north to south, slants to the west. Any square-rigged sailing vessel entering one of those bays or river estuaries could shelter from a south-west wind, but if the wind should change direction and blow from north-west or west, such a ship would, in the parlance of the period, be embayed, and her chances of escape would be negligible.

The duke had undoubtedly consulted his most experienced commanders when he issued the following orders:

> The course that is first to be held is to the North East, until you be found under 61 degrees and a half; and then take great heed lest you fall upon the island of Ireland, for fear of the harm that may happen unto you upon that coast. Then parting from those islands, and doubling the Cape at 61 degrees and a half, you shall run West-South-West to the height of 53 degrees; and then to the South-South-West, making to the Cape Finisterre, and so to procure your entrance into the Groyne [Corunna] or to Ferol, or to any other port of the coast of Galicia.

But some ignored the dire warnings contained in the duke's instructions. They had little choice, for their crews were dying daily of sickness, malnutrition and dehydration due to lack of fresh water, and they hoped to replenish their water casks on the Irish shore. Some survived, but more than twenty vessels of the 1588 Spanish Armada perished on Ireland's rocky coast.

From east to west, across the coast of Ulster, and down the west coast the following losses occurred (although not in this order):

The *Girona* ran onto the rocks near Dunluce Castle; the *Trinidad Valencera* sank at anchor in Kinegoe Bay; the *Juliana* sank near Bloody Foreland and an unnamed ship off Gola Island. One ran onto the rocks to the west of Killibegs harbour, another to the east, and another at the harbour entrance.

On Streedagh Strand near Sligo three great ships, including that captained by Francisco de Cuellar, were cast away, as an onshore wind revealed their shortage of anchors, most of which they had cut when the English sent in the fireships in Calais Roads.

The *Rata Encoronada* was abandoned in Blacksod Bay and burned to the waterline. The *Gran Grin* struck Clare Island, and either sank there or drifted off the rocks to end up on the mainland. At Tirrawley on the Curraun peninsula another ship ran onto a rock and sank — or possibly this was the *Gran Grin* drifting from the island. The *Falco Blanco Mediano* allegedly struck the island of Inishbofin and sank close by, while yet another foundered within sight of the town of Galway.

A great Flemish ship struck on Mutton Island, and on nearby Doonbeg beach the *San Esteban* met her end. In the mouth of the River Shannon the *Anunciada* was in such poor condition that she was set alight, her crew escaping in another Armada vessel. A small *zabra* put into Tralee and, pleading for succour, her crew were all hanged by the order of Lady Denny who, in the absence of her husband could think of no other remedy for a tiresome situation.

Between Tralee and Great Blasket Island on the coast of Kerry, a great Biscayan ship ran into the cliffs, with no survivors. Somewhere north of the Blaskets, the Spaniards scuttled or cast adrift the *San Juan* of the Castilian squadron, after attempting unsuccessfully to take out her artillery. In Blasket Sound, the *Santa Maria de la Rosa* struck a rock and sank within minutes.

The sinking of the Spanish Armada on the coast of Ireland makes a sorry tale. Thousands of seamen and soldiers were either drowned, or had their heads beaten in with clubs and axes as they struggled ashore. Some were hung. There is little evidence to suggest that the native Irish indulged in mass murder of Spanish survivors. The instructions for the massacre of the Spaniards came from Lord Deputy Fitzwilliam in Dublin who, realising that the several thousand Spanish soldiers on board the Armada ships greatly outnumbered the English soldiers in Ireland, took what for him was the only decision he could make. The Spaniards must be killed to a man, lest they foment rebellion and help train an Irish dissident army.

Chapter 3

In Search of the Spanish Armada

Although my film of the Filicudi expedition had been readily accepted by the BBC, it needed extra footage which had to be shot in UK waters, for the BBC could not afford — so they said — the cost of flying a camera crew back to the Aeolian Islands. In due course, therefore, I journeyed down to Cornwall to meet Mike Edmonds and the expedition team at their RAF base at St Mawgan. The BBC camera crew turned up, and a few surface shots were re-enacted in St Ives harbour. After the camera team left, I spent an enjoyable week diving in south Cornwall and Devon, with either Mike Edmonds or another diving buddy, Flight Sergeant Neil Adams.

Adams was a spear-fishing enthusiast, and he also liked to pick up lobsters and crayfish. It was on such a routine dive off a certain south Devon harbour in the autumn of 1962 that we discovered a wreck. We dropped over the side of a hired fishing boat, and swam around in about 60ft of water in relatively poor visibility, eventually losing contact with each other. I was first to surface, and was picked up by the boat. Adams surfaced about fifteen minutes later carrying a sackful of crayfish. We gave one to the boat owner, and the rest went into Adams's refrigerator. That night, in a Cornish pub, Adams mentioned that during our dive he had swum over several bronze cannon. 'It could have been six in all,' he said, 'or it could have been a pair and I perhaps saw them three times — it was hard to establish the number because of the poor visibility.'

Before I left for my home in north Wales, Adams promised to draw a rough plan of what he believed to be his 'cannon area' and post it off to me. I never received it. Shortly after our dive he was posted to Singapore, and on a flight from Singapore to the island of Ghan in the Indian Ocean his Shackleton aircraft ditched into the sea and there were no survivors. I puzzled over his alleged discovery. Had he really seen bronze guns or had he seen discarded sewer pipes? In later years I

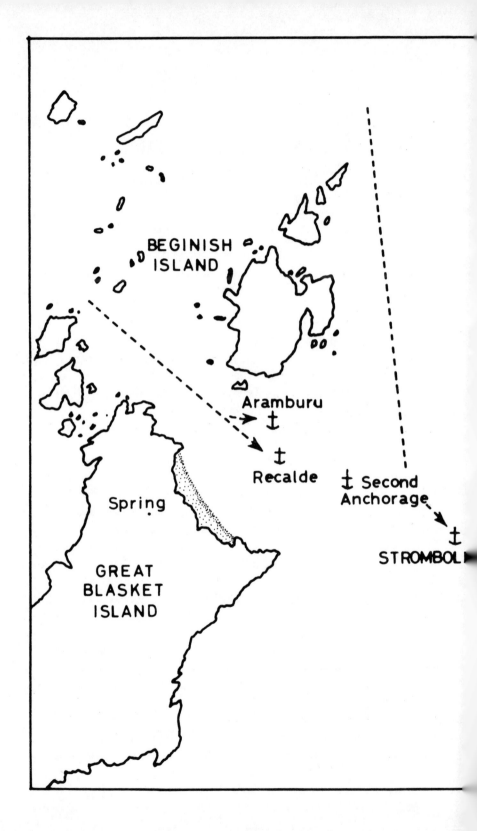

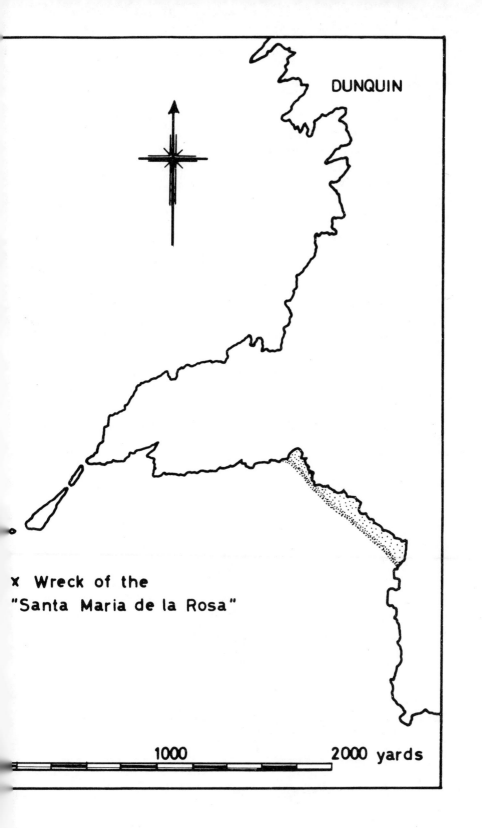

DUNQUIN

x Wreck of the
"Santa Maria de la Rosa"

1000   2000 yards

was to investigate two similar instances, one in Ireland and one in the Azores, and in both cases what was reported as cannon on the seabed turned out to be either iron or aluminium pipes. I was to forget Adams's alleged bronze guns for eighteen years, when my researches in Spain eventually bore fruit. I know now that Adams did see bronze cannon, and that they were not from an Armada vessel, but from a combined Anglo-Spanish fleet of the reign of Philip and Mary; but that is another story which may ultimately form the basis for another expedition.

Meanwhile, as already mentioned, my Spanish Armada researches kept leading me back to one great fighting ship of the Battle of the Narrow Seas — the *Santa Maria de la Rosa* of 945 tons, vice flagship of the Guipuzcoan squadron, and commanded by her owner, Martin de Villafranca of San Sebastian, who had her built and commissioned in Santander only a year before the Armada sailed. She was a stout built *nao*, armed with twenty-six guns, and for the 1588 Armada she was crewed with Spanish, Portuguese and Italian seamen.

The *Santa Maria de la Rosa* is one of the most documented of all the Spanish Armada shipwrecks. She entered Blasket Sound on the Kerry coast of Ireland on 21 September 1588, shortly after which she dragged anchor and, striking a submerged rock, sank with the loss of 499 lives out of the 500 on board; the sole survivor was a boy, Giovanni de Manona, son of the ship's pilot, Francisco de Manona of Genoa. He was washed ashore on a plank and interrogated at Dingle, giving his interrogators a tale of part fact, part fiction. He gave truthful facts concerning the size of the ship, the name of her captain, and of some of the principal dons on board, but also told outright lies to please his captors. After this he, together with survivors from other Armada ships, was taken to Cork and hanged. Manona's claim that the ship carried 15,000 ducats in silver and as much more in gold might or might not have been true; his statement that the Prince of Ascula, base son of Philip II, was drowned in the wreck was a patent falsehood. The prince had indeed sailed with the Armada, but not on the *Santa Maria de la Rosa*. Furthermore, when the Armada arrived at Calais, the prince went ashore to greet the Duke of Parma, where he stayed.

The area of search was indeed extensive, for the sound between Great Blasket Island and the mainland of the Dingle peninsula amounts to more than 6 square miles of unexplored seabed. While I

Fig 1   Blasket Sound. Spanish anchorage in September 1588 and the site where the *Santa Maria de la Rosa* lies

was planning my proposed three-week reconnaissance, the Irish Tourist Board put me in touch with Irish maritime historian Desmond Branigan. Branigan not only explored archival sources for me in Ireland, he took a reconnaissance party to Blasket Sound to 'test the waters'. At one point Branigan was towed across the sound behind a motor fishing-vessel on what was undoubtedly the first search ever for the famed ship. An expedition needs divers, and my friend Joe Casey provided them in abundance through his membership of the St Helens Underwater Exploratory Club — an amateur diving group. Casey also supplied, at no charge whatsoever, a scuba compressor, a van, diving sets, and a great deal of engineering and survey apparatus. The St Helens scuba divers provided a large inflatable boat and outboard motor.

In the early summer of 1963, therefore, we set out for Ireland, to what was to be my abiding passion and quest for the next six years. We found Blasket Sound to be an awesome place. The gap between Dunmore Head on the mainland and Great Blasket Island provides a funnel through which the tides must race, so that the sound can be a terrifying place in anything other than fair weather. Unfortunately 1963 proved to be a poor year for diving conditions on the west coast of Ireland. Day after day we carried our inflatable boat down the cliff path to Dunquin jetty and watched as the seas raged over the reefs and outlying islands in a white fury. Eventually the gales abated and we were able to enter the water. The wind was blowing at about 15 to 20 knots and the build up of waves over the reef areas was a warning sign to us to keep our distance. Off the tiny strip of beach on Great Blasket, known as 'White Strand', I dropped over the side of the boat, towing a surface float, and searched for signs of the Armada vessel. There was no sign either of anchors or wreckage. Two other divers made similar efforts but to no avail. I realised that, with the short time at our disposal and the enormous area of seabed to be searched, we were going to need an awful lot of luck. As it happened, we were to have none.

The weather again closed in for several days, but when the storm lessened we sailed off again, only this time to the area of underwater reefs which runs from Scollage Rock by Dunmore Head out to Stromboli Rock in the centre of the sound. Stromboli was given its name from an English Royal Navy paddle steamer HMS *Stromboli* which struck the rock in the mid-nineteenth century. Later, the damaged ship was towed off the rock and taken to the Royal Navy base at Scattery Island in the River Shannon, where she was repaired. We were to have one more dive in Blasket Sound — my solo drift-dive in a 1 knot current, over the submerged Scollage-Stromboli reef massif. I saw a sandy bottom pass by like a slow-moving conveyor belt until, out of the gloom, the rocky walls of the submerged reef loomed ahead. I swam over the top, passing resting salmon lying amongst the waving kelp fronds, finning just to stay in one position and awaiting the moment when they would swim up the nearby Dingle estuary to spawn and die. Crayfish abounded; I saw them in their dozens. Then the reef dropped away, and within a few minutes I was in 120ft and running out of diving time. Little did I know it, but I had missed the wreck of the *Santa Maria de la Rosa* by about 200yd.

It was now time to cease activities, and my friends from the St Helens club departed, leaving me with one diving companion, Eric Reynolds, who had found that 70lb gold bullion bar with me on the wreck of the *Royal Charter*. We headed north to Ulster, where I had ideas of locating the Spanish Armada sail-and-oar propelled galleass *Gerona*, which had run into the cliffs there when her rudder broke. There were only a handful of survivors, and the local Irish chieftain Sorley Boy O'Donnell and his men helped them. The Spaniards in their gratitude told O'Donnell that there was great wealth on the wrecked ship, and the latter was able to raise three chests of treasure and several pieces of the ship's bronze artillery.

In 1963 nobody in the UK had any clear idea as to who held title to shipwrecks of the Spanish Armada lying in UK waters. Ulster was in the UK and not in the Irish Republic, so UK laws would prevail. Since England and Spain had been at war in 1588, then surely any Spanish Armada vessel lost on part of the UK coast could be deemed to be war prize and therefore UK property. I wrote to the Board of Trade (now the Department of Trade) in London seeking clarification, and to my surprise I was offered a salvage licence for the wreck of the galleass *Gerona*, if I posted a bond of £1,000. Before accepting the terms of the agreement with the Board of Trade, I wanted to be clear in my mind which shipwreck I was going to treat as my number one priority. Was it to be the *Gerona* or the *Santa Maria de la Rosa*? I decided against the *Gerona* because I knew that she had been smashed into splinters when she hit the cliffs of Ulster. On the other hand, the *Santa Maria de la Rosa* had gone down intact, and offered what to me was the greater prize — the prospect of substantial ship's structure to locate and subject to detailed archaeological survey. But although she was not going to be our main endeavour, as we were in the area Reynolds and I decided that we must have a try at locating the *Gerona*. Without a compressor and only one scuba set each, we would be restricted to one dive only. That dive, in an area suggested by the early twentieth-century historian William Spotswood Green, was a failure. With no compressed air in our diving sets, we set out to look at a second site — a cliff area, at the foot of which lay a jutting rock known as the 'Rock of the Spaniards'. Reynolds and I looked down on the rock and decided that, armed only with masks and snorkels, there was no way we could explore the area, and consequently we travelled to Belfast to meet members of the Belfast Sub Aqua Club.

The latter regaled us with a most surprising story. They had been researching the Irish Rebellion of 1798, and had learned that a French ship had been wrecked on the coast of Ulster when trying to land artillery to aid the Irish rebels. Underwater searches of the area proving fruitless, one of the divers mentioned their quest to a local rod-and-line fisherman who asked, 'Why don't you go and look in Cannon Hole? When the water is thin [clear] we can see cannons lying on the bottom.' And so it proved. The club's divers, with a contingent from Queen's University, Belfast, dived where he had suggested, and there were the French contraband culverins lying around in profusion. It was apparent that the French ship *Amitie* had anchored off the coast waiting to make rendezvous with the Irish, when a storm arose and the vessel dragged her anchors until she struck the cliffs. As luck would have it, she must have run straight into the cleft in the rocks which later became known to local fishermen as 'Cannon Hole'. I was invited to the site, and took a number of photographs of the scatter of long-barrelled cast-iron French cannon. Attrition caused by the movement of sand in and out of the hole had worn away a considerable part of the trunnions and cascabels, also any markings such as founder's marks or gun weights. The site was interesting but not inspiring. To me there is a magic in bronze artillery which is never present in iron guns. Bronze guns were usually products of an artist's eye, the mouldings and escutcheons on the breeches and barrels taking diverse forms and shapes. Some Portuguese bronze guns had their barrels fluted to appear like a Doric column, while some English guns were shaped to appear like a Tudor chimney. Cast-iron artillery had little or no place in my scheme of things. But now the *Santa Maria de la Rosa* project lay fallow for four years while I struggled to make the money necessary to launch a full-scale archaeological expedition which would

51

operate for a six-month season and, if crowned with success, would have to have funds for a second six-month season of wreck survey and excavation. I did not feel disposed to bang on doors begging for finance. I was determined to be entirely self-sufficient, for in that way I would have the satisfaction of being my own man, and not have to doff my cap or touch my forelock to anyone. By 1967 I had enough money put together for a six-month expedition the following year.

Meanwhile, as early as 1963 my lawyer in Dublin, John P. King, had approached the Spanish authorities for me through the good offices of the Spanish Ambassador in Ireland, requesting a sole and exclusive salvage licence. Now after four years he learned that the authorities in Madrid had no objection to me searching for the *Santa Maria de la Rosa*. This was hardly the definite response I required, because one does not need a permit to search for ancient shipwrecks in Irish waters, nor to excavate. I was taking, as I still do, a strictly legalistic approach to underwater archaeology, whereby I will not interfere with such a shipwreck without the written, formal approval of those whom I believe to be the owners of the wreck. In the midst of the negotiations, my friend Joe Casey advised me that he and the St Helens group were off to Blasket Sound for a further search for the *Santa Maria de la Rosa*. Two weeks later he telephoned to tell me that the day before, two of the divers, while being towed off Beginish Island by a surface inflatable boat, believed they had seen two bronze cannon on the seabed. I awaited further information.

When I received a full report on the 'sighting' I was far from certain in my own mind that the two divers had in fact seen bronze guns. Working at a depth of about 70ft, just when they were thinking of ascending, one diver thought he saw two cannon on the seabed. He did not let go of the towline, and therefore lost the opportunity to examine his alleged cannon physically. His diving buddy had his mask almost torn off his face by either the force of the current or the speed of the boat's passage through the water — hence the speedy ascent of both divers.

The story reached the press; a great deal of excitement was raised and I was flooded with applications to join my proposed 1968 expedition. I wrote an article for the British Sub Aqua Club magazine *Triton* inviting volunteers, and ended up with more than 240 anxious divers pestering me for a place on my roster. In the event, forty-five divers were to join me in Blasket Sound over the two-year wreck location, survey and excavation seasons, including officers and other

Bronze medio-sacre from the wreck of the *Gran Grifon*, flagship of the 1588 Spanish Armada squadron of Urcas (hulks) located off Fair Isle, Shetlands, by the author and Colin Martin in 1970. On the left, Chris Oldfield, and on the right, Colin Martin

Prince Philip presenting the author with the Duke of Edinburgh/BSAC Annual
Gold Medal Award for achievements in underwater science, 1971, for his work
on the *Santa Maria de la Rosa*. Also present are Alex Flinder of BSAC and the
Council for Nautical Archaeology and Jean Wignall

Off-centre casting of broken off end of Spanish bronze gun from the Armada
flagship *Gran Grifon*

ranks from all branches of the British armed forces (Army, Navy, Royal Air Force and Royal Marines), the Royal Navy providing the largest contingent. Three relatively unknown volunteers have since made considerable reputations for themselves in either underwater archaeology or commercial diving: Colin Martin, who is now the director of the St Andrews Institute of Maritime Archaeology; Jeremy Green, now curator of underwater archaeology for the Western Australia Museums; and Lieutenant Commander (later Commander) John Grattan RN. Grattan became my diving officer, Martin my surveyor and assistant expedition leader, and Green was in charge of artifact detection by means of pulse-induction underwater metal-detectors. Reynolds, who had dived on the *Royal Charter* and the *Amitie* with me, and Edmonds, who had invited me on his Roman wreck expedition, both put in appearances. Joe Casey, as always, proved a stalwart friend in providing compressors, engines, inflatable boat, etc, plus an abundance of engineering equipment and boat chandlery.

Our expedition headquarters was the Kerry town of Dingle. This town had been the headquarters of the English when the Armada ships led by Juan Martinez de Recalde entered Blasket Sound in 1588. It was from Dingle that agent James Trant journeyed to Dunmore Head to observe the Spanish ships lying at anchor between Great Blasket Island and the mainland. I rented two houses for a six-month season, introduced myself to the local head of the police force or *garda*, the Receiver of Wreck in Tralee, and the local newspaper, the *Kerryman*, also based in Tralee. Thus a good relationship was established with the forces of law and order, the official agent for the government in Dublin with reference to ancient shipwreck salvage, and the media. That exercise in public relations was to stand me in good stead when a group of treasure-orientated divers attempted to oust me from the wreck site the following year. In Dublin, my old friend and colleague Des Branigan kept close contact with the relevant authority, the Ministry of Transport and Power; and a new colleague, Peter Start of the Department of Chemistry at University College, Dublin, agreed to assist me with regard to artifact chemical analysis and conservation. My lawyer there never relaxed his pressure on the Spanish Embassy for the much needed exclusive salvage licence.

Grattan and his naval colleagues trained my divers in his adaptation of a Royal Navy search system called the 'swim line'. By this system we were eventually able to search no less than 4 square miles of the seabed in Blasket Sound in a methodical manner. It was in fact to become the largest 'area cover' underwater search ever undertaken by divers, for electronic and acoustical wreck-detection systems did not form part of our capability. The ferrous-metal detecting proton magnetometer would be of no use to us due to the volcanic nature of the rock strata in Blasket Sound, with its high in-built natural magnetic gradients. Likewise, such apparatus as the acoustical side-scan sonar systems then available (which could by reflected and recorded sound pulses identify not only a modern wreck, but also the existence of a wreck ballast-mound) would be of little benefit owing to the fact that sonar cannot see through rock pinnacles or around corners, and there was a strong possibility that the wreck of the *Santa Maria de la Rosa* lay in a gully or crevice in a reef structure. Our instrument of search was therefore what we came to refer to as the 'Diver's Mark 1 eye-ball'.

Our advanced operations centre was to be the small concrete jetty at Dunquin at the northern end of Blasket Sound, from whence we set out each and every morning that the weather permitted. To pack as much search time as possible into our season, cost effectiveness was increased by doing two dives per day. The problem was that with less than six hours between dives, we stood the risk of a 'bend', and as the nearest recompression chamber was at a Royal Navy base several hundred miles away in Northern Ireland, we saw to it that our diving was undertaken within the confines of what is termed the 'no stop limit'. We had a lot of good chaps, and a few duffers. We also had one or two dead beats, and either Grattan or myself politely told them to 'get on their bicycles' with the proverbial 'We don't know how we are going to do without you, but we are going to try.' A tremendous camaraderie burgeoned amongst us to the extent that our expedition became 'the way of life' and the real world was regarded as very effete and unreal. In the early part of the 1968 season we never took a day off, nor did a team member ask for one. Days off happened when we had a Force 8 gale with wind strength of 40 knots. We would search in up to Force 4, gusting 5, hoping that the wind would drop in ferocity. One RAF diver with an unbelievable logbook of quite impressive dives asked for a shore job after his first venture out into the inhospitable Atlantic. Grattan saw him off. Another RAF volunteer arrived in natty reefer jacket and yachting cap. We did not take to him when he asked 'When do you have a day off?' before he had even taken off his cap and put down his duffle bag. We had just gone through a spell of three weeks without a day off; we were weary and tempers were wearing thin. 'Pretty Boy' lasted one dive and, coming ashore quite shaken, admitted that it was not quite what he expected and sensibly packed his bags and left.

The swim-line search system evolved around the principle of placing from six to twelve pairs of eyes on the seabed, spaced equidistant apart, drifting along with the current, and connected to each other by a slim nylon line which the divers held in both hands. The line was attached to a rewindable reel in the dive-boat, and the first diver dropped over the side holding the end of the line. At pre-arranged intervals, as the boat sped through the water, the other divers dropped over the side and, swimming to the line, took hold of it. The swim lines searched a swath of the seabed from 100 to 250yd in width, and the length of the run, determined by the depth, could be anything from 400 to 1,200yd.

My prime area was that in which the St Helens divers had found their alleged cannon. These were soon located and proved to be two pieces of piping which had been jettisoned from a ship. Then, in the main anchorage off Great Blasket, we located two ancient iron anchors, one of which was minus its ring. This rang a bell in my memory, and I repaired to the Spanish records for confirmation of a hypothesis that was building up in my mind, my main source of information being the journal of the Spanish admiral, Marcos de Aramburu, of the squadron of Castille. He had entered Blasket Sound in the galleon *San Juan*, close behind Admiral Juan Martinez de Recalde, and he mentions that Recalde gave him cables and an anchor, and that later Recalde and he himself had dragged anchor and the two ships had collided. Could the anchor minus its ring be Recalde's? Loss of a large anchor could have led to the gift of an anchor described by Aramburu.

The swim-line search areas extended across the sound in the general direction of the mean of the wind and the tide on 21 September 1588. Approximately midway between the main anchorage where we had found the broken-ring anchor and the forbidding reef area to the south-east, we came across more ancient wrought-iron anchors, in what would probably be the place to which both Recalde and Aramburu had dragged anchor before their ground tackle held. We appeared to be heading in the right direction. Further reading of Aramburu's log provided us with more clues:

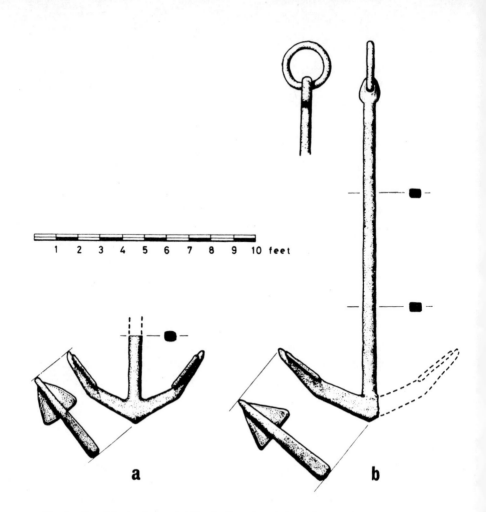

Fig 2   Spanish Anchors: A The half anchor left in Blasket Sound by Spanish
Admiral Marcos de Aramburu; B Sheet anchor of the *Santa Maria de la Rosa*
found hooked foul on Stromboli Reef

At mid day the Nao 'Santa Maria de la Rosa' of Martin de Villafranca, came
in by another entrance near the land on the North West side, and on
entering fired a shot as though seeking help, and another further on. All its
sails were in pieces except the foresail. It cast its single anchor, for it was
carrying no more, and with the tide entering from the South East and
dashing against its poop, stayed there until two o'clock. Then the tide
waned, and as it turned, the Nao began dragging on two of our splicings [a
splicing equals one cable's length, or 200 yards, hence she was dragging 400
yards away] and we with it, and in an instant we saw that it was going down,
trying to hoist its foresail. Then it sank with all on board, not a person being
saved, a most extraordinary and terrifying thing. We were dragging on it,
about to be lost ourselves, when our Lord willed that we might foul in that

place an anchor of medium stock, which Juan Martinez gave us, with a cable. We cast anchor, the Nao [*San Juan*] turned its prow, and we recovered another anchor, finding the stock with half its shank. The rest was broken, its cable scraping pebbles beneath us.

Aramburu was wrong when he stated that there were no survivors; we have seen that young Giovanni de Manona was washed ashore. Manona stated that the Spaniards, with a cry of 'Treason', killed his father Francisco de Manona, the ship's pilot, shortly after the ship struck a rock. This would tie in with Aramburu's log entry concerning the doomed vessel trying to hoist its solitary foresail. If the ship was dragging anchor and badly holed, it would make sense for the pilot or master to cut the anchor and hoist sail and try to beach the ship on nearby Coumenoole Strand to the south–east. The Spaniards, thinking that the pilot intended surrendering to the English, killed him with either sword or dagger. What of the anchor which Aramburu lost, broken in two at the shank, the strongest part of any anchor? We found the lost bottom half of that broken anchor a few days and a few swim lines later. We were definitely on the right track.

It was during this intensely exciting phase of the 1968 season that we experienced a really frightening accident which could have ended in catastrophe. That no lives were lost or physical injuries sustained must bear witness to the strict discipline and close teamwork which had become second nature to us. The incident happened on a day when diving officer John Grattan deemed the weather to be marginal: we would go out in the wind strength of Force 4, gusting 5, and search if the wind dropped, but if it increased we would call it a day and put back into Dunquin. So our two inflatable boats, with six divers in each plus helmsman, motored out of the cove into a large Atlantic swell. We ran broadside on to this, but turned our boats' prows into the weather when a particularly large wave bore down on us. Grattan's boat occasionally vanished into a trough then, seconds later, rode up on a crest way above us.

Midway across the sound all hell broke loose. Sudden squalls or 'williwaws' hit us at about 40 knots; the wind had increased to Force 6, gusting 8. It was time to head back. Grattan gave me the thumbs down sign, and we tried to turn and run for home, but it was not to be. The wave crests now began to curl over and break. There was nothing for it other than to 'butt and dodge', to keep our nose into the waves; then make a starboard turn, open the throttle and make a few yards towards the cove, which was about half a mile away; and then turn the bow of the boat into the next big sea as it towered above us. The wind screamed like a thousand Irish banshees as we struggled to the east. It was an unequal struggle and we had to give up and run south before the wind.

We were now in a fearsome trap. There was no way in which we could run athwart those seas back to Dunquin. On the other hand, running before the weather we were heading south towards the Scollage-Stromboli reef massif, which was a boiling white inferno. My divers were all in their diving suits with twin scuba sets on their backs, for we always went to sea fully kitted up to save valuable time when we arrived at the diving area. I was wearing a Royal Navy dry suit, but without mask and fins. I thought to myself that if we were capsized we could at least keep afloat, but to what purpose, for the current which would take us out into the Atlantic was by now running at about 4 knots and there was no way that we could swim ashore against that. Grattan signalled that we should head to the south-west to try to get under the lee of Great Blasket Island. I realised that he intended that we should try to beach the two boats on the island's White Strand. Every minute or so we had to put about and point our bows to the north, to take a huge wave head on; for if we were pooped and took a big green sea over the stern, the boat would be flooded and the outboard motor swamped and put out of action.

By now we were in mid-stream between the mainland and the island of Beginish, and passing over a submerged reef formation which was not shown on the charts and which we had recently discovered. Over the 'mid-point reef', huge standing waves reared their crests 20ft up into the sky. Then we were amongst the maelstrom, fighting for survival in the biggest seas I have ever experienced in a small boat. Grattan later commented that he could see a sharp pointed rock which at that state of the tide should have been 15–20ft below the surface, and the trough of the wave was about the same distance beneath the newly revealed rock. This meant that we were in amongst waves in excess of 30ft in height.

I lost sight of Grattan's boat and was wondering if he and his team of six had gone under, when an enormous wave bore down on us. I throttled back the engine of my boat and motored slowly up that enormous wave, which seemed as steep as the roof of a house. The crest was about to break, and its top was a translucent green as we mounted it. The view down the other side was both awe inspiring and exhilarating; we shot down the slope as if on a rollercoaster and then up the other side of an almost vertical wall of water. At that moment disaster struck; for the great swell, with its 'long fetch' from hundreds of miles away to the north-west, was being riven by a sudden shift in the wind blowing a sea along the crest at right angles to the direction of the waves. It looked for all the world as if we were in a huge triangle, with a mountain of water coming at us from two directions at once. I remember cresting the main swell with the bow of the boat up in the air and nothing but sky to be seen; then the sea running from the west hit us.

What happened next was all confusion. I saw the boat above instead of underneath me, as the wave flipped us upside down, overturning boat, engine and six men into the sea. The screaming of the wind suddenly ceased, and all was silent and dark green. I looked up and could see the surface coming towards me as the buoyancy in my dry suit sent me up out of that strange ethereal world. When I surfaced, I saw the boat a few feet away. By some miracle or other, after tipping us out, the boat had continued its cartwheel and had landed back in the water right side up.

One diver had remained in the boat, or half in the boat. I could see only his legs and backside, for his head and shoulders were underwater, and the weight of his twin scuba set was just about to complete his descent into the sea. A voice said, 'Grab this!' It was one of our Royal Navy divers, 'Tug' Willson, who handed to me the bow line which I grabbed and pulled myself to the bow of the boat. Other helping hands pushed me from behind as I struggled aboard. The half-submerged diver was Brian Maidment, one of my RAF team and a member of Mike Edmonds's expedition to the Roman wreck at Filicudi. I grabbed him by his scuba harness and dragged him back into the boat with an urgent 'Pull them in as they come by!' For my greatest fear now was that the inflatable boat, at the mercy of a Force 8 gale, would be sped across the surface of the sea at a much faster rate than my five now-surfaced divers could swim, with the result that we would lose contact with each other.

Another huge wave broke over us, completely flooding the boat, as I struggled with the silent outboard motor. It failed to start at the first pull on the recoil starter, and at that moment I was probably the hardest-praying devout practising atheist in Blasket Sound. At the second pull, the engine fired and sprang into life. I motored the water-logged sluggish boat up a huge crest, and then throttled back so that the wind would take me back to where my divers were in the water.

61

Maidment and I grabbed one man and literally threw him aboard. He immediately righted himself and, leaning over the side, grabbed another diver. Within a couple of minutes we were all together again, winded, breathless, but some of us grinning. Colin Martin shouted to me above the screech of the wind, 'Could you please do that again, I'm afraid I wasn't watching?' We had two plastic bailing cans tied to the boat, and both were put to use. Others bailed with their diving masks, as I turned the boat and motored before the weather, to turn again and put the bow into the next big wave. I looked to starboard and about 20yds away, Grattan was grinning at me like a Cheshire cat, from the steering position of his inflatable.

The beaching on Great Blasket Island was executed Royal Navy style. The six divers, fully kitted up, sat with legs astride the inflated tubes of both sides of the boat. I ran in under full throttle and, when in about 6ft of water, the divers slid over the side and hung on. When the wave receded, the divers were under the boat, standing on the draining beach, the boat resting on their shoulders. I sprang over the stern to take the weight of the outboard motor, and we walked ashore with the boat on our backs. Grattan followed us in, and within minutes we were seated on the beach, looking at the white inferno which was now Blasket Sound.

I looked about me. One or two faces were quite drawn; others relieved their tension by somewhat hysterical giggling. I thought to myself, 'What the hell are we doing here, risking our lives for an old Spanish *nao*?' when a solitary voice asked 'What time is it?' I replied 'It's 8.15am', to which the enquirer responded, 'Two minutes silence for all the poor bastards who are commuting into London this morning.' That broke the ice and there was a roar of laughter and a spirit of general agreement.

It took hours for the wind to drop and the seas to lessen. We spent that time exploring the now deserted village on Great Blasket. Eventually the weather improved and we made the journey back to Dunquin. All twelve of us piled into Paddy Bawn's bar in Dingle, still in our diving suits, and a few team members proposed to get drunk to celebrate their salvation from the embraces of Blasket Sound. But the day's diving was not over for all of us. One of the Dingle fishermen was down in the dumps, for in the bad weather he had somehow got his mooring chain wrapped around the propeller of his 60ft motor fishing boat. Two of my divers offered to assist, and three hours later the salvage job, volunteered and without pay, was done. I regarded such activities on our part as a public relations gesture, and an expression of our gratitude for the kindness and warm hospitality we received from the people of Dingle.

When the weather once more improved, we continued our searches towards the reef, and close to Stromboli Rock one of the team, Bryan Woodward, came across a huge anchor, more than 17ft in length. It still retained its ring but was minus one fluke, the other fluke being hooked foul on the reef. We presumed this to be the *Santa Maria de la Rosa*'s solitary anchor, and the broken off fluke would account for her dragging across the sound to the point where she struck a submerged rock close to the charted Stromboli Rock. I had previously hypothesised that the *nao* could not have struck Stromboli itself, for that rock was too deep to have been a danger to a vessel with the draught of the *Santa Maria de la Rosa*. Our detailed swim-line searches were now paying off for we discovered one deadly pinnacle of rock which reached to within 6ft of the surface. The charts were incomplete, and our discovery led to an amendment to the Admiralty Chart for Blasket Sound.

If we had located the main anchor of our ship, then surely close by there should be an anchor of medium stock left behind by Aramburu. Had he not raised a broken anchor, which we had located, and fouled the anchor which saved him from dragging onto the sinking *Santa Maria de la Rosa*? Only one more swim line was required to locate Marcos de Aramburu's missing anchor, which lay only a few yards away from the *Santa Maria de la Rosa*'s main one. Aramburu's *San Juan* had been very close to colliding with the sinking *nao* or striking the submerged pinnacles around Stromboli Rock when that medium-stock anchor held.

Taking the mean of the wind and tide once again, led us to the south side of the reef, over which we ran our swim lines diligently for more than half a mile of reef. The problem now was underwater visibility. In April and May in the northern part of the sound, we had experienced 75 to 80ft visibility. Amongst the kelp and rocks of the submerged reef, the visibility was down to 5 or 10ft. We reduced the distance between divers on the swim line, and consequently reduced the area covered on each dive. It was slow, methodical, painstaking work. By July 1968 we were a very battered and weary team, depleted in both personnel and funds. Grattan had reached the end of his leave from the Royal Navy and as we had covered the whole of Blasket Sound twice and not located the wreck, he was of the professional opinion that we had failed, and that I should fall back on my emergency plan for a search for any one of the three Spanish galleons which were wrecked on Streedagh Strand on the north-west coast of Ireland, near Sligo.

I had to leave Ireland for business reasons, mainly in search of more funds for the expedition and, placing Colin Martin in charge of the now pathetically small hard-core of six divers, advised him to make one or two more searches along the Scollage-Stromboli reef area, and then decamp for the north. No sooner had I arrived in the UK when I received a letter from Martin. Prior to opening it I presumed it was in response to my letter of two days before countermanding my previous orders, and instructing him and the team to stick it out and stay in the reef area, for that was where I now thought the wreck to be. Our letters crossed in the post. In his, he apologised for the action he was about to take in defiance of my previous orders, for he proposed to stay in Blasket Sound and continue searching the reef area. It amounted to two minds with but a single thought.

The emphasis now was on a sighting of a pile of large rocks by one of the divers on a previous swim line. Could it have been a ballast mound, with no sign of cannon, perhaps because the Spaniards had jettisoned the artillery at sea in rough weather? By now my old friend and colleague Squadron Leader Mike Edmonds had joined the expedition, boosting the number to seven. The next swim line located the pile of rocks, which proved in fact to be too large for ballast stones and of natural origin. As the swim line stopped, Edmonds, who was further down the line sank onto a long pile of stones, picked one up and chipped at it with his diving knife. An outer shell like thick black orange peel broke away, leaving an almost perfect sphere of cast iron which exuded clouds of ferrous oxide. Edmonds was holding a 7in diameter 50lb 'whole cannon' shot. The *Santa Maria de la Rosa* had welcomed on board her first visitor for 380 years, though we still had conclusively to confirm her identity.

Chapter 4

Identification of
Two Armada Flagships

What we had found on the seabed, in 100ft of water in Blasket Sound, looked nothing like what we had expected to see if we were fortunate enough to have found the *Santa Maria de la Rosa*. There was no shipwreck identifiable as such, just a long, low mound of ship's stone ballast, higher at one end than the other. The discovery could easily have been overlooked. If Edmonds had not actually settled on the pile of stones, he would probably never have given the 'stop' signal to the swim line as he swam over the barely distinguishable ballast mound. One diver, Chris Oldfield, who had by far the sharpest eyes of any of my team, admitted later that on an earlier swim line he had swum over the same mound of stones, but had ignored it, believing as indeed I did, that the first sight of the ship we were seeking would include a scattering of both bronze and iron artillery. There was no sign of artillery and no sign of a hull. Perhaps we had the remains of an old sailing ship, perhaps one as recent as the late nineteenth century. There was only one way to find out — by detailed survey of the wreck site, followed by excavation.

Four datum points were laid from which our survey began. These were situated at what we believed to be the bow and stern of the wreck site, and at approximately amidships on either side. Base lines of precise measurement were established, and a programme of survey by trilateration got under way. The northern end of the site — the supposed bow — rose up like the back of a sperm whale, the hump of which was made even higher by three huge mounds of cast-iron cannon balls. Amongst the shot and ballast stones we found two sizes of lead shot, which would fit the known bore measurements of sixteenth-century arquebuses and muskets. Amidships, we located several lead ingots, all but one of which were boat-shaped, as if the lead had been poured into moulds made by scooping out sand on a beach. There were stores' markings on the lead ingots, the largest of

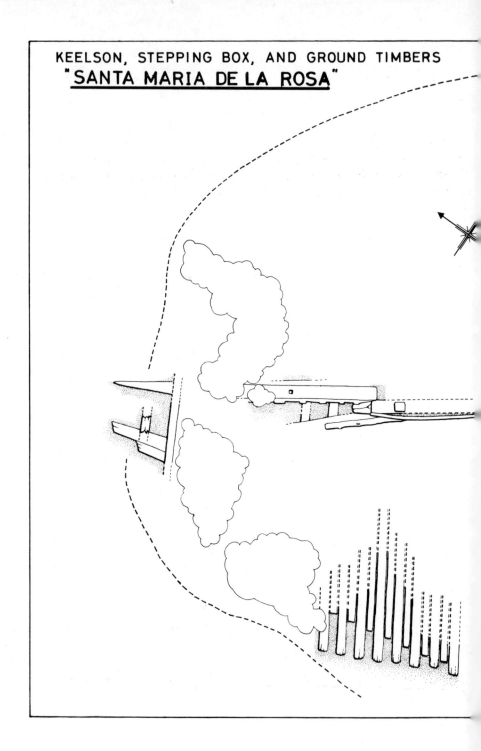

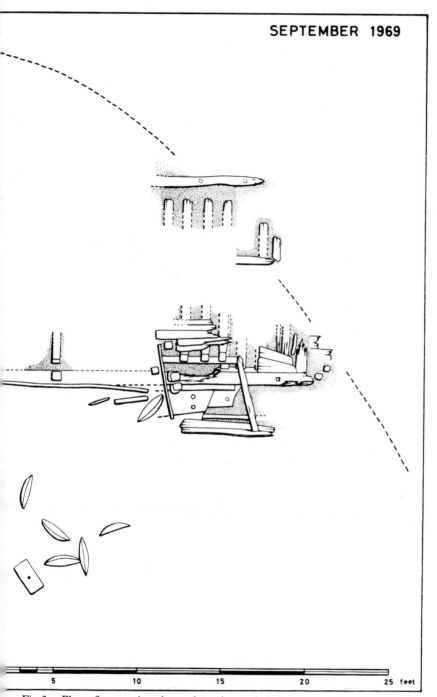

Fig 3   Plan of excavation down through wreck ballast to reach and survey the timbers of the *Santa Maria de la Rosa*

which weighed more than 300lb. There was one rectangular lead ingot with a hole in the centre.

Colin Martin, who was in charge of the survey, located barely visible rectangular timbers protruding through the centre of the ballast mound and running along the axis or spine of the wreck. Excavation highlighted that these were in fact the vertical supports for the lowest deck in a great ship of sail — the orlop deck. These deck supports would be socketed into the keelson, so down into the ballast we went and, lo and behold, we had a huge oak keelson.

Odds and ends of finds included stone Perrier shot beyond the northern end or highest part of the ballast mound. The Duke of Medina Sidonia had instructed infantrymen and their officers to accommodate themselves in the bows of the ships; we excavated just north of the wreck and came across the fragile remains of arquebuses and muskets. The Spaniards had their galleys near the forefoot of the mainmast; so Martin estimated the distance from the hump or bow of our ballast mound to where the mainmast would be situated. We excavated, and there we located typical galley debris, including brush-wood and flints for the galley fire, and a broken and crushed pewter goblet. Further digging in the galley area produced a badly crushed balance pan from a set of scales, on which the crew's rations would have been weighed. A most remarkable find, to both Martin and myself, was an almost complete Brazil nut, its kernel eaten away by marine micro-organisms which had first bored their way through one end of the shell. We found this more exciting than golden ducats or silver pieces of eight.

To the rear of the galley debris, we located the mainmast stepping box — a box of timbers so situated that it would prevent a spill of ballast over the mast block, into which the heel or foot of the mainmast would fit. The stepping box was essential if shipwrights were to have easy access for repairs to the mainmast foot area, or for stepping a new mast. There we found riders, frames, ribs, and part of the ship's keelson. The latter provided all the evidence required to establish that the ship we had located had been subjected to such damage that her last moments would have been very brief. The keelson was broken off, snapped like a carrot. In her last agonies she had broken her back.

The survey and excavation of the shipwreck was to occupy us for the remaining three months of the 1968 season and for almost six months during 1969. In that time we excavated down to the frames, spacers, ground timbers and planking on what we believed to be the port side of the bow quarter of the ship. A surface survey of artifacts on the port side of the wreck gave us the mast truck — the doughnut-shaped circular piece of timber which is situated on the very top of the mast. Our mast truck was complete with the sheave holes through which would be rove the halliards for sending up the ship's signal flags. Closer in to the wreck, we found the 'fid pin' — the great wrought-iron pin which takes the weight of the topmast as it sits atop the mainmast proper. Dr E. T. Hall, director of the Laboratory for Archaeology at Oxford University, very kindly offered the use of one of his new and highly sophisticated pulse-induction underwater metal detectors complete with operator, Jeremy Green, whose dry, almost sardonic humour, made him very popular with team members.

Green's metal-detector survey of the wreck was most revealing. At the stern, where the ballast mound curved away into a thin banana shape, he obtained a powerful signal. We excavated through the ship's ballast, and under only a few inches of ballast and sand intrusion we found the almost complete skeleton of a member of the crew. Across his chest lay a large pewter plate, badly crushed and in a poor state of preservation. On the underside of the plate there was the inscription 'A.H.'. There was also a maker's touch-mark, which we have not yet been able to decipher. Attached to the ribs of the skeleton was a spongy mass of textile material, with something solid inside it. On extraction, this item looked like a small blackened biscuit — obviously a small mass of silver sulphide. Careful cleaning exposed two coins: one a silver 4 reale piece of Philip II which had been hammered in the Mexico City mint, the other a 4 escudo gold coin of Philip II from the Seville mint. All seamen and soldiers in the Armada had received three months pay prior to the departure of the fleet from the Tagus. We had presumably discovered the body of a crewman, or more likely an officer, carrying on him part of his pay.

But how had the wretched man managed to be hidden under the ballast which lies on the ship's bottom timbers? Crewmen do not generally burrow into ballast, then lay a large pewter plate on their chests prior to covering themselves over with the same ballast stones. We can presume that the man in question was not a murder victim, hidden under the ballast by his assailant. If he were, the assailant would have assuredly taken the gold and silver coins. The only acceptable solution also fits the theory concerning the ship's broken back, and the direction in which the ballast tailed narrowly away. If our ship was indeed the *Santa Maria de la Rosa*, and she broke her back on

Stromboli Rock, she would have been under great strain as her single sheet-anchor hooked itself foul on the reef and, as suggested in the last chapter, the pilot would order the anchor cable cut, and would run under storm jib for the nearby beach. Such an attempt to beach the boat was doomed to failure, for the axis in which she lay and her distance from the reef, allied to our knowledge of the direction of wind and tide at the time she dragged onto the reef, suggest that she went down like a grand piano filled with lead shot. This is confirmed by the testimony of the survivor, young Giovanni de Manona: 'The gentlemen thinking to save themselves by the boat, it was so fast tied, they drowned.'

We hypothesised that the fast-sinking ship would have gone down hard by the bow, and that it was when the latter struck the seabed that her keel and keelson snapped and she broke her back. As she settled down onto the hard shingle, the stern half would pull away due to the enormous drag created by her towering stern castlework. As this happened, the ballast would be spilled out, resulting in the slender, slightly curved ballast tail we had found. We further postulated that the crushed skeletal remains were those of a man who had gone down with the ship; who was probably somewhere between decks, in the aft part of the vessel, and who went out of the port side and had the ballast spill over him as the stern of the wreck broke away. This theory was supported by negative evidence — an almost complete lack of artifacts in the stern area of the ballast mound.

The bow area created a sensation when Green's metal detector located two 7in diameter pewter plates. One was contained in a mass of accretions of oxide, stones, sand, seashells, etc, and looked for all the world like a blackened football, from which a wing extended on either side. Careful mechanical cleaning of this mass exposed a demi-culverin 9lb cast-iron shot; the barrel and forestock of a shoulder-held arquebus, complete with ramrod with copper tip, and charge of powder and shot in the barrel; a small religious pewter medallion of the type worn by most Roman Catholic seamen of the period, bearing a relief portrait of the Virgin on the obverse side, and Christ on the reverse; and, most important of all, the pewter plate. The cannon ball had lost nearly half of its original weight, due to migration of iron. As it had deteriorated it had exuded oxide of iron which enveloped nearby artifacts, providing us with a microcosm of life on board a 1588 Spanish Armada ship. And on the pewter campaign plate a name had been inscribed on the underside of the lip — the name was 'Matute'.

The *Mary*, royal yacht of King Charles II, wrecked on the Skerries off Anglesey in 1675

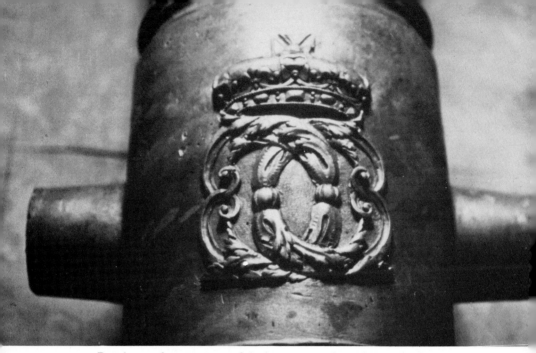

Royal coat of arms on one of the bronze guns from the wreck of the royal yacht *Mary*. Inter-twined letters 'C' for 'Carolo a Carolus' (Charles son of Charles)

Expedition personnel. Angra do Heroismo. Azores. Island of Terceira. Author seated, centre. 1972

This was an awe inspiring moment for us all. Here was history writ large, for we now had the equivalent of a piece of timber inscribed 'Santa Maria de la Rosa, registered A.1 at Lloyds of London'. Further investigations in the bow area of the wreck revealed another identical 'Matute' plate. Giovanni de Manona had stated in his several depositions that 'Matute was the captain of the infantry of that ship'. We had identified our shipwreck beyond any doubt.

Matute's position as captain of infantry disguises the true nature and dignity of his rank. Captains of infantry in the sixteenth century held a position of power far exceeding that of a captain in a modern army; the rank was more equivalent to that of a modern brigadier. His full name was Francisco Ruiz Matute, and he was captain of the Sicilian *tercios* (regiments), regarded at that time as containing the most seasoned fighting infantry in Europe. He would have been a man of quality as well as rank, and would have equipped and outfitted his men mainly from his own resources. But the famed Sicilian *tercios* who sailed under the command of their brave captain Matute on board the *Santa Maria de la Rosa*, were destined never to see battle against the land forces of Queen Elizabeth of England, nor to see their home shores again.

That same night we all met in the local Dingle hostelry where we were wont to imbibe. We charged our glasses and drank a toast to 'To Captain Matute of Philip of Spain's Armada'.

The two-year excavation of the *Santa Maria de la Rosa* solved some problems for us. It also posed several important questions. What, for instance, had happened to the ship's twenty-six pieces of artillery? Presumably they were jettisoned somewhere at sea, to lighten an already stricken, leaking vessel. The Spaniards would retain a solitary small swivel-gun for signalling, for the Duke of Medina Sidonia's instructions stated that any ship in distress should fire a gun, and if in dire distress a second gun. It will be recalled that Admiral Marcos de Aramburu told us in his journal of events in Blasket Sound that the *Santa Maria de la Rosa* 'on entering fired a shot as though seeking help, and another further on'.

Many years ago, a Blasket Island fisherman, fishing close to a reef with a trammel net, found that he had fouled it on a heavy object on the seabed. Hauling it in, he discovered that he had salvaged a small bronze swivel-gun. We can presume that the Blasket islander was fishing just to the south of Stromboli Rock, and that his net had caught on the one gun the *Santa Maria de la Rosa* had retained, for signalling purposes. We know something of what happened to this unique item of ordnance. It was taken to Clonskeigh Castle in Dublin, and lay there until the Easter Rising of 1916, when the English occupation forces, the ill-famed 'Black and Tans', were billeted in the castle. When the British flag was lowered in Dublin, and independence gained for Ireland, the Black and Tans decamped from Clonskeigh Castle and the small bronze swivel-gun vanished with them, presumably to be sold for scrap metal.

And why was the ship's ballast raised so high in the bow? The answer is simple in the extreme, but it took us a long time to figure it out. A Spanish *nao* of the period, with its very weighty castlework aft, would sit in the water with a very pronounced stern-down trim. It made sense that the ballast would be piled higher in the bow, to counteract the weight of the stern.

Why the Spaniards had failed to sink any of Queen Elizabeth's ships in 1588 was a question which increasingly puzzled me, and the 'finds' excavated during our work in Blasket Sound were all-important in reaching a solution. There was not even serious hull damage recorded on any of the English royal galleons, although the Spaniards had shot off most of their 123,000 and more rounds of ammunition. Examination of actual shot seemed a good starting point. I weighed a 50lb, 7in diameter cast-iron cannon ball; it weighed only 18lb. This caused no great surprise. As with the shot adhering to the 'Matute' plate, weight had been reduced due to migration of iron as the sea water inexorably returned the cast iron to its original chemical and mineral constituents. We turned to chemical analysis. Our close friend Peter Start of the Department of Chemistry at University College, Dublin, had tested samples of Armada shot for me and come up with the remarkable fact that the analysis showed a high percentage of sulpher, which was highly deleterious for good-quality iron shot. This analysis, carried even further, showed that the major part of the sulpher content had been introduced by the shot's 380 years immersion in sea water.

Thus the sulpher content of the Spanish Armada shot proved to be a red herring, but it served its purpose by introducing a new train of thought: was it possible that the Spanish Armada had failed not only to sink, but even to inflict hull damage on Queen Elizabeth's ships, because Spanish cast-iron cannon balls of the period were of poor quality? I had half decided to abandon any thoughts of research into what seemed quite obviously a ridiculous hypothesis, when Peter Start telephoned me from Dublin with the words, 'I think you should drive over right away and take a look at something very odd which emerged during X-ray analysis'. I wasted no time in driving the 200 miles from Dingle to Dublin. In the university's chemistry laboratory, Peter Start showed me something very peculiar indeed. On a table lay a piece of 7in diameter cast-iron shot. It was in two halves, one of which had what appeared to be a spherical raised section in the centre, about half the width of the ball, which fitted into a hollow in the centre of the other half of the ball. I commented that it looked as if somebody had popped a 3in shot inside a 7in shot, when it was being cast. Start agreed, but went further, drawing attention to the fact that there were concentric annular rings in the cast iron encircling the 3in shot, for all the world like an orange with three thick skins. He went on:

> That suggests that the Spaniards, either as general practice, or because they were casting shot in a hurry, poured water onto the mould to cool it off quickly, so that they could extract the shot and refill the mould. Those concentric rings are caused by contraction due to cold-water quenching, and would make the ball brittle.

We thought for a moment we had hit upon a solution for the ball within a ball — the Spanish shot-moulders, ordered to increase the shot allowance for the Armada by more than 50 per cent, might have used up unwanted 3in shot by dropping it into 7in diameter cannon-ball moulds. A far from satisfactory solution that proved to be, for, as Start pointed out:

> Drop a 3in ball into an empty 7in mould, and the ball drops to the bottom of the mould, where it would lie as an eccentric part of the whole. There is no way they could suspend the ball in the centre of the mould. I strongly suggest that you continue to research this question of the quality of the Spanish Armada shot.

Thus I started on a quest which was to last to this day, researching Spanish, English, Dutch, Portuguese and Italian iron-founding, and gun- and shot-casting in the sixteenth century.

With the conclusion of the second six-month season on the *Santa Maria de la Rosa* expedition, I found myself almost impoverished. Martin and I discussed demobilising the expedition, but I countered with the suggestion that we have one 'swan song' in the form of a rapid, lightweight reconnaissance up the west coast of Ireland to search for any one of half a dozen Armada wrecks recorded as being lost on the coasts of Clare, Mayo and Donegal. Without more ado Martin and I, accompanied by three others, set off towing a trailer caravan behind a van which contained all our diving gear, a small compressor and one inflatable boat.

Three sites were examined briefly but unsuccessfully; then we thought we had hit success in Broad Haven in County Mayo. Broad Haven was a lair for pirates in the sixteenth and seventeenth centuries, and at one time King James I of England had sent one of his ablest admirals, Sir William Monson, to root them out. Monson warned the local populace against further depredations against shipping, and hanged one of them to discourage the others. No sooner had Monson left Broad Haven than the acts of piracy by the local McCormick clan recommenced.

Our stay in this picturesque harbour was to last no more than four days due to the onset of the autumn equinoctial gales, but in that short time we located the wreck of a vessel armed with cast-iron cannon. Two local farmers advised us that the only shipwreck site they knew of was *Crawn Casta* — Gaelic which they interpreted as 'Twisted Masts'. The wreck allegedly lay close to Rinroe Point, so there we dived, to find it in a matter of minutes. Large lead boat-shaped ingots, similar to our Armada lead ingots, lay in a stack in only 6ft of water. Nearby, cannon lay amongst rock gullies, and the odd artifact was extracted from what seemed like pavements of iron oxide on the gully bottoms. Glass bottles and clay pipes, however, dispelled any idea that our wreck was of the Armada period. The weather broke, and we departed.

The clay pipes were identified by English clay-pipe historian Adrian Oswald as Dutch in origin, and dated about 1675. Did a Dutch ship lie there, or was she a wrecked vessel of some other nationality carrying Dutch clay pipes amongst her cargo? Or perhaps this was further evidence of the activities of the murderous McCormick clan? The mystery still remains to be solved.

The following spring of 1970, I was taking a break from editing the 16mm film I had shot of our two-seasons' work on the wreck of the *Santa Maria de la Rosa* and, sipping a cup of tea and browsing through my morning copy of the *Daily Telegraph*, I noticed that a very rare bird, the great bustard, had landed on Fair Isle, and was being recorded by a Mr Roy Dennis, warden of the bird sanctuary there. Fair Isle, lying between the Orkneys and Shetlands to the north of Scotland, was an island I had always wanted to visit, and mention of it in the newspaper touched a chord in my memory. There was a Spanish Armada flagship on Fair Isle — the *Gran Grifon*, of 650 tons and 38 guns, flagship of the squadron of *urcas*, of which Gomez de Medina was admiral.

Coincidentally, just a few days before, I had received a letter from Colin Martin in which he expressed interest in a third season of excavation on the *Santa Maria de la Rosa*, subject to availability of finance. Having already gone the long and weary road of fund raising, with little significant success, and having therefore financed the two years of effort on that vessel out of my own pocket, I was far from sanguine about funds being available for a third season of excavation other than from our own resources. I therefore suggested a light-weight, comparatively inexpensive reconnaissance to locate and survey, prior to excavation, the wreck of the *Gran Grifon*.

Martin was immediately enthusiastic. He is a true-born Scot, and the offer of wreck excavation in his home waters was one which he would not lightly turn down. He made a short reconnaissance to the island of Fair Isle, where he stayed at the bird observatory with Roy Dennis. The latter was well into local folklore, and was able to tell Martin that the local people had a legend to the effect that the *Gran Grifon* had run herself into a small cove known as Stromshelier. Martin advised me by telephone that we had a fighting chance of locating the vessel and that he strongly recommended that we try.

Our main problem was again that of finance, and we both went heavily into debt to scrape together funds for a lightweight expedition. We learned from Dennis that the Naval Air Command Sub Aqua Club (NACSAC) had enquired about the *Gran Grifon* and that their proposed expedition would be led by Commander Alan Baldwin, OBE, RN, who was known to both Martin and myself as the British forces representative on the Council for Nautical Archaeology. We contacted Baldwin and he offered us support in the shape of the eventual presence of at least a dozen NACSAC divers, along with a large naval pinnace, etc. Furthermore, Baldwin arranged that a Royal Navy aircraft, which was scheduled to fly over the area, would take photographs of Stromshelier for us.

On shoestring finance therefore Martin and I, and his non-diving brother Simon, arrived on Fair Isle. Unlike the *Santa Maria de la Rosa*

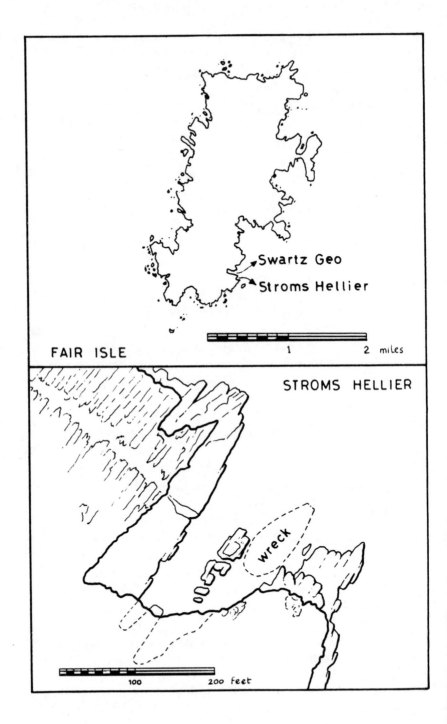

FAIR ISLE

Swartz Geo
Stroms Hellier

1   2 miles

STROMS HELLIER

wreck

100   200 feet

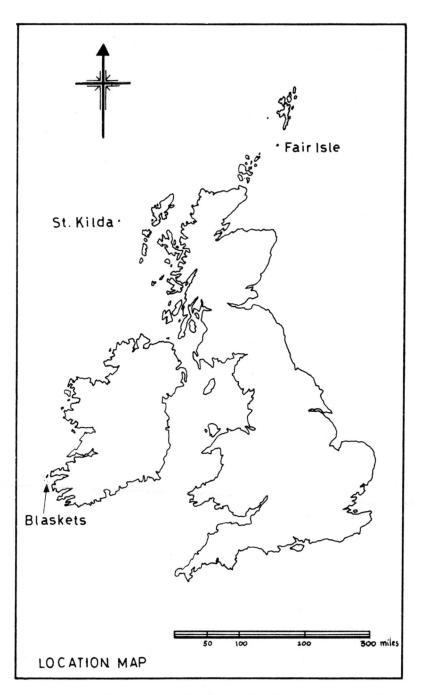

Fig 4   Location of the wreck of the *Gran Grifon*, flagship of the 1588 Spanish
Armada squadron of Urcas (Hulks), on Fair Isle

expedition, we were far from well equipped, and we were under-staffed. We would not be able to enjoy swim lines of six to a dozen divers; on the contrary, our searches would be on a solitary diver basis. We decided that if we did not find the wreck within a couple of weeks, we would not be able to justify a longer stay. Fortunately, on our third dive in Stromshelier Cove, when we had more or less exhausted the 'high probability' area of local legend, Martin surfaced with cries of excitement, for he had only settled on the seabed to adjust his diving mask and felt something sticking into his backside. On looking down, he found he was astride the muzzle of a bronze gun which was protruding at an angle from the seabed shingle.

I put on my diving gear and joined him — this 'find' being my first sight of a bronze cannon underwater. It was, in fact, of a long-barrelled culverin type known as a 'medium sacre'. Reconnoitring further into the gully, Martin located two wrought-iron 'made up' guns of a type which was already obsolescent when the Armada sailed. They were of the breech-loading type, and similar in all details to the wrought-iron guns recently raised from the Henry VIII ship, *Mary Rose*, which sank in the Solent off Spithead in 1545.

We put back to the jetty at South Landing, close to the bird observatory, and broke the news to Roy Dennis. The following day was sheet nectar and ambrosia for Martin and I, for not only were we the first men to have located two Spanish Armada vessels, but both of our discoveries were flagships.

The whole of Stromshelier now had to be searched and, while Simon Martin sat watch in our inflatable boat, Martin and I rummaged amongst the loose stones and rocks in the gullies which led to a submerged cave immediately beneath a great overhanging cliff. Three more iron guns were located, and later, several lead ingots identical to those we had discovered on the *Santa Maria de la Rosa*. The ingots, as before, were of two distinct types: one boat-shaped and the other flat and rectangular with a hole through the centre. This initial success was, however, at all times tempered by the knowledge that we were short on funds, even if high on enthusiasm. Then a valuable contribution to the team arrived in the form of Alan Bax, who had been a member of my 1968–9 expeditions, and who has since established a diving centre at a disused Ministry of Defence fort — Fort Bovisand — at Plymouth. Martin and Bax established survey base lines by the expedient of driving large iron nails into cracks on the nearby cliff face, between which the survey lines stretched. Tape measures were attached to both ends of the base line.

Another member of my 1968–9 expedition, Chris Oldfield, turned up. He was not only one of the most proficient divers I have ever met, he was also a skilled engineer with a bent towards improvisation of equipment on the spot, which might have taken several weeks to obtain through orthodox channels. Oldfield scoured the island for scrap metal, finding some on a disused World War II army camp site and, with the use of his own portable arc-welding set, manufactured a small crane on top of the cliff overlooking the wreck site. The power take-off winch of his Land Rover did the rest, and items up to 300lb in weight, such as lead ingots, were winched up the overhanging cliffs directly from their resting place on the wreck of the *Gran Grifon*.

There was no sign of anchors on the wreck, bearing out the Spanish archives which stated that the *Gran Grifon* jettisoned all her anchors at Calais when the English sent in their fire ships. She had managed to round the north coast of both Scotland and Ireland, whereupon an adverse westerly wind had blown her back on her tracks. With both pumps out of commission, and herself slowly sinking, the *Gran Grifon* came in sight of Fair Isle. Without anchors, the only salvation left to the ship's commander and crew was to beach the vessel. Beaches are hard to find on Fair Isle, and once the ship got under the lee of the island and out of the force of the gale, the decision must have been taken that, on a southward tack, close inshore, the ship could be run into nearby Stromshelier Cove. The Spaniards ran the vessel so far in that her bow must have gone under the overhanging cliff, into a cave entrance where I had come across one of her cast-iron bow chase-guns. There were no casualties, for the Spaniards managed to climb the ship's mast and edge along the spars onto the cliff top. The safe management of the ship into that narrow cove must have been a superb piece of seamanship on the part of the pilot.

I made two trips to Fair Isle during the 1970 season, while Colin Martin, his brother Simon and Chris Oldfield stayed for several months. At mid-season they were joined by Commander Alan Baldwin and his Naval Air Command Sub Aqua Club team, who put in a great many hours at the bottom of the air-lift suction pump, extracting tons of sand and shingle from the site. I managed to complete my third season of 16mm film-making of both the *Santa Maria de la Rosa* and the *Gran Grifon*, the finished product eventually being screened by the BBC on their *Chronicle* programme with the title 'Why the Armada was Beaten'. The title of the film referred to my hypothesis concern-

81

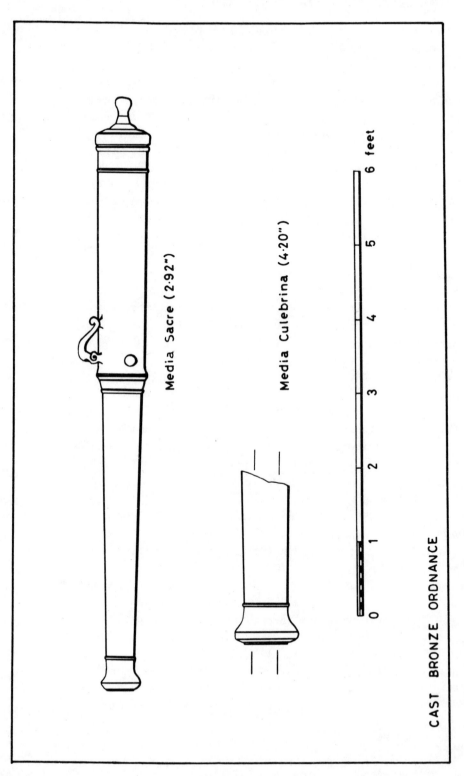

Media Sacre (2·92")

Media Culebrina (4·20")

CAST BRONZE ORDNANCE

0 1 2 3 4 5 6 feet

Fig 5   Bronze guns of the *Gran Grifon*

ing the poor quality of Spanish shot, which I believed was instrumental in the failure of the Armada to inflict any hull damage whatsoever on Queen Elizabeth's royal galleons. The film title was chosen by the BBC and not by me, for I do not believe that the Spanish Armada was defeated in battle.

Martin carried on to establish the St Andrews Institute of Maritime Archaeology at the University of St Andrews, of which he is director. I engrossed myself in the dual tasks of adding to my list of archival material supporting my contention about poor quality Spanish shot, and planning and organising a major expedition to the Portuguese Azores islands in mid-Atlantic, where I hoped to find Drake's former flagship *Revenge*. In the meantime, following Peter Start's surprising discovery, the British Steel Corporation was analysing samples of iron shot from both the *Santa Maria de la Rosa* and the *Gran Grifon* with quite startling results, as will be seen in the next chapter.

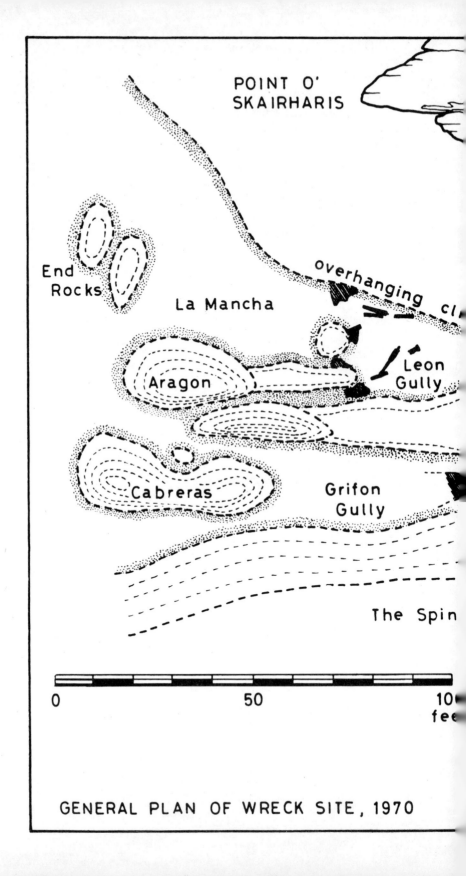

POINT O' SKAIRHARIS

overhanging cl

End Rocks

La Mancha

Leon Gully

Aragon

Cabreras

Grifon Gully

The Spin

0   50   10
                       fee

GENERAL PLAN OF WRECK SITE, 1970

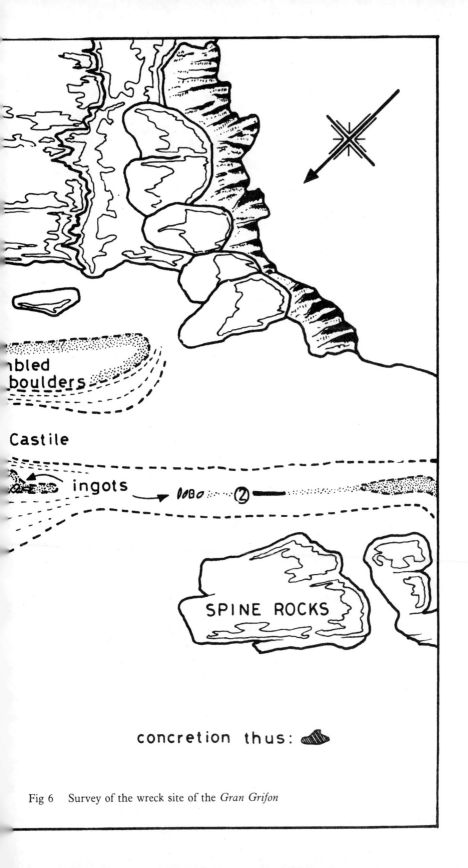

bled
boulders

Castile

ingots ──▶ ²

SPINE ROCKS

concretion thus:

Fig 6   Survey of the wreck site of the *Gran Grifon*

Chapter 5

Why the Armada Failed

Artillery and Shot

General Considerations

The more I pursued my research into the Battle of the Narrow Seas, the more I suspected that all was not well with regard to the generally accepted reasons for the Spaniards' failure. We know that in the earlier part of the battle, the range was open and no serious damage was done to either side.[1] But off Gravelines both sides were presented with an opportunity to force the battle to a conclusion; yet neither side was able to do so, although the battle raged for five hours, ending at point-blank range — no more than a hundred yards. This is confirmed by the testimony of Sir William Wynter on the English side,[2] and purser (paymaster) Calderon on the Spanish.[3] We also know that by this time the Spaniards had expended the greater part of their 123,790 rounds of shot, ships in the thick of the fighting being completely out of ammunition, and those with shot still in their lockers unable to transfer to those in need of replenishment because of the harassing gunfire of the English. But if the Spaniards had fired off what they believed to be sufficient shot for five days, the English were also desperate, for Drake, in a letter to the Council dated March 1588, stated that the queen's fleet would be entering battle with powder and shot for only one and a half days' fighting.[4]

The Spaniards had one advantage over the English in the field of ballistics. All their gunpowder was of the high-quality 'fine corned' or pistol-quality type,[5] whereas most of the English was of the inferior 'Serpentine' variety, which had a much lower maximum pressure when ignited and produced, therefore, a much lower muzzle velocity. This superiority should have been important when one remembers that, as argued early in Chapter 2 when dealing with the tactics by which the Battle of the Narrow Seas was likely to be fought, both sides had guns of similar calibre. Could it be that, for some reason, the Spanish 30lb demi-cannon and 18lb culverin shot, when fired at point-blank range, were ineffective against the sides of well-built English oak ships?

Proof that thick oak planks were no protection from good quality cast-iron shot, fired at point-blank range, was evidenced in a series of tests carried out at the English Royal Artillery headquarters at Woolwich Arsenal in 1651 by Professor John Greaves;[6] at which time there had been no improvement in either smooth-bore artillery or propellent powder. Iron shot, ranging from 32lb demi-cannon down to 9lb demi-culverin, was fired at point-blank range at butts of oak and elm. Three butts were set up, each 19in thick. The distance between butts 1 and 2 was 42ft, and between 2 and 3 it was 24ft. Nearly all the shots fired burst through butts 1 and 2 and struck butt 3, and in every instance the powder charge was less than that used by both the English and the Spaniards in 1588.

Further confirmation of the remarkable degree of shot penetration through ships' timbers is borne out by the fact that during the Napoleonic Wars vessels of the Royal Navy, when 'doubling' (attacking a French ship from both sides), were instructed to reduce the powder charge by 50 per cent. It had been learned by experience that a 32lb ball propelled by a full charge of powder could smash through one side of an enemy vessel, mow down men at their guns, and then smash through the far side of the enemy ship, to effect damage on an English ship 'doubling' on the other side of the enemy.

Armed with this information my initial reaction, when studying English, Spanish, Dutch and Portuguese archives, was that past historians had committed the sin of looking at history from a subjective, not an objective, point of view. The English were victims of their own propaganda, referring constantly to the 'defeat of the Spanish Armada' when it was plain that the battle was fought almost to a draw, and that the Spanish fleet was almost entirely intact and well disciplined at the end of the final engagement. The Dutch Sea Beggars in fact claimed the victory was theirs, due to their pillage of the *San Mateo* and *San Felipe* at Flushing, and to Admiral Justinus of Nassau's success in making sure that Parma could not transport troops across the shallow inshore waters to the waiting Armada. The Spaniards, true to their motto of honour in defeat, were content to draw attention to the valiant way that their men and ships had fought, without apparently questioning the alleged defeat, or seeking reasons for their failure to hurt the English galleons severely. Historians, too, are prepared to state that Portuguese carracks were the largest and best built in the world, Spanish galleons the least handy, and English ships the fastest and most manoeuvrable; that there are good and bad guns and good and bad gunners, and good or poor powder. Why then have they seemed to assume that all cast-iron shot is of the same quality? The British Steel Corporation's laboratory analysis of shot from the *Santa Maria de la Rosa* and the *Gran Grifon* showed that this was far from the case; it told two distinct stories. All samples from the former confirmed Peter Start's theory, that her shot had been quenched in cold water in order to cool off the shot and/or the mould to speed up production. It was therefore brittle. Some samples from the *Gran Grifon*, however, had not been quenched; that shot was of far better quality.

One can advance a reason for this important difference. Both ships we had excavated sailed from the Tagus in Portugal, but both ships were not of the same country. The *Santa Maria de la Rosa* was a Spanish ship launched only a year before the Armada, in Santander. She presumably had taken on her cast-iron shot in Spain. The *Gran Grifon* was a German vessel, on charter to Philip II, and hailed from Rostock on the Baltic coast.[7] As she was already armed with artillery when she left Rostock, she would presumably be carrying cast-iron shot moulded in Germany. This we might reasonably assume was the unquenched shot. In Portugal, the Duke of Medina Sidonia, unhappy with the artillery complement of some of his charges, ordered that bronze guns be cast in Lisbon, to be added to the gun-lists of under-armed ships. The *Gran Grifon* was one such vessel; she took on several pieces of newly cast Portuguese bronze artillery. But now she would suffer from lack of shot, which problem would be overcome by adding Spanish or Portuguese made cast-iron shot to her arsenal — the quenched shot.

We have seen that the duke, shortly before the Armada sailed, was far from happy with the amount of shot available for his fleet's guns. He had pleaded with the king to have the total shot increased from 70,000 to 123,790 rounds. If we average out the Spanish shot weight at about 10lb per ball, we arrive at a total of approximately 240 tons of shot which had to be cast in an inordinately short period of time. The two main foundries at Malaga and Medina del Campo could not have coped with such an order, and taking into account the time needed for the royal command to go out to smaller iron-founders, facilities were so inadequate that new blast furnaces would have had to be erected and lined with bricks.

The end of a hard day's 'swim line' searches of the reefs in the Bay of Vila Nova.
On the left, Signe Klepp, laboratory conservationist at the Oslo Maritime Museum.
In the foreground, John 'Mango' Chetham, and in the background, Joe Vaudrey

A 15ft bronze culverin cast in 1545 by Portuguese royal gun founder Joao Diaz,
located and raised by the author's expedition and donated to the Azores Regional
Museum

Spanish wreck *circa* 1608 off the island of Terceira in the Azores. The diver in the foreground is using a metal detector while the diver in background is measuring a cast-iron cannon

After lighting the charcoal fires a period of no less than three weeks had to elapse before the blast furnace reached the critical temperature, below which it would not be possible to smelt the ore into good quality iron. When the ore had been smelted and the molten iron run into cannon-ball moulds, then cooled, the shot was ready for transportation, which involved carrying it laboriously to the nearest port and thence by sea to the Tagus. Yet the entire production run of 54,000 rounds of shot must have been completed in much less than eight weeks. This would suggest that Spain, a country unable to cast more than 300 tons of iron in any given year, against England's 1,000 tons,[8] was suddenly able to increase production at a rate equal to just over 1,500 tons a year. A seeming impossibility, unless some crafty trick was used to increase the quantity of cast iron, at the expense of quality. Which brings us to an examination of the state of the metal industries in Spain and England, bearing in mind that iron shot was cast by the same foundrymen who cast artillery. Also that, in the early sixteenth century, bronze guns were most in favour and cast-iron ordnance was looked upon with a jaundiced eye. The cast-iron pieces often blew up under proof testing, and any cast-iron gun which stood a proof test was usually of such enormous weight it was unsuitable for shipboard use.

Spanish and English Iron and Bronze Founding
Before dealing with the actual technicalities of manufacture, we must look at the economic and political background against which the Spanish and English foundries existed. Spain's entry into the field of colonial expansion in the 1500s found her with practically no capacity for smelting and casting good quality iron; a state of affairs that was to last well into the seventeenth century. Attempts to establish foundries for gun making were a dismal failure. Medina del Campo was one of Spain's great commercial centres and boasted the largest iron-foundry in the country, but by the middle of the sixteenth century it had fallen into decline. The other large foundry, at Malaga, produced iron of such poor quality that its production fell to almost nothing by 1590.[9]

Philip II, however, had within the boundaries of his various kingdoms some of the finest ordnance founders in Europe, the quality of whose work was second only to that of the English. But none of these master gunfounders lived in the Iberian peninsula and consequently whenever Philip required bronze artillery he was forced to order either from Italy, the Low Countries or, so long as the political situation was favourable, from England. The gunfounders in the Low Countries benefitted most from the steady stream of orders for both bronze and iron guns which were issued from Spain, and they kept the industry in their own country. Predominantly Protestant, they avoided service in Spain owing to their fear of the Inquisition, and only rarely could be tempted, by high wages, to transfer their activities.[10] This by itself might not have prevented the growth of a first-class indigenous Spanish gunfounding industry but the impoverished nature of Spanish iron-founding was linked to Spain's unstable economy. The problem was that there was no commercially minded middle-class in Spain in the sixteenth century. Entrepreneurs did not exist, and gentleman dons woud never involve themselves in anything so demeaning as industry and technology. There was one major cause for this state of affairs — the wealth flowing in from the Americas. The fleets sailing from Panama and Mexico, with the king of Spain's royal fifth of all gold, silver and precious stones mined in the Indies, provided the kingdom with the means to run its internal affairs, prosecute wars with France, engage in colonial expansion and send a huge army to Flanders to try to suppress Philip's rebellious subjects there. But this meant that this enormous wealth was all bespoke in advance, with the result that Philip was to be declared bankrupt three times in his lifetime. At the height of the revolt in the Netherlands, Philip's agents at the Casa de Contratacion in Seville, the regulating house which administered trade with the Indies, were confiscating all private treasure as it came ashore from the plate-fleet galleons, and the indignant merchants were issued with bills of credit at a low interest rate. That the wealth that poured in was quickly spent abroad, is evidenced by the words of the Venetian Ambassador Vendramin: 'This gold that comes from the Indies does on Spain as rain does on a roof; it pours on her and flows away.'[11]

Opposite economic factors brought about the rapid development of both bronze- and iron-founding in England. Henry VIII rapidly dissipated the fortune left to him by his father; as is confirmed by the continental gunfounder Poppenruyter, who cast bronze guns for him and was unable to obtain payment for them.[12] But war with the French forced the almost bankrupt Henry VIII to turn to home industry. The French gunfounder Peter Baude was sent to the Weald of Sussex, the centre of English iron-founding, and there he instructed the master iron-founder Ralph Hogge in the craft of casting ordnance. Hogge cast England's first cast-iron gun in 1543, and

England quickly became noted for the quality of its artillery.[13]

On the contrary, it was not until about 1622 that Spain for the first time was able to produce good quality cast-iron guns and shot.[14] This seems to have been due to the activities of a Dutchman, Jan Andries Moerbeck, who applied to the States General in the Netherlands for a patent to 'cast guns from ore imported from England'. The fact that Moerbeck applied for a 25-year exclusive patent proved that he had discovered something quite new and revolutionary in the gunfounder's craft; presumably he had stumbled on the importance of the tiny grey fossilised seashells present in the English iron ore. In the year 1619 he was granted a 12-year patent.[15] But Moerbeck, employing craftsmen and labourers on a casual basis, would not be able to keep his secret for long. The new technique for establishing good 'grey iron' by precisely monitoring the fluxing stage must have spread throughout Europe. In 1630 a Spanish gunfoundry at Lierganes, near Santander, operated by Germans, was producing first-quality cast-iron guns and shot.[16]

The length to which Philip of Spain had to go to obtain artillery, is illustrated by the following examples. In 1574, the Spaniards, in desperation to obtain good quality iron guns and shot, tried to purchase thirty-eight guns from England, for use in the Netherlands. Queen Elizabeth, supporter of the Low Countries, immediately placed a ban on the export of guns from the realm. The Spanish governor of the Netherlands then turned to the gunfounders of Liège. One of the most prominent of these was Wathier Godefrin, who in 1575 undertook to cast 300 guns and 46,000 rounds of iron shot. Godefrin's guns and shot were delivered on time and all 300 cast-iron guns burst at the breech when subjected to proof test.[17] Godefrin was thrown into prison, his guns were thrown onto the scrap heap — and presumably his 46,000 rounds of cast-iron shot, untested, were taken into Spain's arsenals.

In that same year Spain attempted to correct a situation regarding her workforce which was deteriorating rapidly, and which as early as 1557 was summed up by the Venetian Badoer as: 'I do not think there is another country less provided with skilled workers than Spain.'[18] Spanish emissaries toured the Netherlands bearing offers of high wages and substantial bonuses to any iron-founder who would transfer his skills to Spain. When the mainly Protestant Flemish gunfounders declined the offers, Philip reacted by offering throughout Europe the panic price of £20 a ton for cast-iron guns — double the going rate.

Such high prices brought the inevitable consequence of illicit trade, and in 1587 disloyal English merchants smuggled, from Bristol to Naples, 140 fine English cast-bronze culverins.[19]

In 1603, fifteen years after the Armada failure, a number of Flemish gunfounders did set up industry in Spain at the Crown's expense. The quality of all their products was so poor that the scheme was abandoned with heavy financial loss.[20]

Having sketched the background, we can now turn to actual methods. The Spaniards were influenced by the Italians who brought to Spain their technology, such as it was. The Italians were noted for the beautiful and decorative designs on their cast-bronze guns; the quality of all their work did not, however, quite equal their artistic achievements. Their system for casting iron guns and iron shot is described by Biringuccio in his book *The Pirotechnica*, his recipe for iron shot being most revealing:[21]

> Nearby, have the iron ready for melting. See that you have some of that crude corrupted kind that has been sent through the furnace in order to purify it of earthiness, or some of those old rusty bits of scrap iron.

It is plain from the above that Biringuccio, the master, was of the opinion that high quality was not essential when casting iron shot. A gun was there for all to see, to admire and to comment on. A cast-iron shot, once fired from the barrel of a gun, was never seen again.

It was otherwise in England. As already mentioned, Hogge cast England's first cast-iron gun in 1543, but years of iron-founding in a small way had long before taught craftsmen like Hogge the undesirability of quenching hot cast iron. The English also had a natural accident acting as their ally in good quality smelting and casting processes — an accident which was not appreciated by the English themselves nor by England's Spanish and continental rivals. It consisted of masses of tiny fossilised seashells in the ore, known in the iron-smelting trade as 'greys'; their presence providing the 'flux' that was necessary to extract the maximum quantity of slag from the smelting ore.[22] Thus the term 'grey iron' for good quality cast iron came into use, and is still a common expression in the iron industry to this day. It was described thus: 'Always a fine, genuine, good sort of metal; possessed of every good quality that can be desired.'[23]

The question of the correct flux is of vital importance as regards the quality of Spanish shot. If Spanish shot was poor in quality, how did this come about? A mass of circumstantial evidence suggests that the

Spaniards, having available good quality haematite ore of low sulphur content, must have failed somehow in the smelting, fluxing and the moulding of their cast iron. Iron ore smelted without a fluxing agent was rich in slag and produced a very brittle cast iron which was known in the trade as 'cold short'.[24] It is probable that a great deal of Spain's cast-iron production in the sixteenth century came under this heading, due to either inadequate use of a fluxing agent such as limestone, or not using one at all.

A further improvement was obtained by 'fining' or 'refining' the molten iron as it was smelted, or reheating and fining after smelting. This included the removal of all impurities and dross at the liquid stage. It was learned in England as early as 1496 that it was essential that iron intended for the casting of shot be refined before it was despatched to the shot-moulder, otherwise the unrefined iron, containing many impurities, might produce a poor, brittle shot.[25]

To see what would happen if poor quality cast-iron shot was fired from a smooth-bore muzzle-loading gun, two factors have to be taken into consideration. One is the relative acceleration of the shot due to the action of the propellent forces in the gun barrel — the 'fine corned black powder', which has a high maximum pressure (P Max) initially, and which falls off by 50 per cent before the ball has travelled a distance greater than $1\frac{1}{2}$ times its diameter. The other is deceleration created by the 2ft thick oak side of the ship against which the shot strikes. The high P Max black powder would strike the ball a much harder blow than modern nitrocellulose propellants such as cordite, this massive blow sustained by the shot being to some extent alleviated by the fact that the propellent force is distributed more or less evenly over half the surface of the shot. Nevertheless, if the shot was of poor and brittle quality, its structural integrity might be weakened, for on striking the target the decelerating forces are concentrated over such a small area. From this it seems possible that a badly smelted and moulded cast-iron shot might be so weakened by the massive blow imparted by the fine corned powder propellant, that it would completely disintegrate on hitting the target. There was no magic formula that the English used to cast good 'grey iron', which was the envy of all their competitors. All the practices of the English sixteenth-century iron-founders of the Weald of Sussex are known to us. They weathered their ore out in the open, so that rain could wash out impurities; it was then crushed and washed again. The smelting was, as previously explained, fluxed to a high degree through the presence in the ore of the tiny seashells called 'greys'. All this produced iron free from slag. After smelting, the iron was refined several times by re-heating, and the surface dross and other impurities removed. Then, prior to casting, the gun- and shot-moulds were dried and warmed, with casting carried out at as even a temperature as possible. Cooling of cast-iron objects took place gradually; quenching was avoided, because it made cast iron brittle.

In 1970, Dr W. H. F. Tickle of the British Steel Corporation's ironworks at Shotton in north Wales, asked me for samples of shot from both the *Santa Maria de la Rosa* and the *Gran Grifon*, which he proposed to subject both to X-ray treatment and laboratory analysis. Dr Tickle, a highly respected metallurgist, completed the analysis in late 1970 and a précis of his findings follows. Referring first to the 7in bore whole-cannon shot and 5¼in culverin shot from the *Santa Maria de la Rosa*, he stated:

> Both samples of Spanish shot showed a high graphitic structure. It might be argued that, due to imperfect reduction in the original manufacturing process, ferrous oxide had rehydrated through centuries of immersion in the sea, to furnish the structure examined. This is most improbable even if it is thermodynamically possible. What is more likely is that crushed haematite ore was thrown into the molten iron, making a mush which was finally formed by mould into a cannon ball. This would aid the rate of production but produce an inferior product.

The full implication of Dr Tickle's hypothesis becomes plain when we examine the system used for casting shot. The process of smelting iron is known as a 'campaign', and once the blast furnace is up to temperature, the iron-founders try to keep the campaign in operation as long as possible. Once the campaign has been 'opened' and molten iron run off, there is a consequent drop in furnace temperature which, if continued for too long a period, reaches a point when smelting becomes impossible and the founders are forced to strip out any smelted iron and the unsmelted ore, and start anew. In the sixteenth century, the average time for a blast furnace to reach critical temperature was about three weeks. Consequently, iron-founders sought contracts to cast iron cannon, which needed only brief opening up of the campaign in order to pour the molten iron into the cannon-mould. Shot-founding contracts were far from popular because the campaign had to be opened repeatedly to pour out molten iron into individual shot-moulds. Production rates were low, and attempts to extend production on any given day could reduce the furnace temperature below the critical point, and the entire process of stripping and recommencing would have to be gone through, with a three-week loss of production.

Regarding the whole-cannon shot which appeared to have a smaller shot concealed in its centre (see page 18), Dr Tickle confirmed what Peter Start and I had suspected; there was simply no way that dropping an unwanted 3in ball into a mould would encase it in molten iron so that it lay in the centre of a 7in shot. But Dr Tickle also had the answer to our problem. 'In all probability,' he said, 'the shot-founders, having mixed crushed haematite ore in with their molten iron, would run some of the "mix" into the bottom half of the mould, place the 3in shot on top in about a dead centre position, place the top half of the mould onto the bottom half, and then pour in the molten "porridge mix".' A simple solution for the problem in hand. Neither of us is suggesting that the Spanish shot-moulders acted in a deliberately dishonest manner. Iron shots were iron shots, no matter how you produced them. They looked alike, fitted into the muzzle of a gun nicely, and when subjected to the propellent gas from burning black powder, they flew out of the end of the gun. What more could any gunner want?

That continental shot-founders knew that their product was unsatisfactory, seems clear from reading Biringuccio. It will be remembered that he advised adding 'old bits of rusty scrap iron' to the melt for cast-iron shot. In another paragraph, however, he refers to the wrought-iron shot forged for muskets and arquebuses: 'They are much better than those cast in moulds, and furthermore, they are not brittle because they are made of good soft iron without the corruption of anything malignant to its nature.'

Official Spanish records also bear witness to unsatisfactory shot. In the Archives General in Valladolid lie the list of Armada ships, their guns, sketches of gun carriages, and list of various sizes of shot and the shot weights. All the weights listed are too light for any given shot, and the answer is again to be found in Dr Tickle's analysis and comments that if crushed but unsmelted ore was mixed with molten iron, the resulting shot would be lighter in weight than a cannon ball cast from pure smelted iron.

With England it was different. There could be no doubt in anyone's mind in the sixteenth century, that English cast-iron cannon (and presumably shot also) was superior to that produced in Spain,

Portugal or the Netherlands.[26] By 1628, when the English gunfounder John Browne was able to cast an iron gun lighter than a bronze gun, but which withstood double the normal proof charge of powder, England had led the field in the production of good quality cast iron for nearly eighty years. The proof is still available, for there are in existence today culverins and whole-cannon cast in iron by English gunfounders in the sixteenth century.[27]

Shot Damage to English Galleons
There still remain two other sources of historical information which might prove or disprove the poor quality of Spanish shot. The first is the English state records, the relevant document being the report on the survey of the Navy completed on 28 September 1588, and supervised by the two ablest naval architects of their day, Peter Pett and Mathew Baker.[28] Pett and Baker's survey referred to 'All such ships as were at Chatham, at this instant 28th of September 1588', the rest of the queen's ships were at sea, guarding the entrance to the channel, allowing respite for those vessels in need of repair, the extent of which will show conclusively how much damage Queen Elizabeth's royal galleons suffered during the final point-blank range engagement off Gravelines.

Elizabeth Jonas   In a decayed state, knees to be replaced, and bottom caulked.
Triumph   Decayed timber, needs strengthening and two cracked deck beams replaced.
White Bear   Decayed timbers and new masts.
Victory (Sir John Hawkins's ship)   New bowsprit, mizzen mast and boat. (Small boats were towed astern and cast adrift at the commencement of a sea battle.)
Ark Royal (carrying Lord Howard of Effingham's flag)   New boat and new pinnace, replacement of one cracked deck beam, and caulking.
Hope   Decayed, mainmast rotten, new boat and pinnace.
Elizabeth Bonaventure   Rotten under her sheathing, stern post, fashion piece and rudder much decayed. New bowsprit needed.
Mary Rose   Very leaky due to imperfections in her timbers; decayed stem and stern posts. Mainmast decayed, boat and pinnace need repair.

Revenge (Drake's flagship) New mainmast, her existing one 'decayed
  and perished by shot'. Needs new capstan, boat and pinnace.
And many other vessels were on the list, none of which had been
damaged in the battle.

The striking fact emerging from the above list is that the *Revenge* was
the only ship surveyed which had suffered shot damage. To account
for this it has been suggested by some writers that all shot-holes could
be plugged or repaired immediately after the battle by on-board
carpenters and shipwrights. But this is just not possible. Take away a
ship's outer planking and a huge skeleton of ribs and frames, and deck
beams supported by hanging and standing knees, is revealed. A point-
blank range cast-iron shot, would just as easily bore through a plank
and shatter a frame or a knee as it could dismount a gun; but the
September 1588 report on the state of the queen's ships made no
mention of frames spoiled by shot, or of damage to gun carriages. The
original survey records are there for all to examine, in the Public
Record Office in London. The *Revenge*'s mainmast is the only piece of
timber recorded as damaged by shot; all other references to unsound
timber refer to decay and rottenness. State papers cannot lie; the queen
of England's galleons sustained no hull damage during the Battle of
the Narrow Seas.

The second source concerns the affairs of that great Elizabethan
seaman, Treasurer to the Navy, and loyal subject to the queen, John
Hawkins of Plymouth. In a letter to the Lord High Treasurer of
England, dated 13 November 1587, only eight months before the
battle at Gravelines took place, Hawkins lists the work he has had
done for the better condition of the queen's ships. Only four required
repair above and beyond the resources of the 'ordinary warrant'
(ordinary annual account): the *Elizabeth Bonaventure*, the *Foresight*,
the *Lion* and the *Nonpareil*. The cost of putting them in order was
£4,600 above the ordinary annual refit warrant of £5,714. Hawkins
declared, 'For all which service £40,000 would hardly perform.'[29]
What Hawkins was saying was that for a total expenditure of £10,314,
he had put the queen's fleet in a state of readiness which could hardly
be performed for £40,000. He was no doubt making an oblique
criticism of his dishonest and fraudulent predecessors.

If it cost £5,714 annually to keep in good fettle the queen's entire
fleet, we might expect to see that sum substantially inflated if the fleet
suffered any extensive repairable damage in the channel fight. Such is

not the case, as John Hawkins's accounts for the repair and refit of Queen Elizabeth's entire fleet, dated 23 November 1588, show:[30]

> An estimate of such charges as are already, and will be expended upon Her Majesty's ships within one quarter of the year, begun on the first of October last, and to end the last of December next, over and above that, which the ordinary [account of £5,714] will bear.
>
> For wages, victualling and lodging of a hundred extra shipwrights and caulkers (over and above those which are in work and borne upon the ordinary), working on Her Majesty's ships by the space of 13 weeks, £650.
> For timber, board, plank, iron work, pytche, tarre, tallow, brimstone, resin, okam, reed etc, over and above what the ordinary will bear, £400.
> For the sea store of all Her Majesty's ships on the Narrow Seas, and for the *Antelope* and the *Achates*, appointed presently to be set forth, within this quarter to end at Christmas next, £250.

The estimate of charges was signed by Sir John Hawkins and countersigned by Sir William Wynter, William Gostock and William Borough.

The total cost to the queen, in excess of the annual ordinary account for refit of £5,714, was only £1,300, and this for repair and refit of an entire fleet which had been engaged for several days in a long running fight with the Spaniards up the channel, culminating in a four-hour point-blank gunnery duel off Gravelines, when the range had been down to no more than 100yd.

Anchors

It is not difficult to prove that Spanish wrought-iron anchors of the period were of poor quality. For instance the Netherlanders, as subjects of Philip of Spain, sailed in their thousands in Spanish ships; and it was they who invented the nautical expression 'as meagre as a Spanish anchor'.

Positive identification of several Armada anchors in recent years has provided the physical evidence. During my expedition's search of Blasket Sound, for instance, we located one of Admiral Marcos de Aramburu's anchors, broken in half in the middle of the shank — the strongest part of any anchor. On Stromboli Reef we located the main 'sheet' anchor of the *Santa Maria de la Rosa*, which had one fluke and arm broken off.

It has been suggested that the expression 'as meagre as a Spanish anchor' referred to thin or light construction.[31] The construction of the Aramburu and *Santa Maria de la Rosa* anchors belies this. The anchor of the latter even had its ring intact, although this, being the weakest part of an anchor, should be the first part to break. The next part to break away would be the tip of a fluke or an entire fluke. A well-forged anchor would not break asunder at the crown.

When Robert Stenuit excavated the Armada galleass *Gerona* in Ulster in 1968–9, he located an anchor which had one fluke and arm broken off. Colin Martin's excavation of the Armada ship *Trinidad Valencera* in Kinegoe Bay in 1973 found another with the same damage. In 1972 my expedition to the Spanish plate anchorage off the town of Angra in the Azores located nearly a score of ancient anchors in the roadstead, and many of these were devoid of either a fluke, or fluke and arm. My 1975 expedition surveyed the outer anchorage of the Spanish treasure-embarkation harbour at Porto Bello, Panama, and the story was repeated.

Bronze Artillery — Physical Evidence

If the Spanish cast-iron guns and wrought-iron anchors were inferior to English ones, perhaps this applied also to the bronze artillery cast for Philip II. In fact that seems to have been the case. In 1968, during a break from diving in search of the *Santa Maria de la Rosa*, brought about by bad weather, our expedition visited the site of the Spanish-Papal invasion force of 1580, at Smerwick Harbour on the Dingle peninsula. A survey was undertaken on the spit of land on which the Spaniards had sited their artillery, and Jeremy Green meticulously investigated dozens of metal-detector readings, all of which produced evidence of the Spanish occupation force.[32] A piece of history needed to be rewritten when we located the breech of a Spanish bronze culverin which, badly flawed, had burst on firing. The English claimed to have dismounted a Spanish gun by culverin shot!

In 1970, when Colin Martin and I located the *Gran Grifon* off Fair Isle, one of the finds consisted of the broken-off end of the muzzle of a bronze culverin of a bore of 4½in. The bore of the piece was well out of true; the bore kernel or tube having been fitted out of centre when the gun was cast.[33]

Standard of Gunnery

The standard and practice of gunnery during the 1500s, as related to the small damage usually inflicted on English vessels, has received less than adequate attention. Camden, writing in the sixteenth century, asserted that the Spanish ships were so high out of the water that their cannon shot flew over the tops of the English decks. This is patently absurd. The Spanish ships were only a little higher out of the water than the English vessels where it mattered most — on the lower gun-deck in the waist of the ship. Frobisher's *Triumph* at 1,000 tons was larger than most of the Spanish ships, and we know that he 'mixed it' close in with the Spaniards on more than one occasion; and yet he suffered no damage. The fable of the alleged huge size of the Spanish galleons was due to the very high castlework they carried in the stern, and their relatively high forecastles. The high Spanish superstructure had a purpose, namely to provide platforms for Spanish arquebusiers, musketeers and cross-bowmen. Camden's theory was later repeated by no less a person than Professor J. A. Froude and, as a result, the 'high flying shot' explanation is still a not uncommonly held assumption.

If we examine the recorded broadside gunnery engagements between English and Spanish ships during the sixteenth century, we are in fact presented with massive testimony to the ineffectiveness of Spanish gunnery. The first recorded such battle took place at the Mexican plate-fleet embarkation port of San Juan de Ulua (now Vera Cruz) in 1568.[34] John Hawkins in the *Jesus of Lubeck*, anchored between Spanish galleons and perceiving that an attack was about to take place, warped his ship offshore and opened fire with his main armament. Although greatly outnumbered and armed with only culverins and stone-shot firing perriers,[35] Hawkins put at least sixty shots into the Spanish admiral's galleon, setting her on fire. A couple of his broadsides into the Spanish vice admiral's vessel were enough to make her blow up. Only in the face of Spanish fire-ships, and attempts to board him by Spanish troops and seamen, did Hawkins retreat to a smaller vessel, the *Jesus* falling into Spanish hands.

In 1583 a decisive battle was fought at the port of San Vicente on the coast of Brazil between the English galleon *Leicester* (400 tons) and three Spanish Biscayan ships (300, 400 and 500 tons). Captain Edward Fenton in command of the *Leicester* described how the galleon *Santa Maria de Begona* bore down on him, guns firing as she came, in an attempt to board. The *Leicester* opened fire with her main battery armament, shortly after which the badly holed *Santa Maria* sank, the English ship suffering no hull damage at all. The other Spanish ships drew off to lick their wounds. The engagement is well documented in Fenton's narrative of his voyage,[36] and also in the journal of the

Spanish admiral and hydrographer Pedro Sarmiento de Gamboa, who arrived at San Vicente a few days after the battle and raised several of the bronze guns from the sunken *Santa Maria de Begona*.[37]

One battle above all stands out in this comparison of Spanish and English gunnery. The story of how Sir Richard Grenville in the royal galleon *Revenge* took on the combined might of the entire Spanish Indian Guard of more than fifty ships off Flores in 1591, is told in Chapter 7. But it is worth remembering here that the comparatively small English ship managed to take on galleons of up to 1,500 tons for 16 hours, until, her shot expended, she surrendered.

Our last example, out of many others, concerns a battle of attrition fought between John Hawkins's son, Sir Richard Hawkins, in the galleon *Dainty* and two Spanish frigates, off the coast of Peru in 1593.[38] In that action the *Dainty*, armed with demi-cannon and culverins, fought off the Spaniards armed with culverins, for three days and two nights. Most of the time, according to Hawkins, the fight was at point-blank range, 'the enemy never left us, day nor night, beating continually upon us with his great and small shot'.

Hawkins suffered grave handicaps right from the commencement of the engagement. His master gunner was incompetent and allowed the two Spanish frigates to pass close alongside while that side of the English ship had none of her broadside guns loaded. On another occasion he was seen to place the cannon ball inside the barrel and the charge of powder after it. Hawkins's crew, by his own admission, were intoxicated with wine, and the general level of English incompetence, from which Sir Richard Hawkins cannot be excluded, lost the *Dainty*. She surrendered when there were insufficient unwounded men to load the guns and sail the ship. But her loss emphasises the fact that a badly crewed and incompetently commanded English galleon, could not be sunk by a superior Spanish force even at point-blank range.

This contrast in gunnery skills can perhaps be best appreciated by realising that between 1568, when Hawkins took on the Spanish Indian Guard galleons at San Juan de Ulua, and 1603, when peace between England and Spain was at last declared, not one English galleon was sunk by Spanish gunfire. A terrible and damning indictment of Spanish gunnery, and proof itself that something was severely amiss.

To sum up, it seems likely that the failure of the 1588 Spanish Armada was due to poor technology which in turn affected the standard of gunnery. There is no evidence of any shortcomings in the quality of the Spaniards' seamanship, discipline or fighting spirit.

Notes to Chapter 5

1 State Papers Domestic, English, ccxii, July 1588. Cecil to Walsingham: 'There are few men hurt with any shot nor any vessel sunk, they shoot very far off.'
2 Ibid. Winter to Walsingham: 'When I was furthest off in discharging any of the pieces I was not out of shot of their arquebus, and most time within speech of one another.'
3 *State Papers Spanish*, edited by M. Hume, Vol IV (1899), pp444–5.
4 State Papers Domestic, English, cclx 40m March 1588.
5 C. F. Duro, *La Armada Invencible*, Vol II, No 110 p83.
6 C. Ffoulkes, *The Gun Founders of England*, p97.
7 The mythical bird/beast the griffon was, and still is, the emblem of the town of Lubeck.
8 H. R. Schubert, *History of the British Iron and Steel Industry*, p250.
9 A. Carrasco, *Memorial de Artilleria de Bronze*, p185.
10 J. Yernaux, *Chronique Archaeologique du Pays de Liège*, pp6–13.
11 C. M. Cipolla, *Guns and Sails in the Early Phase of European Expansion*, p36.
12 Ffoulkes, op cit, p109.
13 Schubert, op cit, pp171–2.
14 Carrasco, op cit, p187.
15 G. Doorman *Patents for Inventions in the Netherlands*, p118.
16 Carrasco, op cit, p67.
17 J. Lejeune, La formation de capitalisme moderne dans la Principaute de Liège au XIV siècle, p185.
18 Cipolla, op cit, p33.
19 M. Lewis, *Armada Guns*, p137.
20 Carrasco, op cit, p187.
21 Vannoccio Biringuccio, *The Pirotechnica*, p320.
22 Schubert, op cit, pp171–2.
23 H. Horne, *Essays Concerning Iron and Steel*.
24 Ibid.
25 Schubert, op cit, p233–4.
26 H. R. Schubert, 'The Superiority of English Cast Iron Cannon at the Close of the Sixteenth Century', in *Journal of the Iron and Steel Institute*, 161 (1949), pp85–6.
27 Schubert, op cit, p251.
28 J. K. Laughton, *The Defeat of the Spanish Armada*, Vol 11, pp250–4.
29 J. Bruce, *Report on Arrangements which were made for the Internal Defence of These Kingdoms*, Appendix XXXVII.
30 Bruce, op cit, Appendix XLL.
31 W. J. Van Nouhuys, 'The Anchor', in *Mariner's Mirror*, Vol 37 (1951), p44.

32 J. N. Green and C. J. M. Martin, 'Metal Detector Survey at Dun an Oir', *Prospezioni Archeologiche*, 5, pp101–4.
33 C. Martin, *Full Fathom Five: Wrecks of the Armada*, p174–5.
34 J. S. Corbett, *Drake and the Tudor Navy*, p114.
35 J. M. Lewis, 'Guns of the *Jesus of Lubeck*', *Mariner's Mirror*, Vol xxii (July 1936), pp324–6.
36 Hakluyt Society, *The Troublesome Voyage of Captain Fenton*.
37 Hakluyt Society, *Voyage of Pedro Sarmiento de Gamboa*.
38 Hakluyt Society, *Observations of Sir Richard Hawkins*, p214.

Chapter 6

The *Mary*, Royal Yacht of Charles II

In July 1971, while engaged in research both on the Spanish Armada cast-iron shot and for my forthcoming expedition to the Azores, I received a telephone call from Dr Peter N. Davies of Liverpool University in his capacity as north-west representative of the Council for Nautical Archaeology. He had been approached by two separate groups of amateur divers, both of which had found bronze cannon off the Skerries group of rocks outside the harbour of Holyhead on the island of Anglesey. This mention of bronze guns off the Skerries was very interesting; the Royal Navy had lost King Charles II's royal yacht *Mary* there in 1675.

The *Mary* had come into the possession of King Charles II shortly after his restoration to the throne. In his years in exile in the Low Countries, he had become interested in the Dutch pleasure sailing-vessels they called 'yachts' and, when the English 100 gun first-rate *Naseby* came to the Netherlands to embark Charles for his journey back to England, he sailed to the port of embarkation in a Dutch yacht. The king was so taken with the delightfully ornate and swift pleasure craft, he asked if his English ship architects could have a set of plans; the Dutch were so flattered that they made him a gift of a new yacht, which he immediately named after his sister Mary, widow of the Dutch Prince of Orange.

The *Mary* was galliot-hoy rigged, and armed with two lightweight pieces of ordnance in the bow, both of which were gifts to the king from gentlemen of substance in Dutch maritime affairs. Her gun-ports were circular, their periphery adorned with carved wooden wreaths covered in beaten gold leaf, and shortly after her arrival in England in August 1660, further additions to the decorations were made, six more bronze guns being mounted, three aside, on her main deck. The guns were cast to the order of Master of the Royal Ordnance, Sir William Compton. Compton had been a leading member of the underground

Diver using a metal detector probe invented by the author's colleague, Joe Casey. The detector works on the same principle as the life jacket light which uses sea water as its battery eloctrolite. The result is that the apparatus works only in sea water (not in fresh water) and does not require batteries

Possibly the largest bronze gun ever found in the sea. The author's expedition located this 15ft, 6,300lb Portuguese bronze culverin in 115ft of water. The bay of Angra do Heroismo, Terceira. The gun was cast in 1545 by Portuguese royal gun founder Joao Diaz. The piece was donated to the Azores Regional Museum

royalist movement known as the Sealed Knot Society, and his official position was King Charles's reward to a loyal and faithful servant.

England's naval architects became jealous of the Dutch origin of the king's new toy, in which Charles could often be seen, accompanied by his brother James, sailing down the Thames. The king was persuaded that it would be patriotic for him to order the construction of an English-built royal yacht. And this was done, with the *Mary* sailing in competition with English-built rivals. She was eventually handed over to the Royal Navy as a general-service packet boat, and it was on a voyage from Dublin to Chester that she foundered.

The *Mary* had sailed on this last passage with a crew of twenty-eight officers and men and forty-six passengers, including gentlemen of noble birth, amongst whom were the Earl of Meath, his son Lord Ardee and the Earl of Ardglass. The ship ran into thick fog off the Welsh coast and, constantly using the lead-line to establish the depth of water, it became clear to the *Mary's* master that he was being dragged by the current into shoal ground. Anchors were dropped, but still the speed of the current dragged her on; she struck the Skerries by the stern and very quickly broke up. Thirty-nine passengers and crew managed to scramble ashore, and there they stayed, hungry, wet and miserable, for two days, until the fog cleared and they attracted the attention of a passing ship by igniting dry gunpowder from one of the gentlemen's powder flasks.

It was an interesting story, but I had presumed, like many others, that the wreck would have been extensively salvaged by the Royal Navy shortly after her loss. However, Davies was now asking if I would be interested in visiting the wreck site with a view to advising the divers concerned how to do a survey. The discovery actually amounted to a remarkable coincidence because amateur divers from both the Chorley and the Merseyside branches of the British Sub Aqua Club had chanced on two groups of cannons almost simultaneously. One group of divers, swimming offshore of the rocks, had chanced upon a large iron anchor, close to which lay two bronze cannon. The other group of divers, unbeknown to the first group, yet less than a hundred yards away around a corner in a small rocky cove, came across bronze cannon, masses of cast-iron shot, and lead sheathing. Having gained my wholehearted interest, Davies immediately recruited two expert divers, who were also professional surveyors — John Stubbs and John Smart. (Stubbs was later to join me as survey officer for my 1975 expedition to Porto Bello, Panama.) We sailed out to the wreck with Davies in an inflatable boat provided by the Chorley BSAC divers, and were horrified by the spectacle of at least half a dozen boats anchored there, and divers hauling aboard cannon balls and artifacts in profusion. It was quickly explained that after the two cannon which lay close to the offshore anchor had been raised and handed into the custody of the Receiver of Wreck in nearby Holyhead, the story had broken in the Press and divers from all over the north-west of England were converging on the wreck site like flies to a honeypot.

The sight was depressing in the extreme. Here without a doubt was an important shipwreck, and it was being looted piecemeal by people who had little thought for their country's maritime heritage. Some divers were adopting menacing attitudes to other groups, and on a later occasion knives were drawn; heavy iron shackles were waved under people's noses, and one man arrived with a loaded shotgun which he fired into the air to intimidate his rivals. Stubbs, Smart and I advised Davies that there was no way that an orthodox, academically acceptable, pre-disturbance survey of the wreck site could be undertaken under such conditions. I dived on the wreck in an attempt to identify it, and spent a very miserable half hour being pushed aside, prodded with wrecking bars, and even having a fist thrust close to my diving mask. Eventually, however, eight bronze guns lay in a yard in Holyhead, officially the property of the Crown until such time that the Receiver of Wreck could decide on the cannons' legal ownership. If, after a year and a day, no bona fide claimant put in an appearance, the Receiver of Wreck, who on this occasion was the local customs officer, would be empowered by law to sell off the items, either by public auction or private treaty, after which the salvors would receive a percentage reward.

I had already told Davies and the divers concerned that they might have found King Charles II's yacht *Mary*. But one thing which completely foxed me with regard to identification of the wreck was the large amount of iron shot, some of which were 32lb demi-cannon balls. The *Mary* carried only small light ordnance, and thus the 32lb shot did not fit her guns. To help solve the problem of identity, Davies had recruited the assistance of naval historian Peter McBride, who researched the *Mary* extensively in the Public Record Office in London. Meanwhile, I wrote to the Scheipvart Museum in the Netherlands with details of the high-relief escutcheons on two cannon which were obviously of Dutch origin, having been cast by one of the most famous of Low Country gunfounders, Gerard Coster. These were the two guns found close to the anchor, well away from the wreck. The museum told me that the guns bore the coat of arms of Simon Van Hoorn, once burgomaster of Amsterdam, and that one of the coats of arms on the gun was indeed that of the city of Amsterdam. The gun was dated 1660; it was obvious that the two guns were those presented to Charles II along with the yacht *Mary*. The inscription on the six other bronze guns clinched the matter; it read as follows: 'Wm.Compton. Mª.Ord. Anno Dom.1660'. These could only be the six English cannon cast for the *Mary* on the instructions of the king.

I telephoned Davies to tell him what I had found, and learned that McBride had come to similar conclusions. He had also solved the puzzle of the presence of 32lb cast-iron shot. The *Mary* was a shallow-draught vessel, designed to sail in Dutch shoal waters. Instead of a conventional keel, she was fitted with lee boards on both sides of the ship, and these were raised or lowered into the water to act as keels, as the ship turned from one tack to the other. The Royal Navy did not like 'keel boards' so the Dutch system of maintaining the vessel's stability was removed and, to compensate, the *Mary* was ballasted with many tons of discarded cast-iron shot, hence the presence of the 32-pounder balls which had puzzled me.

Over several years, a more orderly manner of excavation eventually prevailed, under the supervision of Peter Davies. Hundreds of artifacts eventually found their way to the conservation laboratory of the City of Liverpool Museums (now the Merseyside Museums), where the Keeper of Conservation, Keith Priestman, carried out the laboratory treatment of not only the eight bronze cannon, but also gold and silver coins, items of jewellery, and a complete skeleton of a young girl. As there were no females registered on the passenger list of the *Mary*, we can only presume that the poor unfortunate girl was the private doxy of one of the gentlemen who sailed in the ship.

The problem, however, still existed that not only the *Mary* but also a great many other shipwrecks of historical importance were being located and secretly looted around the shores of the British Isles, with little thought given to recording or conservation. The rape of the *Mary* incensed me to such an extent that I decided to write to His Royal Highness the Duke of Edinburgh, drawing his attention to the current appalling lack of protection for ancient shipwrecks in UK waters. Within a few days I received a letter from Commander William Willett RN (ret), Secretary to Prince Philip, asking if I would be able to prepare a short paper on the present legal situation and the legislation which might be needed. I discussed the matter with Dr Peter Davies and also with Professor P. J. Odgers, head of the Faculty of Law of Liverpool University. The latter ventured the opinion that I had been offered a unique opportunity to put forward a case for the protection of underwater archaeological sites while defending the right of the amateur diver, who locates an ancient shipwreck, to participate in the eventual excavation of his or her discovery.

My short paper was completed in less than ten days, and amounted to a draft Enabling Bill, or Act of Parliament. By return post I received a further letter from Commander Willett, thanking me for my promptness, and saying that the views expressed would be of great interest to His Royal Highness. A separate note stated that the commander looked forward to a meeting when I came to Buckingham Palace to receive the Gold Medal award — an allusion to the recent announcement that my 1968 *Santa Maria de la Rosa* expedition had been awarded the 'Duke of Edinburgh/British Sub Aqua Club annual Gold Medal for achievements in the underwater field'. A few years previously, Prince Philip had inaugurated the award in conjunction with the BSAC in an effort to foster greater interest in the scientific aspect of amateur diving.

On 9 November 1971 I arrived at Buckingham Palace accompanied by my wife, and my two colleagues Casey and Reynolds, both of whom had been with me on my first Spanish Armada reconnaissance in 1963. The British Sub Aqua Club was represented by Alex Flinder, a former chairman of the BSAC, an indomitable fighter for the rights of the amateur diver and for amateur involvement in underwater archaeology, and with a proven record of archaeological excavation of ancient harbours and settlements on the Mediterranean coast of Israel. The Council for Nautical Archaeology was represented by Bill St Wilkes, its deputy chairman and a protagonist of amateur diver participation in underwater archaeology, as witnessed by his annual summer schools for young divers from the UK to help survey ancient sunken harbours in Sardinia, under the supervision of the Italian museum authorities. Commander Willett told us that we would have fifteen minutes conversation with Prince Philip, after which the prince would depart. Without more ado the Duke of Edinburgh entered and, after we were all introduced, thanked me for the documents I had prepared. We learned that the draft had been sent off to the Prime Minister, Edward Heath, and that it was to be used as one of the study documents for the forthcoming Protection of Wrecks Act.

The fifteen allotted minutes quickly sped by. Prince Philip ignored the time and launched into a lecture to us all on the importance of our nation's maritime heritage and how it must be protected whatever the cost. Although I had been advised that photographs could not be taken inside Buckingham Palace, other than of the ceremonies pertaining to visiting heads of state, on this occasion the restriction was relaxed. The photographs were taken by Richard Walter, archaeological correspondent of *The Observer*. After chatting to us for forty-five minutes, Prince Philip left, leaving us all in no doubt that we had been in the presence of a man who had a great understanding and knowledge of our subject, and who also possessed a deep sense of history.

Two days later I was in the library of Liverpool University continuing research for my forthcoming 1972 expedition to the Azores, when I received the surprise information that Buckingham Palace wanted to contact me urgently, and would I telephone them. Mystified and a little apprehensive, I did just that, and was put through to Lord Rupert Neville, Treasurer to the Duke of Edinburgh. Lord Rupert informed me that, shortly after I and my colleagues had left Buckingham Palace, the Maritime Trust had arrived. During their visit I had been mentioned to two gentlemen prominent in the shipping world, Sir Alexander Glen and Mr Costas Lemos and, as a result, I could look forward to a contribution towards my Azores expedition. I stumbled through my heartfelt thanks and put down the telephone; three days later I received, from a London shipping agent, a cheque which covered more than a third of my total projected budget.

Chapter 7

The Royal Galleon *Revenge*

To me, the most famous fighting ship ever to sail the seas was the Elizabethan royal galleon *Revenge*, Drake's flagship against the 1588 Armada, and flagship of Vice Admiral Sir Richard Grenville for his last glorious fight against Spanish naval might in the Azores in 1592. Of all the ships which carried the royal standard of Elizabeth of England, none earned greater glory. Before describing my 1972 Azores expedition and its findings, let us examine her history in detail.

My initial interest in the *Revenge* stemmed from the 1588 Battle of the Narrow Seas, in which she was Drake's flagship; her history, however, began eleven years earlier, in 1577, when she was launched at Deptford two years after her keel had been laid down. Her fourteen-year span of life as a queen's ship was marred by much ill-fortune, and Elizabethan seamen regarded her as an unlucky ship. She can be regarded as a forerunner of the 'race built' ships which were inspired by John Hawkins, and which proved time and again to be faster and easier to handle than the great top-heavy High Charged Spanish and Portuguese galleons built by Elizabeth's adversary, Philip of Spain.

The troubled history of the *Revenge* was recorded in 1622 by Sir Richard Hawkins, son of Sir John Hawkins:

As was plainly seen in the *Revenge*, which was ever the unfortunate ship the late Queen Majesty had during her reign, for coming out of Ireland with Sir John Parrot, she was like to be castaway on the Kentish coast.

After the voyage of Sir John Hawkins (my father) in Anno 1586, she struck aground coming into Plymouth, before her going to sea. Upon the coast of Spain, she left her fleet ready to sink with a great leak. At her return into the harbour of Plymouth, she beat upon the Winter Stone, and after in the same voyage, going out of Portsmouth haven, she ran twice aground, and in the latter of them lay twenty-four hours beating upon the shore, and at length with eight feet of water in the hold, she was forced off, and presently ran upon the Ouse, and was cause that she remained there, with three other of her Majesty's [ships] six months until the spring of the year. When coming about to be docked, entering the Thames, her old leak breaking upon her, had like to have drowned all those which were in her.

In Anno 1591, with a storm of wind and weather, riding at her moorings at Rochester, nothing but her bare masts overhead, she was turned Topsie Turvie . . . her keel being uppermost. And the cost and the loss she wrought, I have good cause to remember. In her last voyage, in which she was lost, when she gave England and Spain good cause to remember her. For the Spaniards themselves confess that three of their great ships were sunk at her side, and was the death of above 1,500 of their men, with loss of a great part of their fleet, by a storm which suddenly took them the next day. What English died in her, many living are witnesses. Among them was Sir Richard Grenville, a noble and valiant gentleman; Vice Admiral in her Majesty's fleet. So that well considered, she was a ship loaden, and fraught with ill success.

The *Revenge* was not a large ship by sixteenth-century standards. She displaced between 450 and 500 tons, was 92ft long in the hull, 32ft in the beam, and drew 15ft of water. Her complement of bronze artillery, all bearing the royal coat of arms — the Tudor rose, girdled by a buckled garter inscribed with *Hon y soi qui mal y pense* — was later described by her Spanish captor, Don Martin de Bertandona, as the finest he had ever seen. She was heavily armed for her size, carrying 42 pieces of ordnance when she sailed on her last voyage; but the Spaniards, in their manifest of guns captured on board, refer to gun weights and not bore or shot poundage. However, from the weights they give — 2,000, 3,000, 4,000 and 6,000lb, — we can deduce that the *Revenge* was carrying a full range of demi-cannon, culverin, demi-culverin and sacre.

Revenge's first action was against a Spanish landing at Smerwick Harbour on the Kerry coast of Ireland in 1580. The Spaniards had built temporary fortifications and breastworks on a spit of land which jutted out from the cliff tops into the bay, and English galleons, including the *Revenge*, bombarded the Spaniards from anchored positions offshore. The papal force of Spanish and Italian troops eventually surrendered to the English, who sent in bands of armed men commanded by Sir Walter Raleigh, who massacred all 600 prisoners.

In 1588 Drake was in command of the *Revenge* during the action against the Spanish Armada. It was the *Revenge* which captured the Spanish galleon *Nuestra Señora del Rosario*, and it was on *Revenge's* deck that Drake accepted the sword of Don Pedro de Valdez, in the act of Spanish surrender. But 1589 marked the nadir of Drake's fortunes, and his disgrace in the eyes of his monarch. In that year, in joint command with Sir John Norris, he took a combined sea and land force in an attempt to invade Portugal and set Dom Antonio back onto the throne from which he had been deposed in 1580 by Philip of Spain. Again the *Revenge* bore Drake's pennant; but the attack on Lisbon was a dismal failure, Drake refusing to sail his ships past and under the guns of Fort St Julian on the River Tagus to support Norris and the queen's new favourite — the brave, hot-headed, romantic, thoroughly likeable but militarily incompetent Robert Devereux, Earl of Essex.

A dispirited Drake now took the *Revenge* and the rest of his squadron to the Azores, the place where the Spanish treasure ships from Nombre de Dios in Panama and Vera Cruz in Mexico, stopped for water and victuals. This group of islands, more than 900 miles off the coast of Portugal, was poorly defended and ripe for attack. But Drake sought only plate-carrying galleons and loot, and in this he was disappointed. Damaged by bad weather, the *Revenge*, leaking badly, put back to England.

In 1590 the queen, having rejected Drake as a suitable flag officer for further attacks on Spanish interests, ordered Sir Martin Frobisher to take a fleet to the Azores, where he should lie awaiting the arrival of the annual convoy of treasure-laden galleons, *naos* and *urcas*. Frobisher left Plymouth in the *Revenge* in the spring of that year, accompanied by a small squadron of well-armed ships; but the *Revenge* was no luckier for him than she had been for Drake. Frobisher arrived too late to intercept the fast *gallizabras*, which carried some of King Philip's royal fifth of all treasure mined in the Indies. And as for the plate-fleet, which should have contained the major part of the treasure, it never sailed. Disturbed by Drake's attack on Corunna, the king of Spain decreed that the main treasure fleet should not sail in 1590. Instead, it would wait for another year until new, well-armed, supporting galleons could be sent out to form a great double convoy, which would sail for Spain from Havana in 1591.

The news of Philip's revised plans eventually reached England, and Queen Elizabeth ordered that a strong fleet be prepared over the winter of 1590–1, the intention being to attack and capture the largest and richest treasure fleet ever to leave the Indies for Spain. Unwisely, she placed the command of the English fleet in the hands of Sir Thomas Howard, an officer possessed of no great skill at sea, with no sea-battle experience, and lacking in the one vital quality essential to success in a desperate enterprise against greater odds — courage. Howard was not prepared to take risks, and regarded the safety of his ships and his men as paramount over the expedition's main objective of seeking out the queen's enemy, destroying his fleet, and denying him the wealth with which he could continue his war against the Netherlands.

Philip II's intelligence service in England was no less efficient than Elizabeth's spy network in Spain. There were a great many Catholics in England who longed for a return to papal blessings and the end of what they believed to be a Lutheran heresy. Such religious fervour provided a breeding ground for disaffection, and Philip had his agents everywhere. If England intended to surprise Spain by a lightning raid on the double plate-fleet as it approached the Azores, then Spain would surprise England by putting to sea a huge fleet of fighting galleons, including those newly built for the strengthening of the convoy system to and from the Indies. Thus Don Alonzo de Bazan, Captain General of the Indian Guard, was ordered to take a fleet of fifty-three ships to the Azores to find, attack and destroy Sir Thomas Howard's much smaller squadron, before the double plate-fleet arrived at their rendezvous at the Azores island of Terceira.

Bazan knew the reputation of Sir Thomas Howard and dismissed him contemptuously as an unworthy adversary. But Howard's vice admiral and second in command was a different man altogether — Sir Richard Grenville, cousin to Sir Walter Raleigh, a man of fiery temperament and resolute courage, who would draw his sword and fight a duel, for his own good name or that of a friend, at the drop of a hat. It was Grenville who had organised the first American colony, although Walter Raleigh was later given the entire credit; and his mobilisation of land forces in Cornwall and Devon at the time of the Armada has already been noted. Even his enemies treated him with deference and respect, none more so than Drake himself. Sir Richard provided the stiffening required for his far from resolute overall commander, whose position could be attributed more to sycophancy than to merit. By the time Grenville sailed in the *Revenge*, he had worked his ship, his seamen and his guns' crews to a pitch of battle readiness never before seen in an English royal galleon.

The meeting of the three great fleets — the Indian Guard from the Spanish mainland, the plate-fleet from Havana, the English squadron bent on the plate-fleet's destruction and plunder — moved towards its climax. It was to result in one of the most glorious single-handed sea fights in the history of naval warfare.

The English were the first to arrive at what was to be the scene of battle, namely the deepwater, exposed anchorage off the Azores island of Flores. Here they would lie, their presence unknown, their small speedy despatch boats constantly out reconnoitring to the west, each vying to be the first to cry 'Sail Ho', as the hoped for treasure-laden argosies of Philip II hove into sight. To the west of the Azores, the plate-fleet was not as intact as when it started out. Savage storms had ravaged it, and many ships had been lost after leaving Havana for the Bermudas, whence they sailed to seek the trade wind which would blow them across the Atlantic to the Azores. To the east, the great fleet of Don Alonzo de Bazan had raised anchor and was also bound for Flores. The trap was about to be sprung whereby the queen of England's squadron of seven ships would be caught in a gigantic nutcracker.

The English squadron had originally comprised Howard in the *Defiance*, Grenville in the *Revenge*, the *Nonpareil* and the *Elizabeth Bonaventure*, all about 500 tons. Added to these four main fighting galleons were the *Crane* (250 tons), the *Charles* (60 tons) and the *Moon* (70 tons); but after several months at sea the latter was sent back to England to plead for promised supplies which had not arrived. The *Nonpareil* followed, her crew so ravaged by sickness and disease that there were not enough fit men to work the ship or fight. To Howard's relief he was in due course reinforced by the *Golden Lion* (500 tons) and the *Foresight* (300 tons). The English ships were all by now foul with sickness and disease, with scurvy prevalent; so the vessels were ransacked and rummaged, their holds cleaned out, and the sick men sent ashore to recuperate.

Meanwhile off the Spanish coast George, third Earl of Cumberland, was at sea. Cumberland was that rare bird — a man who spent more on gathering in Spain's riches than he profited by his forays. He and like-minded gentlemen adventurers financed substantial fleets to attack Spanish interests, Cumberland's most spectacular capture being that of the great carrack *Madre de Dios* between the Azores and the mainland in 1592. Even later, in 1598, he was to outdo Drake by completing the task Drake had failed to do in 1595 — the capture of San Juan, Puerto Rico. Cumberland was a man after Grenville's own heart. Now his squadron espied the fleet of Don Alonzo de Bazan and, noting the direction in which the Spaniards were sailing, correctly assumed that they had got wind of Howard and Grenville's presence in the Azores, and were en route to attack the markedly inferior English fleet. The Earl of Cumberland made a quick decision and, hailing Captain Middleton of the pinnace *Moonshine*, bade him proceed under press of sail for the Azores, to give fair warning to Howard and Grenville of their peril. Middleton clapped on all sail and sped westward in an effort to overhaul the Spanish fleet under cover of darkness, and carry the vital intelligence of Spanish movements so that the English fleet in the Azores could make a hasty exit.

Bazan's fleet was indeed a powerful expression of Philip of Spain's maritime might. Huge new galleons had been built, called the 'Twelve Apostles', each of more than 1,000 tons burden and reputedly carrying up to 90 guns. Some of the king's most able admirals sailed with Bazan on that fateful voyage, including Don Martin de Bertandona, Marcos de Aramburu, Sancho Pardo, Antonio Urquiola and Bertholome de Villavicencio. As the Azores came in sight, Bazan ordered Marcos de Aramburu to detach his squadron of twelve ships, seven of which were from the famed Castillian squadron, and sail between the islands to approach the English fleet from the far side of Flores, thus placing Howard and Grenville in a vice, between forty-one ships coming in from the east and twelve from the west. The tiny English squadron of seven ships would not stand a chance.

Ahead of the Spaniards, Captain Middleton could see the island of Flores off his bow, while off his port quarter he could espy Aramburu's squadron of twelve ships, tacking for their planned surprise attack on the anchored English fleet. His tiny pinnace sped on 'with a bone in her teeth', the white bow wave curling along her sides towards the English, anchored under the lee of Flores. There, all was quiet. Grenville had ninety men ashore, and those remaining on board worked with a will to get the ship into fighting trim for the expected plate-fleet which, for all they knew, could appear from the west at any time. Young Philip Gawdy, son of gentlefolk from the county of Norfolk, was on board the *Revenge*, and had recently sent a letter home with the departed *Nonpareil* in which he wrote, 'We stay and pray every day heartily for the Spanish fleet's coming.' The Spanish fleet was coming, but not only the treasure fleet imagined by young Gawdy, whose next letter home was to be penned from a cell in the castle at Lisbon.

Middleton rounded Flores and there at anchor, sails furled, some of the ships partly careened, lay the English squadron of seven vessels. One can only wonder at the incompetence of Howard who, as overall commander, was duty bound to see to it that his fleet was not surprised by the enemy. One ship should have been keeping a watch for the Spaniards, by sailing to the east but staying in signalling distance of the rest of the squadron. The English complacency didn't last much longer. Middleton in the *Moonshine* was soon amongst the English vessels, bearing his tidings of a huge Spanish fleet of more than fifty ships, many of which were fighting galleons.

A council of war was called in great haste, and Howard took what for him was the only decision his mind was capable of making — to flee at once, and forget the sick ashore. Guns were fired to warn those on land who were fit enough to make the journey back to ship that the English fleet was about to weigh anchor; and in very short order, sails were unfurled and anchors raised. At that very moment Aramburu's galleons appeared from the western side of the island, and Bazan's ships came, hull down, from the east. Only Grenville made no move, the *Revenge* staying at anchor as pinnaces plied to and from land. Grenville had no intention of deserting his crew members who were sick ashore; he could not and would not leave them to the far from tender mercy of the Spanish Inquisition.

One by one the English ships began to move, and with their sails filling with the wind tacked away from the double danger of the closing Spanish trap; yet the *Revenge* stayed where she lay, at anchor, as if no danger threatened. Howard managed to elude his opponents due to the superior speed of the lighter English galleon *Defiance*. The huge 1,000 ton Spanish ships could only fire departing salvos at him, some of which registered but did not delay, and in all probability hastened, his departure. Two more English ships ran the gauntlet of Spanish fire to escape, followed by the *Golden Lion* and one of the smaller craft.

Grenville had by now retrieved all his sick mariners, and he gave the order for all canvas except the mainsail to be unfurled. As the sails billowed out, the anchor came up to the 'cat head'. Gun-ports were triced up and guns, loaded with bar shot, were run out. Grenville knew that, outnumbered as he was, his best chance of survival was to damage his enemies' rigging and try to bring them dead in the water. The crew of the *Revenge*, expecting the order to put about and run to escape, were surprised at Grenville's order that they should head straight ahead into the mass of the Spanish fleet. The mainsail was not yet unfurled, and Grenville cried that he would hang any man who cut it loose. He was going to fight a classic gunnery action under minimum 'fighting sail', sailing at low speed, able to direct his master gunners so that every individual gunshot and broadside would find its mark. Grenville must have reflected with sadness on his decision to transfer three guns to another, less well-armed ship a few days before the battle which was now inevitable.

And so the fighting galleon *Revenge*, brave Sir Richard Grenville in command, sailed into action as less than 300 English seamen took on 7,000 Spaniards and Portuguese, and 39 fine pieces of English cast-bronze artillery faced almost 1,000 Spanish guns. The Devon and Cornish seamen and gunners stood to their allotted posts and to their guns as the first of the huge Spanish galleons came up, firing first her bow chase-guns, and then her broadside.

The *Revenge* opened up with a broadside of bar shot, intended to damage the enemy's rigging, and thus make his ship unmanageable and take him out of the fight. And this first opening round of what must be one of the fiercest battles ever fought in the age of sail, gave victory to the English. The great ship opposing Grenville did indeed sheer off, crippled and unable to take any further part in the action. Sir Walter Raleigh, in his narrative of the last fight of the *Revenge*, described the exit of the first Spanish galleon being due to her 'utterly misliking her first entertainment'.

By now, Grenville was in the jaws of the Spanish vice, as enemy ships which had skirted round the west side of Flores, to take Howard on his seaward flank, turned back to attack the solitary English galleon which appeared set on a suicidal course. As the Spanish ships closed in, the last English ship, a small victualling vessel, came in under the *Revenge*'s stern, her master calling up to Grenville, asking what he should do. 'I bid you save yourself, and leave me to my fortune,' Grenville replied. The tiny ship turned and fled. Marcos de Aramburu with his Castillian squadron was now coming up on Grenville's lee bow.

The *Revenge* was at that moment dead in the water, for the great ship which had first accosted Grenville was in fact one of the 'Twelve Apostles', the *San Felipe*, and in her act of attacking Grenville from the windward side this 1,500 ton ship, sails fully spread, had taken the wind out of Grenville's sails. The commander of the *San Felipe* seized this opportunity to try to board and enter the *Revenge*, but his grappling ropes parted and he was forced to sheer off. Bertandona was next in line in the *San Barnabe*, and he managed successfully to grapple the *Revenge*. A third ship crossed the *Revenge*'s stern, raking her with gunfire; a fourth crossed Grenville's bow, boxing him in. By now the Spaniards were executing almost as much damage to each other as they were to the *Revenge*, the smoke from the gunfire obscuring all vision. Nevertheless, the gunners on both sides performed the unbelievable task of loading their guns, sitting astride the muzzles protruding from the gun-ports. The mortality rate must have been prodigious. Gunners were shot off their stations by arquebusiers and musketeers; occasionally, a 16ft pike, thrust at arms' length from the side of a ship, would plunge a gunner to his death.

Ships' sides were now hard against each other. Guns flamed and roared as the shot thudded home, splintering ships' timbers, the broken planks mowing men down by the dozen. Grenville concentrated his small-arms fire on Bertandona's deck, his small breech-loading swivel-guns, or versos, loaded with 'murthering hail', sweeping the Spanish soldiers off their rail as they climbed up to swarm onto *Revenge*'s deck. Meanwhile, Grenville's gunners jammed wooden quoins under the breeches of their guns to depress the muzzles, so that they could fire down through their adversary's sides into his hold. The English guns, double-shotted, had a murderous effect as the 32lb demi-cannon balls smashed through the Spanish galleon's sides, down through her orlop deck, into her hold, and out through her bottom planking. A crippled Spanish galleon grappled to the *Revenge*'s starboard side was cut loose by English seamen, allowing it to drift away through the gun smoke and founder with almost total loss of life. But there was to be no respite for the men on the starboard watch. No sooner had the stricken, holed Spanish galleon turned away from *Revenge*'s side, than another took her place. Yet another came alongside to port.

Now Admiral Marcos de Aramburu thrust his Castillian flagship into the fray, running her into the *Revenge*'s bow, and taking blisteringly accurate gunfire from Grenville's two bow chase-guns. There would be no great honours for the admiral who had fought valiantly against the English in 1588, and who had witnessed and recorded the sinking of the *Santa Maria de la Rosa* in Blasket Sound. One of the *Revenge*'s 32lb shot struck Aramburu's bowsprit which broke like a carrot; the forestay snapped; the foremast, unsupported against the wind, unstepped itself and, falling sternwards onto the mainmast, left the flagship helpless. The wind carried her off to leeward, and Aramburu took no further part in the battle.

Revenge's bow was now relatively clear, but she was increasingly threatened from both sides. The new adversary on the starboard side, pouring in gunfire as she came, had thrown her grappling irons and managed to lash herself alongside. Manned by men fresh to the battle, she sent scores of soldiers swarming over *Revenge*'s top rail. But the most stalwart of all Grenville's adversaries that day was Don Martin de Bertandona, in his flagship the *San Barnabe*. Resolutely hanging onto the *Revenge*'s port side, his men constantly sought more places where they could lash the two ships together, and traded death to exchange broadsides. And, while the fighting raged, Grenville strode around his ship, ignoring the target he presented to the Spanish musketeers who were only yards away from the poop deck from which he directed the battle.

The English gunners, most of them by now wounded, fought their way back across the deck, to be urged forward again by a cry from Grenville. In the ship's fighting tops, English seamen rained down boulders and rocks as big as a man's head onto the Spaniards beneath. Throwing stones from fighting tops was standard procedure once arquebuses and muskets had been discharged, for there was little time to go through the ponderous process of reloading. Amid the chaos Grenville and his fellow officers, swords in hand, led the charge which swept the Spaniards off the *Revenge*'s decks, and back onto their own ship. Suddenly there was a great cracking sound, followed by the graunching of falling timbers as the *Revenge*'s mainmast, cut through by round shot, its stays gone, fell across its own deck and onto the Spanish galleon on the starboard side. This led to a brief respite, for the galleon cast herself off from the stricken *Revenge* — the Spanish commander, his ship and his men had taken all the punishment they could bear. Taking water through her shot-holed sides, the galleon sank a few hundred yards from the centre of the battle. By now the fighting had raged for more than four hours, and more than half of Grenville's crew were dead or wounded. Grenville himself had been struck by an arquebus shot but, refusing to go below, ordered the chirurgeon, or barber-surgeon, to bind the wound while he continued to direct the battle. The *Revenge*'s foremast was the next to go as the chirurgeon, still trying to treat Grenville's wound, dropped dead at his commander's side, killed by a musket shot.

The sun started to go down and at dusk a Spanish *urca*, flagship of Don Louis Cuitino, breasted the *Revenge*'s unopposed side and lashed herself there. She was joined by another ship which in turn lashed herself to the *urca*. The Spaniards were now employing the stratagem of attrition for, with two ships firmly against the *Revenge* on the one side, they could withstand greater losses in men, the fallen soldiers from the first ship being replaced by fresh men from the second.

Night came, and in the darkness the rest of the Spanish fleet, unable to close with the *Revenge*, could only watch as Bertandona on Grenville's port side, and the *urca* flagship together with a 1,200 ton galleon on the *Revenge*'s starboard side, continued to fire into the seemingly indestructible English ship. Few of the *Revenge*'s guns were firing now, most of them having been dismounted from their carriages by Spanish shot. On the Spanish side the slaughter was dreadful, with dead and dying everywhere. Far away, miles to leeward, a ship signalled with lanterns. It was Marcos de Aramburu's flagship of the squadron of Castille, still helpless and dead in the water, trying to summon assistance.

> And the sun went down, and the stars came out far over the summer sea,
> But never for a moment ceased the fight of the one and the fifty-three.
> Ship after ship the whole night long, their high built galleons came,
> Ship after ship the whole night long, with their battle thunder and flame;
> Ship after ship, the whole night long, drew back with her dead and her shame.
> For some were sunk and many were shattered, and so could fight us no more —
> God of battles, was ever a battle like this in the world before?
>
> 'The Revenge', Alfred, Lord Tennyson

During the night, the *Revenge*'s mizzen and bonaventure-mizzen masts fell onto her decks; she was now a nearly helpless, shot-riddled hulk. Fires glowed on her decks, the seamen who quenched them fearful of ignition of the ship's main powder magazine. But her few remaining guns continued to hammer their hellfire message into the surrounding Spanish galleons. Grenville was almost alone now on his poop deck, surrounded by dead and dying seamen, gunners, and his close friends of gentle birth. Perhaps he reflected that, over the past ten hours and with only one of the queen's ships, he had executed almost as much damage to the king of Spain's fleet, and the king of Spain's pride, as the entire English Navy in 1588. The Spaniards, surveying the scene of carnage on their own and the English decks, must have marvelled how that solitary galleon could have survived for so long.

By daybreak, ninety members of the English crew were laid dead on the ballast under the orlop deck; hardly a man was unwounded. The

Expedition personnel at Porto Bello, Panama in 1975. Author third from right standing

Drake's island, Panama, off which Drake was buried in a lead coffin in 1596

From left to right, Mr Robert John (British Ambassador), Dr Reina Torres de Arauz (Director of the Panama Museums), and the author

The customs house at Porto Bello. In the seventeenth century the entire ground floor was piled to the ceiling with ingots of silver, awaiting transportation to Spain

ship's master, Captain Langhorn, took Grenville the unwelcome news that the *Revenge* was down to her last few rounds of ammunition. Grenville paid no heed to those around him who suggested that as they had sunk two ships and mortally damaged several more, were completely dismasted but had all acquitted themselves so well in the service of her majesty Queen Elizabeth of England, that honour was satisfied, there could be no shame in now lowering the *Revenge*'s colours to surrender to the Spanish admiral. Grenville would not countenance surrender and, resolving that he and his men should fight to the last drop of blood, was struck in the head and laid low by a Spanish musket ball. It was a mortal wound. Grenville was dying, and the surviving English seamen knew it. He was carried to his cabin where he was told that the last piece of roundshot had been fired at the Spaniards. The English guns fell silent.

From the *San Barnabe*, Bertandona called for an honourable compact. The English could surrender, be afforded all the honours due to such a brave and resourceful foe and, on reaching Spain, all survivors would be released to return to their homes. It was a generous offer, in the best traditions of naval warfare, and signifying the high esteem that blue-water seamen have one for the other. But Grenville, on having this offer made known to him, sent for his master gunner. He wanted to know only one thing, was there enough powder left in the magazine to blow up not only the *Revenge*, but also the Spanish ships lashed to her sides? The master gunner affirmed that there was indeed enough powder left to blow them all to kingdom come. Grenville then bade him ignite the powder magazine.

The master gunner left Grenville's cot to do his master's bidding, only to be accosted by wounded seamen who asked what the admiral was about. 'I have to blow up the ship,' the gunner replied, at which the disgruntled seamen took hold of him and tied him up. The crew decided that the fight they had put up would satisfy both their own honour, and that of England. They sent a messenger on board the Spanish flagship, the compact was made, and the *Revenge* became the first and only royal galleon of Queen Elizabeth I ever to surrender to Imperial Spain.

The mortally wounded Grenville was now taken on board the *San Barnabe*, where Don Martin de Bertandona and his most senior officers paid their respects to the bravest seaman it had ever been their good fortune to meet. But Grenville, partially revived by glasses of red Spanish wine, downed his last drink on God's earth. He chewed the glass between his teeth, swallowing both wine and broken glass, and sinking back on a Spanish cot, expired. Thus died one of the bravest and noblest of all English seamen, a true and loyal subject of the queen, a gentleman revered and almost worshipped by the people of his native West Country. With all due honours, he was buried at sea by the Spanish victors, and the *Revenge* was taken under tow.

And now, over the horizon, topmasts were seen, as the mighty treasure-laden plate-fleet hove into view, bearing down on Flores after their journey across the Atlantic from Havana. As they luffed up and fired their signal guns in greeting to Captain General Alonzo de Bazan, they looked in awe at the shattered remains of that most famous of all English corsair ships — Drake's fabled *Revenge* — now captive of the Spanish Navy, her commander Sir Richard Grenville dead. As they sailed past, they saw the havoc and destruction on the *Revenge*'s decks, her fallen masts, her scuppers filled with dried blood. Bertandona, on his part, ordered his ships to make emergency repairs to battle damage, in preparation for the passage home to Spain. Aramburu's flagship was taken in tow; but another galleon was scuttled, her damage being so great that she was no longer seaworthy. Another ship was beached to prevent her sinking.

The combined fleet of mainland galleons and Indies treasure ships sailed in convoy, their destination the nearby Azores island of Terceira where, in the roadstead of the town of Angra, the plate-fleet ships could take on fresh water, meat and bread, and the battle-damaged ships could further attend to their injuries. But many a Spanish ship, and hundreds of Spanish seamen were never to see the Road of Angra, let alone their Spanish homeland, for the rendezvous at the Azores coincided with the autumnal equinox and a terrifying storm, the winds reaching hurricane force. More than a score of Spanish ships perished in that storm, at least a dozen of which were dashed against the rocks and cliffs of Terceira. Among them was the *Revenge*. She struck a rock close to Terceira, going down with all hands but one — a solitary English seaman who, having climbed the island's volcanic cliffs, gave news of the last moments of his ship to the local people, whereupon he died. Thus the only Englishmen to survive the *Revenge*'s last fight were those who, like Master Gawdy, had been taken aboard Spanish ships to Spain, and were later released and returned to London.

How did this terrible catastrophe at Terceira come about? For that information we must resort to the remarkable Journal of the Dutchman, Jan Hyghen Van Linschoten, who was living on the island.

Chapter 8

Van Linschoten's Journal and the Azores Expedition

Jan Hyghen Van Linschoten, a native of Enkhysen on the shore of the Zuider Zee, being in his own words 'much addicted to see and travaile in strange countries', left the Texel on 6 December 1576. He sailed in a fleet of eighty ships and arrived in Seville on 1 January 1577. His wish to visit foreign lands was fulfilled when he obtained a place in the suite of the friar Don Vicente Fonseca, who had just been appointed to the bishopric of India.

They left the Tagus for India in the good ship *San Salvador* on which, by lucky coincidence, Van Linschoten's brother was pilot; the *San Salvador* being one of the huge Portuguese carracks of the 'Carreira de India', teak built at Goa in India. These ships were recognised as amongst the best built and sturdiest in the world. The uneventful and tedious six-month journey ended when the ship dropped anchor in Goa on 30 September 1583. Van Linschoten spent five years in India but eventually, seeking relief from the boredom of his official post, requested permission to leave, which request was duly granted.

The post of 'Factor of the Peppers' was vacant on the carrack *Santa Cruz* and Van Linschoten, applying for the job, was delighted to receive the appointment. The *Santa Cruz* sailed from Goa on 23 November 1588, and sighted the island of Flores in the Azores on 22 July 1589, only to be chased away by two English reprisal pirates. It was obvious that English piratical activity was on the increase, so the master of the *Santa Cruz* took the wise decision to put into the island of Terceira, and anchor under the comparative safety of the guns of the fortresses at the port of Angra. In Terceira, Van Linschoten learned of the failure of the Spanish Armada of the previous year, and of the very recent failure of Drake's raid on Lisbon.

The captain of the *Santa Cruz* now wisely decided that if after revictualling his ship he sailed directly for Lisbon, he stood in great danger of being captured by the English, who regarded the Azores as a happy hunting ground, rich with pickings and ripe for plunder. Van

Linschoten's stay on the island of Terceira was thus much longer than he had originally anticipated. He was in fact unable to leave until December 1591, when a vessel from Flushing took him to Lisbon, where he arrived on 2 January 1592. During his stay on Terceira, Van Linschoten gleaned a great deal of information concerning the Spanish plate-fleets and their treasure, and also spoke with Spanish and English survivors about the last fight of the *Revenge*. He also wrote a fascinating and informative Journal, which is now quoted almost in full.

The 25th of August 1591, the King's Armada coming out of Ferrol arrived at Terceira, being in all 30 ships; Biscayans, Portingals, Spaniards and ten Dutch fly-boats that were arrested in Lisbon to serve the King; besides other small ships, Pataches, that came to serve as messengers from place to place and to discover the seas. This navy came to stay for, and convoy the ships that should come from the Spanish Indies, and the fly-boats were appointed in their return home, to take in the goods that were saved in a lost ship from Malacca, and convoy it to Lisbon.

The 13th of September the said Armada arrived at the island of Corvo, where the Englishmen with about sixteen ships as then lay [incorrect, there were only seven ships], staying for the Spanish fleet; whereoff some of the most part were come, and the Englishmen were in good hope to have taken them. But then they perceived the King's navy to be so strong, the Admiral being Lord Thomas Howard, commanded his fleet not to fall upon them, nor any of them once separate their ships from him, unless he gave commission so to do.

Notwithstanding this, the Vice Admiral, Sir Richard Grenville, being in the ship called the Revenge went into the Spanish fleet and shot among them, doing them great hurt, and thinking that the rest of the company would have followed, which they did not, but left him there, and sailed away, the cause why could not be known; which the Spaniards perceiving, with seven or eight ships, they boarded her [the Revenge], but she withstood them all, fighting with them about twelve hours altogether, and sunk two of them, one being a double fly-boat of 1,200 tons and the Admiral of the fly-boats, and the other a Biscayan.

But in the end, by reason of the number that came upon her, she was taken, but to their great loss, for they had lost in the fighting, and by drowning 400 men, and of the English were slain about a hundred. Sir Richard Grenville himself being wounded in the brain, whereof afterwards he died.

He was borne into the ship the St. Paul wherein was the admiral of the fleet Don Alonzo de Bazan; where his wounds were dressed by the Spanish surgeons, but Don Alonzo would neither see nor speak to him. All the rest of the Spanish gentlemen and captains went to visit him, and to comfort him in his hard fortune, and wondering at his great courage, and stout heart, for that he showed not a sign of faintness nor changing of colour. But feeling the hour of death approach, he spake these words . . . Here I die, Richard Grenville, with a joyful and quiet mind, for I have ended my life as a true soldier ought to, that hath fought for his country, his Queen, and his religion and honour, whereby my soul most joyfully departeth out of this body, and shall always leave behind it an everlasting fame of a valiant and true soldier, that hath done his duty, as he was bound to do. When he had finished these and other such words, he gave up the Ghost, with great stout courage, and no man could perceive any true sign of heaviness in him.

This Sir Richard Grenville was a great and rich gentleman in England, and had great yearly revenues of his own inheritance, but he was a man very unquiet in his mind and greatly affected to war, insomuch as of his own private motion he offered his service to the Queen. He had performed many valiant acts, and was greatly feared in these islands, and known of every man, but of a nature very severe so that his own people hated him for his fierceness, and spake very hardly of him; for when they first entered the fleet or Armada, they had their great sail in readiness, and might possibly have sailed away for it was one of the best ships for sail in England. The master perceiving that the other ships had left them, and followed not after, commanded the great sail to be cut [loose] that they might get away; but Sir Richard Grenville threatened both him and all the rest that were in the ship, that if any man laid hand upon it, he would cause him to be hanged, and so by that occasion they were compelled to fight and in the end were taken.

He was so hard a complexion, that as he continued amongst the Spanish captains while they were at supper with him, he would carouse three or four glasses of wine, and in a bravery take the glasses between his teeth and crush them in pieces and swallow them down, so that often times the blood ran out of his mouth without any harm unto him and this was told me by diverse credible persons that many times stood and beheld him.

The Englishmen that were left in the ship, as the captain of the soldiers, the Master and others were dispersed in diverse of the Spanish ships that had taken them, where there had almost a new fight arisen between Biscayans and the Portingals; while each of them would have the honour to have first boarded her, so that there grew a great noise and quarrel among them, one taking the chief ancient, and the other the flag, and the captain and everyone held his own. [The captors evidently fought each other for possession of the English flags and pennants.]

The ships that had boarded her were altogether out of order, and broken, and many of their men hurt, and whereby they were compelled to come into the island of Terceira, there to repair themselves; where being arrived, I and my chamber fellow to hear some news went aboard one of the ships, being a great Biscayan, and one of the Twelve Apostles, whose captain was Bertandona. He seeing us, called us up into the gallery where with great courtesy he received us, being as then set at dinner with the English captain [of the Revenge] that sat by him, and who had on a suit of black velvet, but he could not tell us anything, for that he could speak no other language, but English and Latin, which Bertandona could a little speak.

The English captain got license of the governor that he might come on land with his weapon by his side, and was in our lodging. The governor of Terceira bade him to dinner, and showed him great courtesy. The master [of the Revenge] likewise with a license of Bertandona came on land, and was in our lodging, and had at least ten or twelve wounds, as well in his head as on his body, whereof after being at sea, between Lisbon and the islands [on his way back to the mainland], he died.

The captain wrote a letter, wherein he declared all manner of the fight and left it with the English merchant that lay in our lodging, to send it to the Lord Admiral of England. This English captain came into Lisbon, was there well received, and not any harm done unto him, but with good convoy sent unto Sentual and from whence sailed to England, with all the rest of the English prisoners.

The Spanish Armada stayed at the island of Corvo until the last of September, to assemble the rest of the fleet together; which in the end were to number 140 sail of ships, partly coming from the Indies, and partly of the Armada, and being altogether ready to sail into Terceira in good company, there suddenly rose so cruel and hard a storm, that those on land did affirm, that in man's memory there was never such seen or heard of before; for it seemed that the sea would have swallowed up the islands, the water mounting higher than the cliffs, which are so high it amazeth a man to behold them, and living fishes were thrown onto the land.

This storm continued not only a day or two with one wind, but seven or eight days continually, the wind turning round and about, in all places of the compass, at least twice or thrice during that time, and all alike, with continual storm and tempest most terrible to behold, even to us that were on shore, so much more then to such as were at sea. So that only on the coasts and cliffs of the island of Terceira, there were above twelve ships cast away, and not only on the one side, but all around and about it in every corner, whereby nothing else was heard but complaining, crying, lamenting, and telling, 'Here is a ship broken in pieces against the cliffs, and there another, and all the men drowned.' So that in the space of twenty days after the storm, they did nothing else but fish for dead men, that continually came driving on the shore.

Among the rest was the English ship called the Revenge, that was cast away upon a cliff near to the island of Terceira, where it brake into an hundred pieces and sunk to the ground, having in her 70 men, Gallegoes, Biscayans, and others, with some of the captive Englishmen, whereupon one was saved that got upon the cliffs alive, and had his body and head all wounded, and being on shore brought us the news, desiring to be shriven, and thereupon presently died. The Revenge had in her diverse fair pieces of brass [artillery] that were all sunk in ye sea, which they of the island were in good hope of weighing up again the next summer after.

On the other islands the loss was no less than in Terceira; for on the island of St. George there were two ships cast away; on the island of Pico two ships; on the Island of Graciosa three ships; and besides those there came every where around about diverse pieces of broken ships, and other things fleeting towards the islands, wherewith the sea was all covered most pitiful to behold.

On the island of St. Michael there were four ships cast away, and between Terceira and St. Michael three more were sunk, which were seen and heard to cry out; whereof not one man was saved.

The rest put into the sea without masts, all torn and rent; so that of the whole fleet and armada, being 140 ships in all, there were but 32 to 33 arrived in Spain and Portugal, yea, and those few with so great misery, pain and labour, that not two of them arrived there together, but this day one, and tomorrow another, next day a third, and so one after the other to the number aforesaid. All the rest were cast away upon the islands, and overwhelmed in the sea, whereby may be considered what great loss and hindrance they received at that time; for by many men's judgements it was esteemed to be much more than was lost by the army that came for England; and it may well be thought, and presumed, that it was no other but a just plague purposely sent by God upon the Spaniards and that it might truly be said, the taking of the Revenge was justly revenged upon them, and not by the might and force of man, but by the power of God, as some of them openly said in the isle of Terceira, that they believed verily God would consume them, and that he took part with the Lutherans and heretics; saying further that so soon as they had thrown the dead body of the Vice Admiral Sir Richard Grenville over board, they verily thought that as he had a devilish faith and religion, and therefore the devils loved him, so he presently sunk into the bottom of the sea, and down into hell, where he raised up all the devils to the revenge of his death; and that they brought so great storms and torments upon the Spaniards, because they only maintained the Catholic and Romish religion. Such and like blasphemies against God, they ceased not openly to utter, without being reproved of any man therein, nor for their false opinions; but the most part of them rather said and affirmed, that of truth it must needs be so.

As one of the Spanish fleets put out of Nova Hispania [Mexico], there were 35 of them by storm and tempest cast away and drowned in the sea, being 50 in all; so that but 15 escaped. Of the fleet that came from Santo Domingo there were 14 cast away, coming out of the channel of Havana, whereof the Admiral and the Vice Admiral were two of them; and from Tierra Firma [South America] in India there came two ships laden with gold and silver, that were taken by the Englishmen; and before the Spanish army came to Corvo, the Englishmen at times had taken at least 20 ships, that came from Santo Domingo, India, Brazil, etc, and all were sent to England.

From the foregoing it will be readily apparent that not only was the English royal galleon *Revenge* lost on Terceira, but also at least a dozen other ships, some of them of the double plate-fleet from Havana, others from Don Alonzo de Bazan's escort fleet of galleons from mainland Spain.

Having studied the Journal and a great deal of other relevant material, I was now ready for the second part of my plan to locate not only vessels from the 1588 Spanish Armada, which I had done, but also ships lost at the trans-Atlantic plate-fleet revictualling haven in the Azores, and possibly, if fortune smiled on me, Grenville's flagship the *Revenge*. Having established that the latter had ended her somewhat chequered, but finally glorious, career on the island of Terceira accompanied by no less than a dozen of Philip of Spain's ships, including a galleon or two from the double 1590–1 plate-fleet, I was determined to take an expedition to the Azores for the summer of 1972. The Council for Nautical Archaeology, London, at the request of my friend Dr Peter Davies, gave their support to the project. I made two reconnaissances to Lisbon and to the Azores to establish contact with the ministries on the mainland of Portugal and with the Regional Museum of the Azores, whose curator was Dr Manuel Baptista de Lima.

Dr Baptista de Lima was most enthusiastic about my plans, and gave me a letter of introduction to Professor José Teixera, who taught naval history at the Portuguese Naval Academy in Lisbon. By a coincidence, the professor's daughter was at that time studying for a Master of Arts degree in history, and her thesis concerned the last fight of the *Revenge*. I was able to assist by obtaining primary archival material from the Public Record Office and the British Museum, saving her the trouble and expense of visiting London. Professor Teixera contacted both the Ministry of Marine, which is responsible for all surface and underwater activities in Portuguese waters, and the Ministry of National Education, which holds responsibility for administration of Portugal's recently enacted laws pertaining to seabed antiquities.

The Ministry of Marine had no objections to my plans, and a few days after the initial enquiries were made a cinema auditorium was booked, and I showed to an audience of government officials a copy of my 1968–70 film of the Spanish Armada expeditions which I had made in conjunction with the BBC *Chronicle* programme. The Ministry of National Education explained that the letters of support from the CNA and the curator of the Azores museums would ensure that the appropriate permits would be issued in due course. The terms of reference would be that I could search for, survey and salvage items from the *Revenge*, but if I located vessels other than the *Revenge*, I would have to apply for a further permit.

I had already started recruiting my team, its backbone consisting of keen young divers who were undergraduates from half a dozen UK universities. John Tayless, who was at that time teaching marine biology at the University of Bristol, had ideas about a 'shark behaviour' study. His theory was that the free-swimming pelagic sharks in mid-Atlantic would be 'opportunity feeders' and that they could go without a good meal for up to a month at a time. Tayless hypothesised that even in a somewhat hungry state, sharks may not attack a victim until their feeding responses have been stimulated by something like a flash of light reflected from the under-belly of a mackerel. Sharks are notoriously short-sighted, and hunt their prey via a combination of acoustic ranging and smell. Their apparent predilection for light objects led, in the nineteenth century, to the seaman's belief that 'sharks don't eat niggers'. In point of fact a shark will sit down to as happy a lunch off a black man as a white one; the problem is that he sees the white man more easily, therefore involving himself in a form of underwater, gastronomic racial discrimination.

The next part of Tayless's scheme was a trifle hazardous, or so I thought. He had prepared a long list of underwater visual tests, and suggested that as I would have the Associated Television camera crew with me, they should join in the experiments and film the sharks either ignoring or eating my divers. The survivors would record everything that was happening with still and cine cameras, and with writing slates.

I was still far from certain about all this when, on a visit to Spain, I called on my friend Peter Winter who was skipper of a charter boat based in Palma, Majorca. Peter had on board a young lady of twenty-one summers. She was English, very quiet, very attractive, could scuba dive, and had recently taken out a 75ft survey boat, skippering it as if she was an old salt. I was most impressed by this slip of a girl's handling of a large twin-screw motor yacht in the confines of a crowded marina, and was even more impressed when she told me that she had recently obtained the English Department of Trade yacht skipper's certificate. Her name was Jill Corbett-Thompson. Peter and his wife hinted that Jill would very much like to go on an underwater archaeological expedition, to which I countered that I had never included any women, that they would get in the way, argue a lot, and be subject to moods and bloody mindedness. I forgot about the young lady and returned to the UK.

Three additions to my team were Pat Baker, Brian Richards and John 'Mango' Chetham. All had been on Jeremy Green's Oxford University expedition to the Cape St Andreas peninsula in Cyprus, where Green and his team had surveyed a considerable portion of the seabed, locating and recording many ancient anchors. All three were keen underwater photographers, Baker and Richards in a professional capacity, and Chetham a dedicated amateur. They were elated with the success of their expedition to Cyprus, and told me tales of warm-water good-visibility diving, friendly Greek and Turkish citizens, and cheap Cyprus brandy. They also lobbied for the participation on my expedition of Signe Klepp, a Norwegian girl diver, who had been one of the mainstays of the Cyprus project. I gave them a flat 'No', and had no intention of relenting — until Baker informed me that she was a conservationist on the staff of the Maritime Museum in Oslo. That tipped the scales since we did not have a laboratory conservationist, and the staff at the Regional Museum in the Azores, although skilled in conservation of artifacts in general terms, had no experience in treating items from the sea.

The die was cast, and I invited Miss Klepp to join us. She accepted, whereupon I, not wishing to have one young lady amongst about fifteen young single men, wrote off to Spain to invite Jill Corbett-Thompson. It was a decision I was never to regret. Those two girls more than pulled their weight. They even volunteered to visit the local market at 6.30am to select food for that evening's dinner, arriving back for breakfast just as the male contingent were turning out of their beds. The girls worked as hard and dived as often as the boys, never shirked any task presented to them, and often undertook work they saw needed doing, and which had not been scheduled by me for action.

Tayless wanted to know why I had reversed my 'no females' rule, and I replied:

'You said you wanted to find out if sharks are attracted to light colours, so I thought perhaps two light-skinned girls in bikinis might excite their feeding responses. We could have the film crew underwater recording your team of observers, who in turn would be watching the sharks' reactions to the girls.'

'What if the sharks attack the girls?' Tayless enquired.

'You can always trust a scientist to cloud the issue. Surely it'll interest you to see if it takes a shark one minute or five to bite off a leg?' I replied.

'Sounds fine to me,' commented Tayless, 'I've checked up and there are at least six species of shark in Azores waters, including mako, hammerhead, nurse, tiger, bull and white-tipped reef.'

A further reconnaissance to Lisbon and the Azores now ensued, and on this occasion I was accompanied by my wife, Jean. In Lisbon we

136

met Jorge Albuquerque, head of the Portuguese amateur-diving organisation Centro Portuguese de Actividades Subaquaticas (CPAS). The CPAS headquarters in Lisbon was most impressive, consisting as it does of an old civic building converted into a complex which contains lecture theatres, diving store, compressor room, offices, and a magnificently stocked aquarium. The fish and crustaceans in the aquarium were all caught by members of the CPAS, mostly in the waters of the Cape Verde Islands off the coast of Africa, to which the CPAS sent a marine biological expedition every year. To add to their scientific accolades, the members had identified a considerable number of unknown species of sea creatures. This was diving with a purpose, and something which I heartily admired.

Jorge Albuquerque enquired if I would like to have their active support in the form of participation of his members; this I welcomed. We then worked out a roster by which twelve of the best of the CPAS divers would join my expedition in groups of four, spread over the proposed six-month season. Albuquerque accepted my standing invitation for him to visit us as often as he wished. Thus I established a good liaison with the Portuguese amateur diving fraternity, the Portuguese Navy via Professor Teixera, and the museum authorities via Dr Baptista de Lima.

I had already invited amateur American divers from the US base at Lajes Field on Terceira to join us in their spare time. The more divers we could train in our search systems, the better chance we had of finding the wreck of the *Revenge*. Dr Baptista de Lima assigned Dr Diocliciano Mario Silva to the expedition as museum liaison officer. The young doctor, whom we all came to know as 'Dino', was a charming young man, an expert diver, and an Anglophile. We became very close friends.

Back in England, Joe Casey supplied me with a 15 cubic ft per minute capacity scuba compressor, and a great deal of diving and yachting equipment. Avon Inflatables Ltd let me have three inflatable boats on long-term loan; Chrysler supplied four new 40hp outboard motors; and Ellerman & Papayanni Shipping Company offered to transport all my equipment from the UK to Portugal free of charge. An old diving buddy from as far back as 1961 — Peter Dick — had just returned from a job as a chief diving instructor on the Kenyan coast, and he immediately accepted the post of expedition diving officer.

The preparations nearly completed, in the spring of 1972 the vanguard of my expedition assembled at Terceira in an old Portuguese farmhouse which I had rented for the six-month season. The lease included a part-time gardener and his plump, smiling wife, Maria, who became our cook. The farmhouse could sleep about ten people, but as I had up to twenty divers at a time, the overflow was accommodated in large safari tents in the farm garden. A dog went with the house — an old gnarled mastiff, who appeared to be *in extremis*. Being unable to run, he walked with his two front legs, dragging his back legs behind him. As we were unable to pronounce his Portuguese name we called him Grenville, after the English hero whose flagship *Revenge* we had come to seek.

For the initial mobilisation phase of the expedition, there were only five of us on the island: Peter Dick, Siggy Klepp, Guy Wilkinson, Joe Vaudrey and myself. Miss Klepp proved not only to be a museum conservationist, she was also a scuba diver, yachtswoman and ex-merchant marine radio operator; in fact she could turn her hand to just about everything including splicing ropes. A shipping-container of equipment, our compressor on a road trailer, and my 24ft boat, all arrived at the port of Praia de Vittoria at the eastern end of the island. The problem of shifting them halfway across the island to Angra was solved when the commanding officer of the American base at Lajes Field offered to pack everything except the boat on board a landing craft, which motored from one port to the other as an exercise for the troops. I mention 'troops' because, surprisingly enough, in the Azores the US forces' boats are run by the US Army, not the navy. As one officer explained to me, 'Here at Lajes, the Army drive the boats, the Navy fly the planes, and the Air Force drive the buses.' Our farmhouse became a very popular visiting place for both local Portuguese residents and members of all branches of the US forces.

By now, all of the team were present, so we launched our boats and commenced our search for the *Revenge*. My prime spot for underwater exploration was the Bay of Vila Nova. At the outer limits of this, there boiled a reef, and on stormy days it made an awesome sight. Dr Baptista de Lima had informed me that, some years earlier, divers had carried out an illegal operation in locating two or more bronze guns on the reef, carrying them ashore at night, then smuggling them by boat to the mainland for sale to a private collector. The guns reputedly had a crest on the breech, and this crest was a flower. This I hypothesised could be the Tudor rose, which is always present on guns cast for Queen Elizabeth I. So, for many weeks, we regularly searched the reef area off Vila Nova Bay.

One would have thought that a thousand miles out into the Atlantic, pollution of the sea would be minimal. This was not so; for there was never a day in which we did not espy patches of sticky gooey oil from the cleaned-out bottoms of oil tankers, some of whose owners seem to care little or nothing for the fish and bird life which consequently suffer. On some days, we were all plastered with oil. It covered our wet suits like a slimy black sludge; it smeared all over our boats as we re-entered after a dive; it was on our hands, our faces and our bodies.

Oil was not the only hazard. There were the jellyfish; and I had never before seen so many. On some days, when we launched our rubber boats off the tiny jetty in the bay, the sea had the appearance of a semi-solid surface of the creatures. If one went out to sea for a mile or so there they were, those amorphous floating bags in their thousands, with hardly enough space for a diver to drop off backwards from an inflatable boat without getting stung. On the worst day of all I put eight divers in the water on a swim line, Jill and Siggy taking their share of the underwater search chores. There were few jellyfish to be seen at the commencement of the dive, but after about thirty minutes, with the divers swimming along in shallow water, an onshore wind brought huge shoals of them right into our path. I motored my inflatable boat slowly along, zig-zagging in front of the three surface buoys which the divers towed with them — one at either end, and one in the middle of the swim line — and watched the buoys snagging jellyfish tentacles until each buoy-line was towing about twenty fat, bloated jellyfish bodies along.

One of the male divers was first to surface. He shouted, 'I can't take any more of this, I'm stung all over.' With one diver off the swim line, the gap created was sufficient for the others to pass near to, but not see, cannon on the reef rocks; so I gave the required signal via the buoy-lines to the centre man, to call them all up. All were badly stung, but none more than Jill and Siggy. Siggy had what looked like a bad first-degree burn on her ankle; she had been stung by a Portuguese man-of-war, and bears the scar to this day. Jill had been stung on her forehead, around one eye, and on her lips. Within minutes her face began to swell, her left eye became almost closed, and her lips began to puff up.

I got everyone into the two inflatable boats, and we started back to the jetty, and our usual lunch of local homemade bread and cheese, fresh fruit including wonderful succulent pineapples, cold tea or lemonade and, if no more diving was contemplated, some good rough Terceiran red or white wine. The price of the wine was unbelievable.

A palatable red could be bought for about 15 US cents a bottle, and an excellent white for 20 cents.

Over lunch Jill, who was unable to eat anything, came over to where I was munching away at my bread and cheese and, prodding me in the chest with a finger asked in her usual very quiet voice, which I could hardly understand due to her swollen lips, 'Are we not going in again today?'

'No we are not,' I replied, 'everyone is too shattered by those bloody jellyfish and you, young lady, are in no fit state to take further punishment.'

It's not all that bad,' Jill mumbled as she walked off with a disappointed look on her face. I wondered at her quiet determined courage, and was far from surprised when she and Siggy got their heads together, and Siggy approached me with, 'Jill and I think that we haven't achieved enough today and there ought to be another dive.' I shook my head, to the complete and utter relief of the six young male divers who had taken all the jellyfish stings they could handle. I was very proud of those two girls as of that moment, and it was probably at about that time that I reduced (albeit involuntarily) my male chauvinist piggishness somewhat.

Days off from diving owing to bad weather were filled with 'make and mend', and equipment and boat overhaul. I spent my time in the museum with Dr Baptista de Lima, researching his records. My photographers and surveyors — Chetham, Baker and Richards — were now joined by another very talented underwater surveyor and archaeological illustrator, Sean Whittaker, who was a graduate of Salford and Bristol universities, and who also had been a member of Jeremy Green's expedition to Cyprus. Chetham, Baker and Richards photographed cannon in the courtyard of the museum, while Whittaker sketched the guns, and the fine detail on their breeches and barrels.

Apart from a miscellaneous collection of cast-iron guns, the museum also possessed some fine pieces of bronze artillery including Portuguese, Spanish and French guns, and one English piece. All were of sixteenth-century origin, and all had been immersed in the sea and were suffering from 'bronze disease'. The doctor told me how his museum came by the guns. Apparently, some years ago, amateur divers swimming at a depth of over 100ft on the west side of Monte Brazil — a huge rock mountain which stands proud of the sea on the outer edge of the harbour of Angra — had found the entire collection lying at the foot of the cliffs. It was presumed that the guns had been thrown into the sea from the fortress at the top of the cliffs, by a great nineteenth-century seismic disturbance. The Portuguese Navy lifted the guns, and they were transported to the museum.

The English gun fascinated me. It was a shortened culverin of a type cast by the English at the time of the Armada. It was undated, it had no gunfounder's name on it, but it had the English royal Tudor Rose emblem on its breech, encased in a garter, with the legend 'Hon y soit qui mal y pense', the whole surmounted by a crown. I examined the records of the bronze artillery on the island of Terceira in the year 1583 when the Marquis de Santa Cruz — having defeated the fleet of the French admiral Strozzi, occupied the islands and taken them into Philip of Spain's domain — ordered that every piece of bronze ordnance on the island be listed. It was possible to identify French and Portuguese guns in the museum yard as being listed by the Spaniards in 1583, but there was no sign of the English shortened culverin. It had evidently not been on the island in 1583. My supposition was that here lay a gun which had been on board the *Revenge* in her last battle against the naval might of Spain in 1591. Van Linschoten had said that the local people hoped to raise her guns out of the sea the year after her sinking. Sadly, no records appear to exist which would establish without doubt where the shortened culverin came from.

The study of sixteenth- and seventeenth-century muzzle-loading bronze artillery has been my abiding interest for the past twenty years. My enquiries into the strange holes which can be found around the breech of bronze guns that have lain in the sea for centuries — the 'crown piece' holes — led to eventual publication of a paper on the subject. Mentioned in the Bibliography, it seems to be the only one to date on what is to me a fascinating aspect of bronze gunfounding, and which has been ignored by historians for nearly 400 years.

Bad-weather days therefore were never wasted but, whenever it was at all possible, we continued our underwater search. The camera crew from ATV of London arrived and set up their headquarters in a rented house. Both the producer Robin Brown and expatriate Hungarian cameraman Ernie Vincze had learned to scuba dive so that they could record our expedition on film. Brown actually directed several sequences on the seabed. They accompanied the team of divers while they searched, my 24ft twin-screw motor launch becoming the expedition 'camera boat'. Failing to achieve success in the Bay of Vila Nova we proceeded to work our way around the island, dropping overlapping swim lines into the water. In the event we had covered about one third of the coastline of the island by the end of the 1972 six-month season.

In the Bay of Angra we located a galleon wreck close inshore. There was a scattering of cast-iron cannon, together with pavements of ferrous oxide cemented to rocks and covered in a thin layer of sand. Spanish coins of the mid- to late sixteenth century had been washed ashore from this wreck over the years, and presumably she had been extensively salvaged by the Spaniards shortly after she sank. There was no sign of bronze guns, all of which the Spaniards would have raised, their value being very many times that of cast-iron guns. There were no anchors, so presumably the ship's master had dropped his bower, kedge and sheet anchors in an effort to avoid dragging to destruction at the foot of the cliffs. The water was shallow and this allowed us ample time to establish that little of archaeological value remained to be excavated. Researches in Spain suggested that this was possibly the flagship of Juan de Salas, which was lost against the cliffs in the Bay of Angra in 1608.

In the middle of the Bay of Angra, in the main anchorage, we located another shipwreck or, more accurately, a scatter of cast-iron cannon with no evidence of anchors, artifacts or ballast stones. The depth of 75ft suggested that we should at least have found a ballast mound, under which timbers would be pinned. I came to the conclusion that we had located evidence from one of the threatened or doomed galleons of the 1592 plate-fleet, which had jettisoned her iron guns in the bay due to her leaky state. Another hypothesis, which bears consideration, is that this could have been where one of Bazan's Spanish fighting galleons, holed beneath the waterline by Grenville's *Revenge*, had jettisoned guns to bring the cannon shot-holes above the waterline.

Dr Baptista de Lima was informed of our discoveries, and we continued with our searches. My permits from Lisbon stated specifically that I could locate, survey and excavate the *Revenge*, and that if I located other wrecks and wished to excavate them I would have to apply for further permits. This I did not wish to do, for Dr Baptista de Lima had informed me that he proposed to have young Azoreans trained on the mainland in scuba diving and wreck survey techniques, so that the Angra museum could continue the marine archaeological programme which my interest had engendered. It seemed good manners and politically expedient to leave these two

Part of the completed expedition village at Porto Bello

Part of the expedition's self-constructed village at the water's edge at Porto Bello. Palm thatched 'bolio' at rear accommodates eight personnel. In the foreground, the compressor shack and aqualung store

Expedition catamaran heading for the Salmedina Reef galleon wreck site. The long white tubing forms part of the 'air lift' suction pump, used to extract excavated coral from the wreck site. The air lift compressor is situated in the centre of the boat

Professor Harold E. Edgerton of Massachusetts Institute of Technology. 'Doc' Edgerton, inventor of the strobe light and specialist in high speed photography, has also developed highly sensitive underwater sonar systems for wreck detection. 'Doc' is seen operating his sonar apparatus for the sub bottom detection of shipwrecks in the harbour of Porto Bello, taken on board the US Canal Zone survey vessel hired by the expedition

shipwrecks for the museum to excavate at a future date. Taking my cue, the doctor applied successfully to the Ministry of National Education and the Ministry of Marine in Lisbon for the whole of the Bay of Angra to be declared the underwater archaeological domain of the Angra museum. His application was agreed within a matter of weeks — the protection of the maritime heritage of the Azores island of Terceira was in very good hands.

In the meantime, Tayless was plodding away with his shark study or, more accurately, his attempt at a shark study. On more than one occasion we dropped the two girls into the water, surrounded by divers with cameras and recording slates. On every occasion that the ploy was tried, the sharks in the area turned tail and fled. Tayless never could fathom what went wrong. I suggested that perhaps the girls were using the wrong deodorant. We did not even get close enough for a photograph of a shark. Their lack of interest in our girls still remains a mystery to us all.

Unfortunately, after nearly six months of continued diving and underwater search, the remains of Grenville's *Revenge* likewise eluded us. Time was running out, as were our limited funds. The location of two Spanish galleons in the Bay of Angra was insufficient success to my way of thinking, for I had my mind set on the eventual discovery of a complete complement of bronze cannon. Meanwhile, the effect that the expedition had on its members was quite remarkable. The 'brotherhood syndrome' which had been a feature of my Spanish Armada expedition in Ireland, was equally strong in the Azores. Jill Corbett-Thompson had arrived on Terceira filled with the exciting news of her engagement to a young Englishman whom she had met in Spain. I was a bit miffed to learn from her that she proposed to leave the expedition for good in early August to get married, and told her that she was behaving in an irresponsible manner, and that she should have better things to think about than wedlock. Long before August, Jill confided that the expedition completely occupied her conscious moments more and more and, as it did so, the young English fiancé was thought of less and less. She eventually cancelled her return airline ticket to Spain, and wrote to break off the engagement.

Joe Vaudrey went down with a peptic ulcer halfway through the expedition, and the local doctor's advice was that Joe should leave the expedition immediately, and return to the UK for proper medical treatment and a thorough rest. We were sorry to see him go, but Guy Wilkinson drove Vaudrey to the airport and promised to be back for

145

the next dive. In the event Wilkinson returned with Vaudrey, who had also cancelled his airline ticket on the grounds that he could not leave a job half done. It is said that hardship builds character; if my assessment of the young people who staffed my expeditions is correct, this dictum certainly applies to all those whose service, hard work and unquestioning loyalty I have been privileged to command.

It was time to set in motion plans for demobilising the expedition, and I agreed with my team that the following day would be our last in the underwater world of the island of Terceira. The team set off to carry out a search around the foot of the cliffs of Monte Brazil, while I remained behind to pack my personal belongings. In the late afternoon, Wilkinson burst into my room with the cry, 'We have found the largest bronze cannon you have ever seen.' As I had not seen the gun in question I was in no position to argue! It appeared that in the last five minutes of the expedition's last dive, in 115ft of water, Joe Vaudrey had come across a huge bronze gun lying on a rocky seabed, completely exposed, and covered only with a thin white layer of calcareous marine growth. The following morning, I dived on the gun, and it was quite the largest piece of bronze artillery one could ever expect to find in the sea, measuring 15ft in length. The bronze lifting-rings atop the breech suggested that the piece was of Portuguese origin; the Spaniards and the Dutch invariably decorated their guns with dolphin lifting-handles. There were markings and escutcheons present, but they were indecipherable due to the thin covering layer.

I notified Dr Baptista de Lima of our find, and proposed to lift the gun and donate it to the Angra Regional Museum as our last act on the island of Terceira. The Portuguese law on antiquities would have allowed 50 per cent of market value reward if I had made a salvage claim. But such a claim, in law, would have led to the gun being disposed of at public auction, where it would undoubtedly have been purchased by either the naval or the military museum in Lisbon. By declining a reward, I could donate the gun to a museum of my choice, with the result that our expedition won the hearts of 300,000 Azoreans. The culverin, however, had yet to reach the museum, for it was still at the bottom of the Atlantic and I did not have the means to salvage a piece of ordnance which would tip the scales at 6,000lb. How were we to get such a large piece of artillery out of the sea? The answer seemed to lie with our friends at the US base at Lajes, so I telephoned the base and spoke to the deputy commanding general, an officer in the US Air Force. After hearing what our needs were, the general said tersely, 'Sounds good to me Syd, why don't we do it tomorrow?'

When tomorrow dawned, I and my expedition members were off the east side of Monte Brazil in our three inflatable boats and my 24ft cruiser. The first team of divers placed heavy-duty rope strops around the gun, and a second team waited on stand-by for the arrival of the American contingent. Soon afterwards, the US armada steamed into view, consisting of a 40ft launch containing senior air force, navy and army officers, and a large landing craft, crewed by army men, on the deck of which stood a 30ft high crane, which had been driven aboard at the US Army boat facility at Praia. It took less than fifteen minutes for the landing-craft skipper to run his vessel's bow into the cliffs, in a very skilled display of pilotage — and for the crane to drop its hook right where Joe Vaudrey, from his vantage point in an inflatable boat right under the bow of the landing craft, signalled for it to drop. On the seabed, my second team of divers hooked the cannon strops onto the hook and signalled for the lift. In no time at all a huge bronze gun came up out of the ocean depths to be laid on the deck of the landing craft. The gun was carried ashore, and Dr Baptista de Lima arrived to shake warmly the hands of all concerned. A nearby weighbridge registered that the gun weighed 6,300lb, and it was taken to the museum and set up on wooden blocks in the main front courtyard.

Several days of patient cleaning of seabed accretions and calcareous growths revealed a bronze culverin of infinite beauty. The gun was designed so that if stood on end it would look for all the world like a Doric column. It had fluting along the breech, and the muzzle was flared to look like a capital on top of a marble column. We quickly ascertained the date when it was cast — 1545. There was also a designer/founder's monogram on the barrel, and it read IODIZ. This was the sign of Joao (John) Diaz, the most famous of all sixteenth-century Portuguese gunfounders. There was also the royal Portuguese coat of arms, and the globe of Prince Henry the Navigator. Our culverin had the strangest breech-face I had ever seen, proving that the gun was for castle defensive works, and not for shipboard use. Guns used on board ship usually had a cascabel on the breech in the form of a knob, or sometimes a ring, to which the breeching-rope was attached. Our gun had a flat breech-face on which, in high relief, was a portrait of the head of a young man wearing a Renaissance-type helmet called a 'morion'. It was perhaps a portrait of the reigning monarch in Portugal in 1545 — King Joao III.

A party was held that night, and the salvage of the Joao Diaz culverin was duly celebrated by the expedition members, our Portuguese and American friends and Robin Brown and his ATV camera crew. The wine cellar of our rented farmhouse held a goodly store of several hundred gallons of wine, both white and red, of rough but palatable character. There were some sore heads the next day.

The only unhappy blot on that otherwise happy and tranquil Azorean landscape in 1972, was the unwelcome appearance of a party of British underwater treasure hunters who left the UK in secrecy and arrived at Terceira unannounced. Lacking the requisite archaeological permits, they later tried to recruit the support of the Council for Nautical Archaeology in London, which was already supporting our expedition. The CNA declined to become involved with the newcomers, so they travelled to Lisbon and tried to obtain the support of Jorge Albuquerque and the CPAS, and were met with a blank refusal. Foreign tourists are allowed a stay of no more than two months in Portugal without a visa, so the unofficial English were treated as foreign tourists, with the result that when their two months were up they were told to pull up their anchor and get out of Portuguese waters, which they promptly did. When they returned to the UK to face dissatisfied financial backers, the would-be wreck hunters had to have an excuse for their sudden return, and this they gave in a newspaper interview, attributing their shortened season to 'shoals of man eating sharks and gale force winds'. As it so happens 1972 was the warmest, driest summer in Terceira for nearly forty years; the incidence of gales was far less than in any average summer and, as for the 'man eating sharks', it would appear that our Misses Signe Klepp and Jill Corbett-Thompson had more courage than those who had made such an ignominious retreat.

As for ourselves, we had failed to find the *Revenge*, but had had a fair degree of success with our other shipwrecks and the bronze culverin. I immediately began thinking of how to raise funds to search the remaining unsurveyed coastline of Terceira for Drake and Grenville's flagship. In London, ATV edited the film of the expedition and it appeared nationwide in the UK in early 1973 with the title 'Search for Revenge', and was later distributed throughout the world by ATV. Home again in Wales, I began to pick up the pieces of my neglected home life and marriage, and promised once again to a long-suffering wife (with little conviction), that I regarded the Azores project as my last expedition.

In the principality of Wales, amateur divers were locating shipwrecks by accident and looting them piecemeal. Only rarely were Welsh divers the culprits; the majority of latterday underwater grave robbers came from England, on their annual vacation or just for a weekend's diving. The Welsh Association of Sub Aqua Clubs appointed me adviser on underwater archaeology and I immediately proceeded to draw up a 'Code of Conduct for Underwater Archaeology for Amateur Divers'. This code of practice was printed by WASAC and distributed to all the amateur diving clubs in Wales. The Association was definitely moving along the right lines, in fact the WASAC code of conduct came as a surprise to the far larger British Sub Aqua Club, which had not at that time contemplated such a move.

At the University College of North Wales, in Bangor, Dr D. Cecil Jones of the Department of Extra Mural Studies announced that he proposed to organise summer schools in underwater archaeology and I accepted his invitation to be a regular speaker. Cecil Jones provided the catalyst which was to bring together both divers and academics in north Wales in an attempt to educate the amateur diver in his responsibility towards a unique maritime heritage. Jones and I worked together and, with the aid and encouragement of my old friend Joe Casey, I started to put together what was to be the most ambitious undertaking of my life.

Chapter 9

Cold Light on Drake

With the quest for Drake's former flagship behind me, I concentrated on Drake himself. I was now planning an expedition to locate the lead coffin in which Drake was buried at sea off Porto Bello, Panama. The reason for this fascination with Drake's remains can only be explained by analysing Drake's turbulent career and enigmatic personality.

No English seaman, not even the immortal Horatio Nelson has had so much written about his life than Sir Francis Drake. But the wealth of material available about his great voyages has led historians along a path which, confined to the narration of Drake's heroic actions and the brilliance of his seamanship, ignores the psychological and moral make-up of the man, to the extent that Drake has come to be regarded as something of an omnipotent god-like figure, standing four-square as representative of all that was fine and decent, brave, adventurous and patriotic in the world of Elizabethan England.

Much that has been written about Drake is either palpably false or distorted, orientated towards preserving his image; in fact the situation has been reached when someone has to have the courage to say, as in the tale of the emperor's clothes, 'the king is naked!' The king in point of fact did wear clothes, but not the raiment cast upon him by generations of flatterers. Drake was a great man, but aspects of his character, his honesty — perhaps at times even his courage — can be called into question if we seek diligently for the truth. Dr Kenneth Andrews in *Drakes' Voyages* (1967) was one of the first historians to cast doubt on Drake, but he failed perhaps to take his argument to the point of detailed analysis of many events in Drake's life which cast a shadow over his personality.

Drake (c1545–96) was not born with a silver spoon in his mouth. His background was that of the son of an honest seaman who had 'found God', and had as a result become a lay preacher. Thus in Drake's embryonic years, we find the father guiding the young boy along what he believed to be God's chosen path. It was Edmund Drake's teachings and influence that moulded the son into a man who was so religious that his adherence to the Protestant faith bordered almost on fanaticism. Other elements in Drake's sometimes inexplicable behaviour in later life suggest that he was to some degree a megalomaniac. He certainly had delusions of grandeur, and also nursed suspicions of betrayal against some of his closest friends, executing one in a mockery of a trial, and sentencing another to death in his absence — a sentence Drake was later unable to carry out due to the victim's influence at Queen Elizabeth's court.

Drake saw God's hand and guidance in his every action, so much so that on his world circumnavigation he declared himself to be God's representative, chained up the ship's padre and, as we shall see, personally excommunicated him. Drake could be kind and gentle. He could also be extremely volatile, and utterly vindictive towards anyone who opposed or questioned his viewpoint. His hospitality and graciousness towards Spanish dons who fell into his hands, such as Don Pedro de Valdez during the Armada, and the captain of the *Cacafuego* which he captured during his circumnavigatory voyage, contrasts strangely with his resentment or even hostility towards Englishmen of more noble birth.

That Drake was possessed of superb qualities as a seaman, there can be no doubt. His feel for the handling and good husbandry of ships and their crews was to draw men to his side. The common seamen of Cornwall and Devon regarded him as their hero, for he was of their stock, and had sailed before the mast when a mere lad. He had the ability and also the instinct for navigation in unexplored uncharted oceans; as a navigator he was to become the greatest English seaman of them all.

His early undistinguished voyages, first as a crewman and later in command of small vessels, brought him to the attention of his kinsfolk, the Hawkins family of Plymouth. John Hawkins, intent on a slaving voyage to the Guinea coast of Africa in the old and leaky *Jesus of Lubeck*, invited the young Francis Drake to join him. They sailed from Plymouth in 1567. Towards the end of the voyage, Hawkins had promoted Drake to master of the small bark *Judith*. It was in the *Judith* that Drake accompanied Hawkins on an expedition to the West Indies. At San Juan de Ulua, Mexican embarkation point for the Spanish plate-ships, Hawkins's squadron, in need of repair and replenishment, put in and requested temporary accommodation. The Spaniards, lacking the means to defend the port adequately, acquiesced, and Hawkins's ships tied themselves stern to quay on the inner side of the breakwater. To the delight of the Spaniards on shore, and the distress of Hawkins and his men, a Spanish fleet came into view — the annual *plata flota*, come to collect treasure and to land the new Viceroy of Mexico, Don Martin Enriquez. After an exchange of pleasantries, the Spaniards moored their ships between Hawkins's vessels, the English smelling a trap — a trap which was prematurely sprung when a Spanish visitor who was enjoying Hawkins's hospitality accidently let a knife fall from the sleeve of his coat, where it had been concealed.

Amidst a hail of gunfire from shore batteries, and attempts to board and enter by Spanish infantry, Hawkins and his men managed to warp the *Jesus*, the *Judith* and the *Minion* off the shore. In the ensuing battle, Hawkins sank one Spanish ship and blew up another; but the pressure on his vessel was so great he was at last forced to leave the deck of the *Jesus* (which by now was swarming with Spaniards), and take to the much smaller *Minion*. This much-battered vessel, Hawkins now in command, managed to clear the harbour where she hove to so that Hawkins could attend to his wounded and count his dead. Of the *Judith* there was no sign; but she was referred to by John Hawkins as 'which bark . . . forsook us in our great misery'. The two vessels made their separate voyages back to England. And Drake was to bear for many a year the suspicion that he had deserted his commander, thereby breaking one of the cardinal rules of naval warfare when faced by a well-armed enemy who commands a superior force, namely 'mutual support'.

A later journey which tells us a great deal about Drake's character came in 1572–3, when Drake embarked on a voyage of reprisal piracy on the coast of Panama. Planning an attack on the mule train carrying silver and gold bullion on the Camino Reale, which ran from Panama City on the Pacific coast to Nombre de Dios on the Caribbean, Drake had insufficient manpower and resources to undertake the venture. He was, however, joined by the French corsair, seaman and hydrographer, Guillaume le Testu, who provided nearly 60 per cent of the manpower. Marching stealthily through the night, Drake and le Testu and their men lay in wait for the mule train, two and a half leagues from Nombre de Dios. The attack was successful; but in the ensuing pistol, arquebus and sword fight le Testu was wounded, the defeated Spaniards fleeing the field of battle. Drake and his men took as much of the treasure as they could carry, and buried a fortune in silver in a nearby river bank, hoping to return for it later. The

The author seen holding latten spoons, while leaning on a cannon. Orange Cayos wreck, *circa* 1681, near Porto Bello

Latten 'Apostle' spoons, trade goods from the *circa* 1681 wreck at Orange Cayos

Divers using the air lift to suck up broken coral which has been hand excavated on the *circa* 1746 galleon wreck. Gold and silver jewellery and silver coins were beginning to appear

Diver Tom Morrow uses a pulse induction metal detector on the Salmedina Reef
wreck off Porto Bello

Poor boat handling resulted in the expedition's Ingersoll-Rand air lift compressor being jettisoned in 70ft of water off the Salmedina Reef. It was raised and flushed with fresh water, after which it functioned perfectly

wounded le Testu was left to his own devices, one of his officers staying by his side. The following morning, Spanish reinforcements arrived; le Testu and his companion were captured. The latter was tortured to reveal where the buried treasure was, and le Testu was beheaded on the spot. There seems no reason why Drake could not have left behind a few silver bars and carried away his wounded French comrade. One is led to the inescapable conclusion that, in a theatre of war, Drake was not the sort of man one would wish to be back to back with in a foxhole.

Drake's conduct next comes into question during his voyage of circumnavigation of the world in the *Golden Hind*. At the time of sailing in 1578, Thomas Doughty was one of the closest of Drake's friends. During the early part of the voyage they appeared to have differences, mainly because Doughty was an adherent of the 'peace party' which was headed by the queen's treasurer, Lord Burghley; and Burghley had presumably instructed Doughty to try to restrain Drake should the latter act contrary to his express instructions from the queen — to seek Terra Australis. Burghley had his own agents abroad, and there is little doubt that he had wind of Drake's intention of attacking Spanish possessions in pursuit of treasure. At Port San Julian on the coast of Patagonia, Drake had Doughty arrested and clapped in irons, later to be taken ashore and accused of mutiny. Parson Francis Fletcher, the ship's padre, in defence of Thomas Doughty records that 'he was a man of gifts very excellent for his age, a sweet orator, a pregnant philosopher, a good gift for the Greek tongue and a reasonable taste of Hebrew, a sufficient secretary to a noble personage of a great place, and in Ireland an approved soldier and not behind many in studying law'.

Drake's charges against Doughty all revolve around a suspicion, nothing more, that Doughty had acted in a manner treacherous to Drake's expedition. To quote Fletcher again:

> Then it fell upon farther talk that Master Doughty said that my Lord Treasurer had a plot of the voyage. No, that he hath not quoth Master Drake. The other replied that he had. How? quoth Master Drake. He had it from me quoth Master Doughty. Lo, my masters, quoth he, [Drake] what this fellow hath done, God will have his treacheries all known, for her Majesty gave me special commandment that of all men my Lord Treasurer should not know it, but to see he his mouth hath betrayed him.

From this we can perceive the basis of Drake's accusation of treachery against Doughty. Drake says that the queen knew of his plans, but she did not want her Lord Treasurer Burghley to have any intelligence of them; Doughty has informed Burghley of Drake's plans, so Drake now asserts his right to condemn Doughty to death and to behead him. But one could hardly regard communication between a gentleman of Elizabeth's court and her lord treasurer as a treasonable offence against the state. If there was treachery — and there is no proof extant that there was — it was against the personal interests of Drake, who thereupon decreed the death of a close personal friend. On shore, Doughty at no time appealed for his life, although Parson Fletcher, Doughty's brother and others interceded with Drake.

A strange side to Drake's personality now appears, as he tries hard to find other crimes he can lay at the door of the hapless Doughty. An accusation of incitement to mutiny brought by Drake, and for which Doughty might justifiably be brought to trial and executed if found guilty, becomes overshadowed by specious allegations by Drake that Doughty had connived at an attempt to poison the Earl of Essex.

One of Drake's makeweights against Doughty was that the latter was involved in witchcraft and necromancy; in fact he left no stone unturned in his efforts to disgrace Doughty in the eyes of the officers and men present at the trial. The main evidence of Doughty's alleged incitement to mutiny came from one Ned Bright, whose testimony was declared suspect by some of those present when it was pointed out that only lately had Bright come forward with this evidence against Doughty, although Doughty's alleged attempts at mutiny had apparently been made long before. It came out that Bright held a grudge against Doughty because the latter had earlier impugned the honour of Bright's wife, stating that 'she had an ill name in Cambridge'.

In view of Drake's assuming such great powers of judgement over Doughty, it is curious that, when Doughty enquired as to Drake's royal commission for his expedition, the existence of which Doughty suspected was a figment of Drake's imagination, Drake replied, 'I warrant you my commission is good enough.' But he did not produce his royal commission, nor did he ever refer to it again. There is in fact no evidence that Drake ever held the queen's commission for his 1578–80 voyage.

After the trial and sentence of death, Drake and Doughty dined alone together and took communion. A little later Doughty placed his neck on the block and, after the bloody deed was done, Drake picked up Doughty's head and held it aloft for all to see, with the cry, 'Lo! this is the end of traitors.'

The voyage now continued. The Straits of Magellan safely passed, the treasure ship *Cacafuego* taken, Drake sailed on to the East Indies calling at Ternate and, close to the Greyhound Strait, the *Golden Hind* ran onto the Mulapatia Reef. She was eventually freed by the stratagem of jettisoning six guns and a considerable amount of cargo which had earlier been looted from Spanish ships — the treasure of the *Cacafuego* was not of course jettisoned.

Shortly after the *Golden Hind* had freed herself Drake, in a fit of rage, ordered Parson Fletcher to be fastened by the leg, with a staple and padlock, to the fore hatch, passing the following judgement: 'Francis Fletcher, I do here excommunicate thee out of the Church of God and from all the benefits and graces thereof, and I denounce thee to the devil and all his angels.' He also charged Fletcher never to come before the mast, stating that he would hang him if he did. Drake's apologists have looked upon this weird episode as being an illustration of Drake's excellent sense of humour. But no credence is to be placed on such excuses. Fletcher was an ordained minister of the Church, and such denigration and indignity could only be deliberately intended to reduce Fletcher in the eyes of the crew of the *Golden Hind* to a figure of fun. More probably Drake's reasons had their origins in two things — Drake's religious imbalance which encouraged him to act as if he was God's messenger, prophet and agent; and Fletcher's objections and probable continued reference to Drake's semi-judicial murder of Thomas Doughty at Port San Julian. There would undoubtedly be some form of enquiry when the expedition returned to England, so the protesting Parson Fletcher had to be vilified and made to suffer indignity, in order to discredit him. It was also possibly a warning to the rest of the officers and men on the lines of Voltaire's reference to the English execution of Admiral Byng: 'The English now and again shoot an admiral to encourage the others.'

No, there was no sign of humour in Drake's treatment of Parson Francis Fletcher. Try as one can to be charitable, nowhere in the published works on Drake, nor in the extant original manuscripts which deal with his life, do we see any evidence to suggest that Drake was possessed of even the remotest glimmer of a sense of humour. It is well to reflect on the difference in humanity and spirit between Drake and Hawkins. On the journey which ended so disastrously at San Juan de Ulua, one of Hawkins's officers, in a spirited argument with his commander drew his sword, Hawkins suffering a slight wound. The incident had all the ingredients of an open and shut case of mutiny at sea. It was treated as such, and the officer was found guilty and sentenced to death. At the point of execution, Hawkins stopped the proceedings, embraced the miscreant and forgave him, thereby gaining the undying support of a former opponent.

But to return to the voyage of the *Golden Hind*, leaving the Indies she made the long journey across the Indian Ocean and up the west coast of Africa. Nearly three years after setting out, Drake returned to England with a treasure equal to the whole of Queen Elizabeth's annual revenue from taxation and rents from royal lands. Queen Elizabeth allowed Drake to take a reasonable share of the treasure, and the entreaties and complaints from the Spanish ambassador were conveniently ignored. Drake was safe from any form of prosecution for the execution of Thomas Doughty; the treasure in the Tower of London saw to that. But for many years Doughty's family tried to obtain legal redress for the sorrow and tragedy they had suffered, and for Drake's unjustifiable stain on their family honour. Drake himself received a further reward when the queen, accompanied by the French ambassador, paid a visit to the *Golden Hind* as she lay in dock and made him a knight of the realm. Elizabeth, not wishing to further offend the king of Spain, invited the French ambassador to dub Drake knight. Her act of choosing not to dub Drake herself might also be construed as a degree of repugnance on her part to touch the seadog whom several members of her court regarded as a common pirate. But everywhere Drake's world circumnavigation was hailed for what it was — only the second ever made and the first by an Englishman. It was an amazing achievement.

In 1585 war broke out between England and Spain, and Drake was put in command of a fleet which sailed for the Spanish Main. In 1586 he made a raid on Spain's American possessions. This great raid has been described as a failure because it did not show a profit, the queen in fact losing heavily in the venture. But, viewed against the strategic considerations of Anglo-Spanish rivalry, the voyage achieved some degree of success; Spanish ports and settlements were attacked, ships and cargoes burned, and Spanish morale lowered, resulting in pleas to King Philip for stronger defences. Viewed against the impending Spanish invasion of England, the timing for Drake's raid was also right. Only one episode detracted from his success — his visit to the recently established English colony at Roanoke, Virginia. There, after listening to the complaints of the settlers, who regarded themselves as neglected, Drake offered them the choice of staying on to await a supply ship from England, or returning home with his fleet. The disgruntled colonists opted for England and sailed off with Drake; their relief ship arrived at Roanoke barely a week after the colonists had left. Thus Sir Richard Grenville's endeavours, and his cousin Sir Walter Raleigh's inspiration and vision, counted for naught. A more far-sighted man might have told the colonists to stand fast and await reinforcements and supplies, and this error of judgement on Drake's part added fuel to the fire of Grenville's implacable hostility towards him.

Drake's greatest naval success was undoubtedly at Cadiz in 1587 when his small squadron entered the outer harbour and destroyed a considerable number of Spanish ships. For this operation, Drake did hold the queen's commission. He had royal galleons and royal funds; he also had a collection of merchant adventurers tied to his coat-tails, some of whom courageously sailed with him in a quest for profit, while others sat back in the comfort and security of their London counting houses, eagerly anticipating a good return on their investment. Spain's naval might and her maritime commercial interests were to be harried, but there had to be a financial reward in it. To achieve both aims, Drake in the *Elizabeth Bonaventure*, with one Robert Wignall as his pilot, took the calculated and enormous risk of entering the outer harbour of Cadiz. Had the wind suddenly veered around to the north-west, Drake would have been embayed, and at the mercy of the Spaniards. His luck held and in the outer harbour Spanish galleys, operating in what for them should have been ideal conditions — a confined space in which, by clever manipulation of their oars, they could wheel about in standing turns, or stop dead in the water — found themselves at the mercy of English galleons. The latter appeared to be able to turn on a single piece of eight, their broadside guns loaded with grape and canister shot mowing the rows of galley slaves off their benches.

With the galleys repulsed, Drake went on to capture a huge galleon belonging to the Marquis de Santa Cruz himself. The fight raged all afternoon and into the night, and at first light Drake and his men, in a handful of pinnaces, braved the inner harbour where they set light to over a score more Spanish ships. This, for Drake, must have been his finest hour; his penchant for tactical strokes, supported by his loyal Devon seamen, could not be faulted at Cadiz.

Unfortunately, no sooner had Drake left the scene of his victory, than a serious dispute arose between him and his vice admiral, William Borough. Drake reasoned that if he was to stay on the coast of Spain and harry and intercept coastal traffic, then he must have a shore base close at hand where he could careen and clean the bottoms of his ships, and revictual and take on water. But this grand design was impractical for several reasons. For one thing he did not have enough troops to hold such a shore base even if he could capture one; secondly, no arrangements had been made in England for any such plan, and without support from England such a land base could not survive. Drake had his way, a landing was made, and Borough was accused of mutiny; whereupon Borough, in a perfectly reasonable letter to Drake, set out all the problems which would result from the attempted establishment of a land base. That letter was Borough's undoing for, although there was nothing insubordinate in the letter, as Dr Kenneth Andrews commented, 'Drake's response suggests precisely the touchy arrogance that Borough and others found insufferable'. Drake had Borough arrested and imprisoned on board the latter's own flagship, the *Golden Lion*.

The land base was short-lived, as was the grand design for harassing Spanish coastal trade. Drake got wind of a great carrack, allegedly laden with treasure, which was due shortly in the Azores. Off went Drake and the fleet, the gentlemen adventurers' minds as intent as Drake's on turning a highly successful naval exercise into a profit-making commercial venture. The crew of the *Golden Lion*, however, mutinied in support of their vice admiral, took over the ship and released Borough who, on being offered command, immediately accepted. The *Golden Lion* sailed for England, where Borough recounted his tale of victimisation. Drake, hearing of Borough's escape, sentenced his vice admiral to death in his absence. One cannot help but feel that if Drake had been able to apprehend William Borough at that moment, the latter would undoubtedly have suffered the same fate as Thomas Doughty on the coast of Patagonia.

On his return to Plymouth, Drake indulged himself in a personal vendetta against Borough, even to the extent of trying to have him arrested and executed. But William Borough and his family had powerful friends at court and Drake was unsuccessful. This did not, however, deter Drake from many years of persecution.

The events of the following year, the year of the Spanish Armada, are very revealing as regards Drake's conduct as a commander. As already mentioned in Chapter 2, on 21 July Lord Howard of Effingham on board the *Ark Royal* had ordered that, during the hours of darkness, the English fleet should keep together by each ship following the stern lantern of the one in front, the whole led by Sir Francis Drake on the *Revenge*. We also learned that the crippled *Nuestra Señora del Rosario* was wallowing helplessly, far behind the other Spanish vessels. Effingham's plan was a sound one, but sometime during the night Drake's stern light disappeared from view and, as the weather was fine and clear, it must have been deliberately extinguished. When the sun rose on the 22nd, there was a scene of confusion. It appeared that the galleons in the English van had inadvertently followed the wrong lanterns, due to Drake's dowsing of his, and Effingham, to his horror, found the English fleet scattered to such an extent that some of them were only mast tops on the distant horizon. He himself was almost hard against the rearmost Spanish ships and in danger of encirclement, and only the skill of the master of the *Ark Royal* saved him. Of Drake there was no sign.

Why had Drake deserted his post and disobeyed Effingham's instructions by suddenly vacating the lead position in the English fleet, and made no attempt to signal his movements to any other English vessel, which, since he took an escort vessel — the *Roebuck* — with him, he could have easily done? The answer lies with Pedro de Valdez in his stricken *Nuestra Señora del Rosario*; the latter woke to find the feared 'El Draque' lying only a musket shot away. The helpless Spanish flagship, in no position to fight such an unequal battle, was forced to strike her colours and surrender to Drake. One of the latter's first actions was to have his prize crew search for treasure, and this was found in a huge wrought-iron strongbox in the great cabin aft in the captured ship. Drake then transferred the treasure and the captive Pedro de Valdez to the *Revenge*, where he entertained him in a most cordial and gentlemanly manner. Meanwhile the *Nuestra Señora del Rosario* with prize crew aboard, thereby ensuring that Drake and his crew would receive a share of the prize money based on the value of the vessel and its contents, was taken into Dartmouth by the *Roebuck*. Drake himself sailed on again to rejoin Effingham but, thanks to his dereliction of duty, the English were in no position to fight that day, and many valuable hours were lost.

Drake later made the excuse that, in the night, he had seen sail to starboard, and thought this might be part of the Armada slipping to the English rear to attack by surprise at dawn. He had put his helm over and, with the *Roebuck*, had followed the strange sail, only to find that they were harmless German Lübeckers. Having lost sight of the English fleet, he could only return to his original course, hoping to catch up with the queen's ships at sunrise. But at sunrise, to his surprise there was this great Spanish galleon, wallowing in the waves, partially dismasted and helpless. He did the right thing and took possession of their ship. If Drake's story were true, it would still illustrate the actions of a man who is irresponsible and lacking in discipline. There was nothing to prevent Drake sending his accompanying ship after the suspected Spaniards, with instructions to fire guns and alert others of the queen's fleet if the night marauders did turn out to be enemy vessels.

The only knowledge we have of Drake's activities in the later actions of the Battle of the Narrow Seas is that when Effingham ignored his own instructions for he himself to lead the attack on the Spaniards after they were scattered by the fire ships off Calais, Drake led the first attack on the Spanish fleet. We cannot be sure if he took any further action after that initial encounter off Gravelines; there are no records extant. But we do have the testimony of the recently knighted Martin Frobisher who accused Drake of cowardice, stating in front of witnesses that Drake, after going up to the Spaniards off Calais, firing his bow chase-guns and his broadside, sheered off and took no further part in the battle. Frobisher made other, equally damaging, accusations against Drake to a senior member of Drake's crew, Mathew Starke, and what is more, saw to it that he had no less personages than Lord Sheffield and Sir John Hawkins as witnesses. Starke immediately repaired either to the *Revenge* or to his lodgings, and there set down all that had been said by Sir Martin Frobisher, calling in a Mr Grey, master of Effingham's flagship, another Mr Grey, master of the *Revenge*, and captains Spindelow, Platt and Vaughan, to witness his deposition.

Mathew Starke's deposition in its entirety is as follows. Modern historians tend to gloss over it, hinting that Frobisher was a mercurial character, and something of a fire-eater. This he undoubtedly was, but he was also sincere and very brave, giving his life in his queen's cause at Brest in 1594.

Mathew Starke's Deposition

A note of certain speeches spoken by Sir Martin Frobisher at Harwich in the presence of diver persons, as followeth; Sir John Hawkins; The Lord

William Parker of Plymouth, reprisal pirate, who knew and recorded where Drake lay in his lead coffin. The original painting was destroyed in a fire at a National Trust property. The church is St Andrews, Plymouth. The scene at top left is of Parker's exit from Porto Bello in 1601, with the great castle of San Felipe de Sotomayor on the left and a small forteleza on the right. The battle scene on a bridge, bottom left, illustrated the most critical part of Parker's taking of Porto Bello in 1601. Note that the portrait subject has his left arm in a sling. Parker stated in his journal, 'I was shot in at the elbow and out at the wrist by a musket ball from the Wester shore'. The original painting hung in Saltram House, Devon, the subject of the portrait and the scenes in it unidentified by the 'Parker's of Saltram' until the mystery was unravelled by the author in 1975 (*By courtesy of the Courtauld Institute of Art*)

Bronze breech blocks from small breech loading swivel guns from the Salmedina Reef galleon wreck

Silver 'pieces of four' from the Salmedina Reef galleon wreck

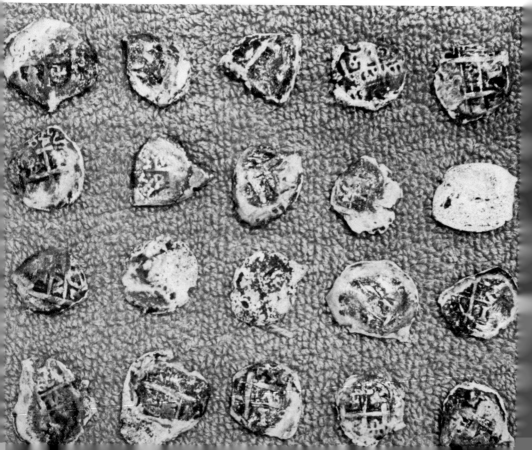

Sheffield, with others, whose names I cannot recite.

The 11th day of August, 1588, I arrived at Harwich, and delivered the letter sent by the Lord Admiral [Effingham] unto Lord Sheffield, whom I found in bed in the house of Mr. King. First, after I had delivered my Lord's letter, the Lord Sheffield bade me depart, and so I did according to his commandment. Then he immediately sent for me again; at which time of my return I found there Sir John Hawkyns, Sir Martin Frobisher, with divers others, who demanded of me in what surety the ships were in, and whether they were all at Margate or not. Then Sir Martin Frobisher began some speeches as touching the service done in this action; who uttered these speeches following, saying; Sir Fra, Drake reporteth that no man hath done any good service but he; but he shall well understand that others hath done as good service as he, and better too.

He [Drake] came bragging up at first, indeed, and gave them [the Spaniards] his prow and his broadside; and then kept his lowfe [sailed off] and was glad that he was gone again, like a cowardly knave or traitor. I rest doubtful, but the one I will swear. Further, saith he, he hath done good service indeed, for he took Don Pedro. For after he had seen her in the evening, that she had spent her masts, then like a coward, he kept by her all night, because he would have the spoil. He thinketh to cozen [cheat] us of our shares of fifteen thousand ducats; but we will have our shares, or I will make him spend the best blood in his belly; for he [Frobisher] hath had enough of those cozening cheats already.

He hath, saith he, used certain speeches of me, which I will make him eat again, or I will make him spend the best blood in his belly. Furthermore he said, he reporteth that no man hath done so good service as he. But he lieth in his teeth; for there are others that hath done as good as he, and better too.

Then [Frobisher] demanded of me if we did not see Don Pedro over night or no. Unto which I answered, 'No'. Then he told me that I lied; *for she was seen to all the fleet*. Unto the which I answered, I would lay my head that not any one man in the ship did see her until it was morning, that we were within two or three cables length of her [400 to 600yd]. Whereupon he answered Ay Marye, saith he, you were within two or three cables length; for you were no further off all night, but lay a-hull by her. Whereupon I answered No, for we bare a good sail all night, off and on.

Then he ask me to what end we stood off from the fleet all night; whom I answered that we had scryed [seen] three or four hulks, and to that end we wrought so, not knowing what they were. Then said he; Sir Francis was appointed to bear a light all that night; which light we looked for, but there was no light to be seen, and in the morning, when we should have dealt with them [the Spaniards], there was not above five or six [English galleons] near unto the Admiral, by reason we saw not his light.

After this and many more speeches, which I am not able to remember, the Lord Sheffield demanded of me what I was, unto which I answered, I have been in the action with Sir Francis in the Revenge, this seven or eight months. Then he demanded of me, What art thou? a soldier? No and like your honour, I am a mariner. Then saith he, I have no more to say unto you, you may depart.   by me . . . . . . Mathew Starke.

All this written on the other side I do confess to be true, as it was spoken by Sir Martin Frobisher, and do acknowledge it in the presence of these parties whose names are hereunder written

Captain Platt; Captain Vaughan; Mr. Grey, Master of the Ark [Royal] John Grey, master of the Revenge; Captain Spindelow.

Moreover, he [Frobisher] said that Sir Francis was the cause of all these troubles, and in this action he showed himself a coward.

by me, Mathew Starke.

It is obvious that when Lord Sheffield summoned Starke to again appear before him, Sheffield, Frobisher and Hawkins had been getting their heads together. Note that Hawkins, whose presence is acknowledged, never at any time attempted to contradict Frobisher's accusations against Drake. Also that Starke, deeming the matter to be of no small importance, saw to it that he had very credible witnesses to his signature, as he set down whatever he could remember whilst it was still fresh in his mind. Yet Drake did not take up the challenge, nor is it recorded that he ever made any comment about the matter, although he must have known of the deposition.

Frobisher's claim that Drake had 'cozened' them out of 15,000 ducats is interesting. For information we must consult both Spanish and English records concerning the chest of treasure taken by Drake from the captured *Nuestra Señora del Rosario*. There is a document in Drake's own handwriting in which he admits to having 25,300 (ducats?), and another bearing Drake's signature in which he testifies to having transferred 3,000 pistolets to Lord Howard of Effingham. But Spanish testimony states that there was a chest on board the *Rosario* containing 50,000 ducats 'of which don Pedro has one key, and the Duke the other'. What happened to the 15,000 (referred to by Frobisher) or 25,000 missing ducats we do not know. Drake's tally of coin did not match that of the captured Spaniards themselves.

Starke's deposition in full can be found in J. K. Laughton; an extract can be found in A. E. W. Mason's life of Drake, but no mention of Starke's statement, surprisingly enough, can be seen in Michael Lewis's account of the battle, *The Spanish Armada*. J. S. Corbett mentions suspicions as to how Drake landed up a-hull overnight by the *Rosario*, but quotes only part of Starke's deposition without naming Starke or providing any references. In other words it seems to have been near heresy to question Drake's honesty, courage and major part in the defeat of Medina Sidonia. In reality the whole story of Drake against the 1588 Spanish Armada is shrouded in myth, common assumptions and very little fact, and what fact there is suggests that Drake's part in the fight from the Lizard to Gravelines was no greater than anyone else's; certainly less than Frobisher's — unless we count that mythical game of bowls on Plymouth Hoe!

If Drake's judgement was suspect in 1588, it was decidedly faulty in the following year when he and Sir William Norreys undertook a massive combined-operations offensive against the Spanish and Portuguese mainland. The total number of ships, great and small, at Drake's disposal was about 150; Norreys, in charge of proposed land operations, commanded 10,000 men. It was indeed an imposing array of English naval and military might; enough one might have thought to come between King Philip and his sleep. The official Elizabethan policy of divided command led as it did before, and would many times again, to disputes between land and sea commanders and rivalries between the various services, resulting almost in chaos, and ending invariably in defeat. Such was the case with the 1589 English Armada against Spain.

The 1589 expedition was financed on a joint-stock basis by gentlemen adventurers, who participated in the voyage with an eye to profit, and the queen's own purse. The original estimates were far exceeded and the final bill came to almost £150,000, of which £50,000 was provided by the queen. Elizabeth also subscribed six royal ships, and promised an artillery siege train. The latter promise was not kept, and it was that lack of siege artillery which was eventually to doom the land operations to failure, as the English troops stood in front of the gates of Lisbon.

Drake's instructions included, as first priority, an attack on the remnants of the Spanish Armada lying at anchor at Santander. Philip of Spain's fleet was not in good fettle after its losses of the previous year; a considerable number of the ships at Santander were undergoing refit, with their topmasts unstepped and their artillery either ashore or laid on the ballast. There could be little doubt that a determined attack on that port could have almost completely emasculated Spain's naval might. The second priority was to place the pretender Dom Antonio onto the throne of Portugal. The death of Dom Sebastian in 1580, making the royal family extinct in the male line, had led to a power vacuum in Lisbon, and Philip of Spain seized the opportunity presented to him for a unified Iberian peninsula under one flag by sending a force of Spanish troops under the command of the Duke of Alva to occupy the country. The pretender to the throne, Dom Antonio, was a weak-willed, far from intelligent man, whose court in exile in England was riddled with agents of Philip of Spain. As Drake and Norreys's plans were passed on to Dom Antonio and his advisers so these agents, via contacts in the Netherlands, made the king of Spain and Portugal privy to Queen Elizabeth's grand design for an attack on Lisbon. In due course, the mightiest armada England had ever launched departed on what could have been a turning point in the war with Spain, and a great strategic victory. It was to be nothing of the kind.

Off the northern coast of Spain, Drake, commanding the *Revenge*, gained intelligence of a great fleet of merchant ships at Corunna. Ignoring the possibility of destroying the almost helpless Armada ships at Santander, Drake made for the more westerly town, to learn on his arrival that there was only one large galleon there, and a few smaller craft. An English force, weakened by the defection of twenty-five ships, attacked and took the lower part of the town, and destroyed the shipping in the anchorage. The English land forces, unable to breech the main battlements of the town, spent their energy in an orgy of looting and drinking. There was little profit at Corunna for either the private investors or the queen, so Drake and Norreys turned to the next part of their plan, and completely disregarded the possible attack on the Armada at Santander.

Military historians of the period have never ceased to be amazed by the English landing of the main battle force of infantry and cavalry at Peniche, 45 miles north of Lisbon. If an attack on Lisbon was planned, why did they not make their landing on the north side of the River Tagus, within sight of the capital? The decision to land at Peniche is, in fact, inexplicable, defying as it did the cardinal rule of 'never divide your forces in the face of the enemy'; for Drake took all the ships to the Tagus with the idea of supporting Norreys as he appeared at the gates of Lisbon.

The English fleet and military arm had been somewhat strengthened by the timely appearance of the queen's new favourite, Robert Devereux, Earl of Essex, accompanied by the diminutive Welshman Sir Roger Williams, who shares with Lord Mountjoy the distinction of being the two ablest soldiers of Elizabeth's reign. Essex had brought the royal galleon *Swiftsure*, and another six ships, to add to Drake's fleet. But the march from Peniche to the gates of Lisbon was contested every inch of the way by companies of Spanish skirmishers, so that the 45 mile land journey took Norreys, Essex and Williams and their men six days to cover. Short of food and minus the promised siege train, they made their attack on the walls of Lisbon eight days after their disembarkation at Peniche. Thus the element of surprise, if there was ever any hope of one, was thrown to the wind by gross incompetence, for which both Norreys and Drake must accept the greater part of the blame.

The two elements, land and sea, of the English forces, had now lost contact with each other. Drake's duty was clear to all on board the English fleet, and that was to go in under the guns of the Spanish forts, engaging them with artillery, until his ships' broadside guns could bombard the city of Lisbon. Drake was not short of skilled seamen. There were many in his fleet who would have cheerfully sailed within range of the Spanish shore batteries, to get through to Norreys. Robert Wignall for instance, pilot of the *Elizabeth Bonaventure*, Drake's flagship for the attack on Cadiz harbour, was with him again, only this time promoted to master of the queen's royal galleon *Nonpareil*. Spanish and Portuguese shipping lay at anchor in the Tagus, all at the mercy of the English, yet Drake did not move. Drake has been excused on the grounds that he was right not to risk his ships in trying to pass the guns of the shore battery; but this ignores the fact that his passage up the Tagus to Lisbon was in the plan discussed and agreed before Norreys, Essex and Williams set foot ashore at Peniche. Drake's own excuse for not supporting Norreys was that 'the sickness and weakness of the mariners and soldiers was so extreme as they were not able to handle the tackle of the ships'.

It is meaningful to compare Drake's inactivity with the actions of the commonwealth admiral Robert Blake and his vice admiral, Captain Richard Staynor, who in 1657 took the English fleet into the anchorage at Santa Cruz on the island of Teneriffe, to attack more than a dozen Spanish ships which lay at anchor. Blake took on the shore batteries at close range while Staynor, ignoring the fortress guns, took his ships right up to the anchored Spaniards. Disdaining to pass them in line ahead — thereby offering the shore guns a series of moving targets — he anchored his ships just off the Spanish galleons and, warping his ships by means of springs attached to fore and aft anchors, was able to concentrate his fire on any part of the Spanish ships he wished. All the Spanish ships were sunk and, depending on whose journal one believes, this means that Staynor sank at least twelve and possibly fifteen Spanish vessels, anchored only 200yd from the forts. Staynor suffered severe damage to all his ships, and the mainmast of his own flagship, the *Speaker*, was so weakened it seemed possible it might collapse at any moment. In 1801, Nelson executed another such heroic task when he took the English fleet into the anchorage at Copenhagen, ignoring the gun batteries ashore, to destroy the Danish fleet completely.

For the English force in Spain, however, there was nothing left but to withdraw, to be picked up by Drake's ships. At this point a despatch vessel arriving from London brought a letter from the queen which made it abundantly plain that she was angry at their failure to destroy the surviving Armada vessels at Santander. Drake now some-how forgot that his crews were too sick and weak to man the ships, and sailed off to the Azores in search of a valuable prize or two. Bad weather dispersed the fleet, and the *Revenge*, leaking badly, turned for home, and disgrace and humiliation for Drake. Drake appeared to have lost his magic touch. The élan and spirit he showed in his superlative attack on Cadiz only two years before, had apparently evaporated. Some say that Drake had lost his nerve. Perhaps Frobisher was right in his accusations of Drake's cowardice. The queen summed up the activities of her officers on the Lisbon raid quite succinctly when she commented that 'they went to places more for profit than for service'. Drake stayed in Plymouth to ponder over his failure at Lisbon, ignored and neglected.

By late 1594, Drake was champing at the bit again, wanting to return to the scene of his earlier successes in the Spanish possessions in the Americas; and in 1595 he and Sir John Hawkins sailed on what was to be the last voyage for both of them. The grand design was to sail to the Caribbean and sack the rich ports of Cartagena and Nombre de Dios.

This last voyage was a large undertaking, and a very costly one; and again Elizabeth's system of joint command created problems, Drake and Hawkins falling into early disagreement and fierce argument. No sooner had the fleet of more than a score of ships, including the royal galleons *Defiance* and *Elizabeth Bonaventure* sailed, than Drake was complaining to Hawkins that he had taken on board his ships 300 more men than he could victual. A far cry this from his voyage of circumnavigation, when a small crew achieved so much, due to her commander's eye for logistical detail.

Drake insisted that the problem be solved by calling at the Spanish island of Grand Canary, to attack the town of Las Palmas, sack it and take on water and food. Hawkins argued that this diversion from the original plan could place the whole project in jeopardy. In the event, the sage old mariner John Hawkins was to be proved right, but Drake would have none of Hawkins's objections, and so the English fleet attacked the town, to be repulsed without one man setting foot ashore. Drake's ships managed the next leg of the voyage without those extra victuals and water that Drake had said were indispensible to him. But the journey now was to San Juan, Puerto Rico, for Drake's ships had captured a small Spanish vessel, whose captain told Drake that a rich plate-fleet galleon had put in there for repairs.

No sooner had the English left Grand Canary than the Spanish admiral Don Pedro Tello de Guzman arrived with a squadron of fast sailing *fregatas*. The latter now had a stupendous piece of luck for, as Drake sailed on to Puerto Rico, he detached his smaller scout vessels to sail ahead; two of these blundered into the *fregatas*, and in a short but spirited fight, one English ship was captured. She was a brand new ocean-going pinnace, built for Drake from his own funds and named the *Francis* after him. Her captain was none other than Robert Wignall, who had left the queen's service to join Drake's force shortly before the fleet sailed. Robert Wignall and his men were probably subjected to torture, for it is difficult to see how else Pedro Tello de Guzman could have found out Drake's destination. It is hardly likely that one of Drake's officers, and also a close personal friend, would have volunteered the information. Of Robert Wignall we hear no more. After serving Drake so splendidly in conning the English galleons in and out of Cadiz in 1587, and commanding the *Elizabeth Bonaventure* in the raids on Corunna and Lisbon in 1591, he may have died on the rack, or on a rowing bench in the Spanish galleys. But Tello de Guzman, armed with his new intelligence of Drake's movements, pressed on with all sail and, having passed Drake in the night, reached San Juan in time to alert the defences.

Matters were not going well for the English. On 12 November, just as their fleet came in sight of the island of Puerto Rico, Hawkins died, and was buried at sea. The Spaniards scuttled several of their ships in the harbour entrance, two of them on top of each other, to deny access to the English deep-draught galleons. This was to be no Cadiz for Drake. The English seamen and soldiers, denied the support of ships' gun batteries, made several sorties in small boats and pinnaces, to be badly cut about by the Spaniards who, firing down on the English from the high sides and fighting tops of their galleons, must have had a field day. Suffering heavier casualties than they could afford, the defeated English were eventually forced to withdraw. Drake had now been repulsed at Las Palmas, Grand Canary, and also at San Juan, Puerto Rico.

Putting a brave face on it, Drake repaired to the coast of Tierra Firma, telling the captain of the *Elizabeth Bonaventure*, Thomas Maynarde, 'I will bring thee to twenty places far more wealthy and easier to be gotten.' Arriving at Rio de la Hacha, he took the small pearling town and, dissatisfied with the ransom offered, which was small, put the town to the torch; then went on to do the same at the small town of Santa Marta. Thus more than three valuable weeks had been spent in taking worthless prizes while the numbers of fit men were decimated by sickness and disease. The Spaniards were not idle, and any chance Drake had of achieving surprise at his old haunt of Nombre de Dios was wasted. Pedro Tello de Guzman took the opportunity to send a fast ship to Panama, and the news of Drake's presence on the coast was soon in the hands of the governor in Panama City. Don Alonzo de Sotomayor placed the city of Panama on an alert, and sent a small force of men over the Camino Reale across the isthmus to meet Drake's men should they venture to attack Panama City from Nombre de Dios.

At Nombre de Dios, all was quiet. The Spaniards had fled, leaving no spoils for Drake. And Drake, for reasons which are difficult to understand, did not reason that his best chance of an attack on Panama City would be to sail to the entrance of the Rio Chagres, and despatch his men across the isthmus by small boat, and then by land, as did Henry Morgan in 1670. Instead Drake decreed that Sir Thomas Baskerville, in charge of land forces, should take a now depleted army across the spine of the isthmus, over the mule track on which Drake had captured the treasure in 1573.

On the summit ridge of Mount Caparila, a greatly inferior Spanish force, commanded by Captain Conabut, met and completely defeated Baskerville and his men. The Spaniards had the dual advantages of surprise and good use of ground. Dr Kenneth Andrews, in his book on the last voyage of Drake and Hawkins, makes the mistake of suggesting that the English were met at a place where there was a steep drop on one side, and a rock face on the other. But I have visited the spot and examined it closely. Conabut set up temporary

Wreck artifacts from the Salmedina Reef wreck (*circa* 1746). On the left, Spanish wrought-iron dead eyes and chain plates prior to mechanical removal of seabed accretions, and on the right, after cleaning and prior to laboratory conservation treatment

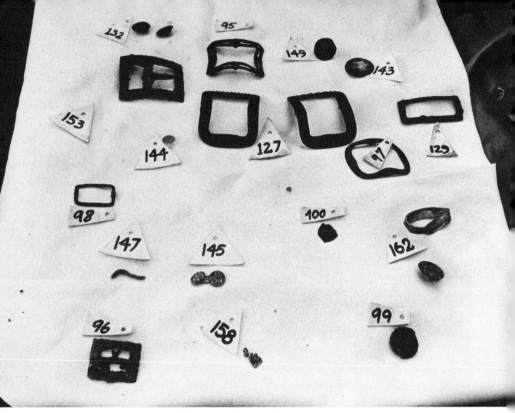

Brass belt buckles, and a sprinkling of gold and silver jewellery, buckles and coins from the Salmedina Reef wreck

Divers tying slings to an unidentified lead artifact off Drake's island

Assembling sonar apparatus for the search for the *Bonhomme Richard* in 1976 on board the survey vessel *Decca Recorder*. On the left is the author and on the right, a Decca Survey Company technician

The fight between the *Bonhomme Richard* and the English *Serapis* off Flamborough Head in September 1779. Captain Richard Pearson in the Royal Navy vessel *Serapis* surrendered to the American John Paul Jones. More than 30 hours later, Jones' *Bonhomme Richard* sank, due to damage sustained in the action

A late medieval clinker built boat found buried under peat during the draining of Lake Peris, north Wales by the Central Electricity Generating Board. The wreck was surveyed and excavated for the National Museum of Wales by the Welsh Institute of Maritime Archaeology and History. In the centre is the site director, Owain Roberts, and on the bottom right, the author, both of whom are trustees of the Institute

earthworks, which can still be seen, and attacked the English as they advanced in close order along a narrow depression in the ridge. Unable to escape either to left or right, the English decided to charge the Spanish position. So narrow was the field of fire that the Spaniards could shoot straight into the mass of the English, or harry their leading men at 'push of pike'. A decision was soon reached, and the retreating English ran pell-mell down the ridge, into the jungle beyond, some of them losing their shoes which were sucked off by the jungle mud. It was a weary, dispirited, defeated English force which returned to Nombre de Dios, and to Drake's waiting ships.

The fleet now stood off for Porto Bello, and one last attempt to gain something of value from a project which by now had all the trappings of a great financial disaster. But Drake was ill with the 'bludie flux' (amoebic dysentery) and, as the *Defiance* came in sight of the entrance to the harbour of Porto Bello, he breathed his last.

The Spaniards were busy erecting artillery platforms for a new plate-fleet embarkation point at Porto Bello, and they quickly decamped when the English fleet sailed into the bay. Sir Thomas Baskerville put the township to the torch, demolished the gun platforms, threw the iron guns into the sea, and took the bronze pieces on board his ships. There was no treasure of any kind.

The next morning, Drake's body, in a hastily constructed wooden coffin covered with sheet lead, was taken outside the harbour where, after a brief formal ceremony, it was shot over the side of the royal galleon *Defiance*. An anonymous Englishman recorded the ceremony thus: 'His corps being laid into a coffin of lead, he was let down into the sea, the trumpets in doleful manner echoing out this lamentation for so great a loss, and all the cannons in the fleet discharged according to the custom of all sea funeral obsequies.'

It is difficult to sum up a character as complex as Sir Francis Drake's, but death-bed statements often reveal the man, and those of the two great Elizabethan sea dogs, both of whom carried their flag in the royal galleon *Revenge*, are no exception. Grenville's come from the Journal of Jan Hyghen Van Linschoten as quoted in Chapter 8, but worth repeating here:

Here I die, Richard Grenville, with a joyful and quiet mind for I have ended my life as a true soldier ought to, that hath fought for his country, his Queen, and his religion and honour, whereby my soul most joyfully departeth out of this body, and shall always leave behind it an everlasting fame of a valiant and true soldier, that hath done his duty, as he was bound to do.

179

Drake's last recorded words come from Thomas Maynarde's Journal, like Van Linschoten's later published by the Hakluyt Society:

> It matters not, man; God hath many things in store for us; and I know many means to do her majesty good service and make us rich, for we must have gold before we see England.

Perhaps in these two quotations we have the measure of both men.

Chapter 10

A Quest for Galleons and Drake in his Coffin of Lead

As my researches into the life and character of Sir Francis Drake developed, I began to wonder whether, if Drake had lived in our own times, the reason for his excessively turbulent nature would be attributed to his chromosomic structure. I had been reading about recent investigations into the chromosomes of people incarcerated in prisons, and these disclosed that those with the very rare YYX chromosomes were inclined to occasional outbreaks of violence, which were apparently triggered off by events which did not justify violent acts. Furthermore, YYX chromosome individuals were always sterile.

By a curious coincidence Drake had no progeny, even though he was twice married. It is of course possible that both Drake's wives were barren, but most unlikely. The problem was that Drake was dead, and buried at sea just outside the harbour of Porto Bello on the isthmus of Panama.

I wondered, too, if sufficient human remains would still survive after nearly 300 years in the sea for a chromosome investigation to take place? Past experience had highlighted that human skeletal remains can survive several hundred years' sea immersion if covered by an overburden of sand or silt; Drake was buried in a lead coffin, and dropped over the side of the English galleon *Defiance* onto a sandy or silty seabed. A search for Drake's coffin seemed well worth contemplation.

Finding I was thinking along these lines, my colleague Dr Peter Davies, introduced me to Professor Harrison, head of the Department of Anatomy at Liverpool University. Professor Harrison, a pathologist of world-wide renown, had recently published a paper on the blood group of the Pharaoh Tutenkhamen, and he readily endorsed my plans. If I could obtain the approval of the Panamanian authorities, mount an expedition, and locate Drake's lead coffin off Porto Bello, Professor Harrison would fly to Panama to carry out an autopsy on any remains surviving. All he required for the establishment of Drake's chromosome structure, was a small sample of bone marrow.

I had recently been introduced to Dennis Hamber of Billericay in Essex, who owned a magnificent 175 ton three-masted schooner, *Jylland.* Hamber had purchased the hull of this former Baltic trader where she lay derelict, without masts, on a beach in Denmark. He and his brothers — Howard, Dennis, William and Brian — completely renovated her into a very fine luxury charter yacht. Dennis Hamber offered me the use of the ship for a six-month season, and further offered to pay my expenses for a trip to Panama to tell the Panamanian authorities of the plans for which I needed formal approval. Armed with letters of support from the Council of Nautical Archaeology of London, and from departments of both Liverpool University and the University College of North Wales, Bangor, I flew to Panama for the first of three reconnaissance trips. The end result was that thanks to the support of the British Ambassador, Dougal Malcolm, and American historian on Drake, Dean Edwin C. Webster (who was resident in the Canal Zone), I was eventually granted the very first permit to search for, survey and excavate shipwrecks of antiquity ever issued by the Panamanian Government. My contact in Panama was Dr Reina Torres de Arauz, head of the Panama museum body, the Institute of National Culture. My permit specifically mentioned the quest for Drake's coffin.

There were shipwrecks in profusion awaiting location along the Caribbean coast of Panama, and three of specific interest inside the harbour of Porto Bello itself. One was the caravel *Vizcaina*, scuttled inside the harbour by Columbus during his last voyage of discovery in 1503 shortly after he discovered Porto Bello, and whose ribs and frames protruding from the shallows of the inner part of the bay were seen by a Spanish explorer some twenty years later. There were also the two vessels scuttled by Drake's senior surviving officer, Sir Thomas Baskerville, shortly after Drake's death and sea burial — the barque *Elizabeth* and the pinnace *Delight*. Yet, search as I might I could not find any written works which dealt extensively with the history of the plate-fleet haven of Porto Bello. This seemed somewhat surprising, bearing in mind the fact that all the treasure from Peru was transported from there from the year 1598 onwards. Dean Webster, who had published a paper 'The Defence of Porto Bello', came to my rescue, and I am indebted to him for permission to extract from that publication.

Anyone visiting Porto Bello would be struck as I was by the fact that the harbour can easily be defended by the establishment of forts on either side of the entrance. For unexplained reasons, the king of Spain originally decided that the plate-fleets carrying the Peruvian silver should sail from Nombre de Dios, not Porto Bello; and so the isthmian fleets commenced their annual sailings to Seville from Nombre de Dios via Havana and the Azores in 1520. By the 1590s it became obvious to the Spanish mariners that Nombre de Dios, with its open entrance, attacked and seized by Drake with impunity, and prone to northerly gales, was far inferior to Porto Bello. King Philip's principal fortification engineer, Antonelli, visited the town, and drew up plans for a transfer. By 1595, when Drake was embarking on his final voyage, the Spaniards had constructed a small village at Porto Bello, to house engineers and slave labour, with gun platforms at strategic points along both sides of the harbour entrance. When Drake's men entered the town in January 1596, work was still in progress, and the later castles and fortresses were still only in the planning stage. The Spaniards were chased from the area at 'push of pike' and their buildings razed to the ground; the bronze cannon established on gun platforms were seized, and the platforms demolished.

The year after Drake's last expedition had departed from Porto Bello, 1597, marked the official founding and inauguration of the newly built city, called by its founder Francisco Valverde y Mercada, 'San Felipe de Porto Bello'. Commencement was made in that year on the largest of all the Porto Bello fortresses, the great castle of San Felipe de Sotomayor, on the north side of the harbour, commanding its entrance. In 1601, when Captain William Parker took the town, he commented that the great castle which commanded the harbour entrance had '25 pieces of brass and 50 soldiers' — a remarkably small number of men for so many pieces of artillery. On the southern side of the harbour entrance, a small fortress or *fortileza* called St Iago was built, almost opposite the castle of San Felipe. Nearer to the town on the south side, stood the castle of Triana. Parker took the latter, but wisely did not attack the more formidable San Felipe, which he called the 'iron castle'. This William Parker was, in fact, to provide me with the vital clue as to where Drake's coffin lies; his part in the story of Porto Bello is therefore of importance, and will be referred to later.

Meanwhile, during another of my reconnaissances to Panama, I made a journey north to visit the Massachusetts Institute of Technology and the illustrious Dr Harold E. Edgerton. 'Doc', as he is called, is an internationally famous physicist whose invention of the strobe light and whose pioneering in the fields of high-speed photography and underwater sonar systems have earned for him a niche in the hall of fame. He listened to my plans and without any further contemplation said, 'O.K. I'll join you.' A further diversion to Austin, Texas, to meet Dr Tom Muir of the university's Applied Research Laboratories, recruited another expert in sonar to my ranks. I also called on Dr Dee Anne Story, Director of the Texas Archaeological Research Laboratory. It was then that we joined together to create a new organisation in the field of underwater archaeology. Anglo-American in concept, dedicated to the ideals of the transatlantic alliance of World War II, it was decided that it should be called the Atlantic Charter Maritime Archaeological Foundation. I was elected director, Doc Edgerton became president, and Dee Anne Story chairwoman. It was in the name of that body that the contract with the Panamanian authorities was signed.

Financial problems were solved (temporarily) when Dennis Hamber informed me that a friend of his, Grahame Bonney, who was well known as a television entertainer in West Germany, would put up the £45,000 expedition budget in return for a share in TV rights of a proposed film of the expedition. I recruited John Stubbs from north Wales as my surveyor, and Richard Price as my deputy; the latter had spent several seasons excavating the Dutch East Indiaman *Kennemerlandt* off the Skerries rocks on Shetland. Dr E. T. (Teddy) Hall, Director of the Research Laboratory for Archaeology at Oxford University signified that he would join us for a month with his highly sophisticated proton magnetometer wreck-detection apparatus. Professor Hall (as he now is) is an internationally respected physicist whose work in the field of exposing archaeological and art fakes includes that of the so-called 'Drake plate', which he proved was made of modern brass, and could not possibly have been the plate left at San Francisco Bay by Drake on his world circumnavigation. Mike Atkinson, who had been with me in the Azores, was now the skipper of the schooner *Jylland*. Two photographers who were with me in the Azores — John Chetham and Brian Richards — added to our growing ranks. Richards was an expedition 'nut' who had taken part in seven expeditions in five years. He later joined became a member of staff of the Western Australia Museums. I needed a medic, and our contacts in Scandinavia sent to me a young lady in her final year at medical college, Swedish Karen Skallsjo. There were many other participants both part and full time.

My biggest headache was that of the laboratory conservation of salvaged artifacts. As marine archaeology was a new and untried science as far as the republic of Panama was concerned, the National Museum in Panama City did not have any staff trained in the skills required. This problem was overcome by sending Adele St John Wilkes — daughter of Bill St John Wilkes, deputy chairman of the Council for Nautical Archaeology — to the Texas Archaeological Research Laboratory where Dee Anne Story and the laboratory's conservator, Donny Hamilton, gave her tuition in archaeological conservation; this was followed by a further course at Liverpool Museum, arranged by her father.

My UK contingent flew to Panama in May 1975 to be accommodated in the American controlled Canal Zone by Dean Webster and his family friends. I learned that the Hamber brothers and the *Jylland* had already sailed into the port of Colon at the Caribbean side of the Panama Canal a few days prior to our arrival. In due course we all met and proceeded to unpack several tons of equipment which had been transported to Panama by sea in a British container ship. From Colon to Porto Bello was only a few hours' sail. By road it was even less, no more than one and a half hours, but what a journey! Five years prior to our expedition's arrival, there had been no vehicular access to Porto Bello; now there was a road — of sorts. Maintenance of this road, which branches off the American-maintained trans-isthmian highway, is undertaken by the Panamanian authorities on a meagre budget; it is full of pot-holes and a real boneshaker, so much so that the sight of stranded vehicles with broken suspension was commonplace. We called it the 'Burma Road'.

I had planned to be out of the docks near Colon, and established at Porto Bello, within a week. In the event it took nearly a month. One of our main problems was that of accommodation. There was no way that twenty-five people could sleep on board a schooner which had accommodation for ten plus a crew of three. My numbers had been swelled by the addition of four members of the Panamanian Guardia Nacional, and an inspector from Deni — the plain-clothed security police. We sensed a certain hostility at first from our Panamanian contingent. This it later appeared was due to animosity felt towards continued American occupation of the Canal Zone. To Panamanians, all people with white skin are 'gringos'. It soon became obvious to the Guardia Nacional team that we were not all Americans when, hearing them refer to me in Spanish as 'another gringo', I retorted, 'I am not a gringo, I am British and therefore a super gringo.' This brought a roar of laughter from my Panamanian friends, and the ice was broken. From that moment on, we worked as a team of English, Welsh, Swedes, Panamanians and Americans, to which we later added one Colombian and the expatriate Englishman-turned-Australian, Jeremy Green, now Curator of Underwater Archaeology, Western Australia Museums.

Thanks to Panamanian intervention we resolved the problem of finding space for a camp site on shore; it consisted of the entire headland on the south side of the entrance to Porto Bello bay. There were a couple of native *bohios*, palm-frond roofed huts, on the site, which we immediately rented from their owners. This led the ever dynamic Dennis Hamber to announce that he and his four brothers were going to build a village for the expedition. Scepticism on the part of my expedition members turned to undisguised respect when Dennis, Howard, Brian, David and William Hamber peeled off their shirts and set to, with native help, to clear a huge area of jungle at the water's edge.

Cement was mixed and foundations laid for several buildings. In no time at all vertical supports and roof timbers were erected, and a Porto Bello hired labour force climbed palm trees which they stripped of fronds, to construct three-layer, completely waterproof roofs. One *bohio* was 30ft long and 25ft wide. This was to be our mess-come-living room, with cookers, breakfast bar, two huge tables, and bench seats to accommodate at least twenty-five people at meal-times. Our largest 'bedroom *bohio*' accommodated eight men; the Guardia Nacional had their own in which all five of them slept. I had one as my sleeping accommodation and expedition office; there were also engineering workshop and compressor-room *bohios*. The Guardia Nacional provided us with two-tiered metal bunks and mattresses, and the US Army in the Canal Zone donated mosquito nets, and even provided us with a huge 50KVA diesel powered generator on loan. The Hambers built a water-tower, topped with four interconnected 55 gallon oil-drums, which were kept filled by a piped water supply from a nearby spring. The final pieces of luxury were a shower cubicle and a flush toilet. Apart from the heat, humidity, sand flies and mosquitoes, our expedition village had all the appearances of a tropical film set.

We possessed five expedition boats, consisting of two ex-British Royal Marine aluminium assault craft, and three large high-speed

The bronze bell dated 1677 from the unidentified wreck off Harlech, north Wales. The wreck carried 26 cannon, several swivel guns and a cargo of Italian Cararra marble

Wrought-iron swivel gun from the 'Bronze Bell Wreck'

inflatables on loan from Avon Inflatables. We immediately experienced difficulty in launching and retrieving our boats due to the presence of a submerged coral reef which lay close to our camp. The reef did afford us protection from northerly gales, but it also grounded and damaged our boats. Dennis Hamber again proved himself to be man of the moment when he declared that he was going to build for me a 100ft long jetty. In less than a week the work was completed, the supports for the jetty consisting of surplus 55 gallon oil-drums filled with concrete, on which were bolted surplus railway ties, or sleepers. The railway timbers formed the foundation on which planks were in turn fastened to provide a 100ft long continuous walkway to the 10ft wide jetty at the offshore end. I felt as we all did, that the Hambers had done their share of the work.

The last act in the establishment of our expedition village was to erect flagpoles along the edge of the jetty walkway, from which we flew the national flags of all participating members. I also included a flag bearing the personal coat of arms of Sir Francis Drake and, in recognition of the participation of faculty members of the University of Texas, the American Confederate States flag.

Expedition activities were now divided into three separate spheres. Doc Edgerton commenced his side-scan and sub-bottom profile sonar searches inside the bay of Porto Bello. My head of survey, John Stubbs, and a young American university undergraduate, Tom Morrow, worked as Doc's assistants. The sonar fish was streamed from an aluminium Royal Marine assault boat, and Doc searched for anomalies which might protrude from the harbour-bottom mud layer. Professor Teddy Hall operated his proton magnetometer from an inflatable boat, with me as his assistant. The third party consisted of divers of considerable and lesser experience who worked up our diving search techniques amongst the outlying reefs and islands.

The proton magnetometer search was to be our first casualty. The rock strata in the area of Porto Bello is in the main basalt, which is volcanic in origin. The built-in magnetic gradients of the Porto Bello rock strata proved to be of a considerable order of magnitude, so much so that any signal Teddy Hall's magnetometer recorded from ferrous items on the seabed, such as anchors, cannon and shot, was completely masked by the natural magnetic properties of the underlying rock layers. Teddy Hall commented, 'You could hide a German U-boat down there, and it could quite easily escape detection.'

The next problem was that of precise-fix navigation. There would be little use in locating a buried shipwreck if we could not relocate the position of that wreck for subsequent diving operations. Stubbs erected a number of shore markers, one behind the other, as a system of 'marks' or 'transits'. We would have preferred to use natural marks, such as the proverbial 'line up the third window on the left-hand side of the post office, with the spire of the church behind it'; the problem was that there were few 'marks' of that quality around the bay of Porto Bello. There were trees by the hundreds of thousands, and they all looked alike. But Stubbs's marks allowed Doc Edgerton to make runs which could be recorded on the chart, and American Canal Zone surveyor Paul Shacklette let us have a theodolite with ranging poles, to enable our surveyors to fix the start and end of the track taken by Doc's survey boat. This system is slow but accurate. I would have preferred to have a radar range-finding system such as Decca Trisponder, or the American equivalent such as Cubic or Motorolla. These latter-day navigational aids consist of a mobile transmitter station on board ship, and two or three shore-based transponders, which are located on known land survey-datums. The angle of the two signals is plotted on a chart at frequent intervals, and one's precise location is known at any point in the survey. Lacking such sophisticated and expensive apparatus, we had no choice other than to stay with 'transit marker' combined with theodolite survey.

In the meantime, Doc was picking up anomalies or 'targets' on the bottom of the bay. The first anomaly lay in shallow water only a few hundred yards from the village of Porto Bello. It was quite obvious from the reflected sonar pulses which showed up on Doc's paper roll-chart that we had indeed found a shipwreck. A group of divers went down to examine the find, and our first shipwreck turned out to be a wooden ship, with just a foot or two of her timbers lying proud of the seabed. The underwater visibility was poor, due to the influx of sediment from the nearby Rio Cascajal, and wreck identification was carried out by feel more than visual examination. It soon became obvious from the number of iron fittings on the upper part of the wreck that our initial find was in all probability a late nineteenth-century or early twentieth-century trading vessel.

Doc continued with his searches and started to pick up strange anomalies on the bottom of the harbour, which he referred to as 'hollows'. This I disbelieved, knowing that the river sediment settling in the bay would provide a uniform flat coverage. Again we put down divers, and Doc in his infinite wisdom was of course right. There were holes or hollows in the mud, made by large groupers which had finned to make a shape somewhat like a large shell crater, in which they settled down to await an unwary prey in the form of small fish which might swim over the hole. By simply sucking water through its cavernous mouth, the grouper swallowed its prey.

It was at this stage in the proceedings that Stubbs and Doc told me that they were having trouble in relocating, or in the jargon of survey 'retrieving', anomalies that had been highlighted by sonar the previous day. It was obvious that sunken shipwrecks do not move around the ocean floor. Something was wrong, and the error appeared to be in both the US Navy charts of Porto Bello, and the Panamanian Government ordnance survey of the bay. The shore of the bay as shown on the American charts had presumably been accepted by the Panamanian survey authorities as completely accurate, and they had transferred the American survey to their own maps. It was apparent to Stubbs, the professional surveyor, that the American survey was far from accurate as far as the shoreline of Porto Bello bay was concerned. Lest we accuse the US Navy of producing inaccurate charts, let me hasten to explain that naval charts are designed to aid navigation, and these Porto Bello charts were perfectly adequate for coastal navigation. They were just not accurate enough for us to pinpoint a seabed anomaly.

There was only one thing for it — the entire bay of Porto Bello had to be re-surveyed, and we had to do the job ourselves. Stubbs and Morrow, aided by one of my other professional surveyors, John Chetham, marched, struggled, waded and climbed their way around the entire periphery of the bay, setting up Shacklette's theodolite and taking the angles of ranging poles established on the opposite side of the water. Two walkie-talkie radio sets simplified the problem of communication from shore to shore. When I asked Stubbs how long it would take him and his team to complete the survey he replied, 'It's a good month's work but we'll do it in two weeks if it kills us.' As it so happens, the trio of indefatigable surveyors completely redrew the shoreline of the bay of Porto Bello, and refixed the position of a small rocky island — which later became the centre piece of our search for Drake's coffin — in eight days flat; after which all three were in a state of almost complete physical collapse.

The re-survey of Porto Bello has to be seen against the geographical and meteorological problems encountered in the work. The south side of the bay was easy to survey, having a cleared area on which ran the

'Burma Road'; the eastern end contained the Rio Cascajal, with mud flats, mangrove swamps, and rumours of alligators (although none were seen). The north-eastern end of the bay contained the 'careening cove' in which the Spaniards had careened their ships for bottom-cleaning in the seventeenth and eighteenth centuries. The north side of the bay posed the greatest problem because it consisted entirely of sub-tropical jungle, which ran right down to the water's edge. In the daytime, sand-flies flew in abundance on the north shore, their fierce itchy bites causing a great deal of discomfort. Humidity was usually about 90 per cent, and resulted in continual perspiration and loss of body fluids; the rainfall was prodigious, averaging 220 inches a year. I could imagine the hardship and suffering of my brave trio, trying to survey in what I likened to an Indian monsoon, only worse.

Thanks to my weary survey team we were able to tighten up our survey patterns. Stubbs paid for his endeavours by getting an infectious insect bite which caused his left arm to swell up like a balloon. He had to make several trips to an American hospital in the Canal Zone, to have the fluid drained from his arm. Morrow, a young 'Eagle Scout' whom I had accepted with misgivings because of his youth and lack of experience, turned out to be perfect expedition material. I found him one day on the edge of the jetty, sitting with his feet in the water and his head in his hands. 'Tom,' I asked, 'when did you last have a day off?' Young weary Morrow, without looking up replied, 'I haven't had a day off since we arrived, there is too much to do.' In my concentration with overall administration I had overlooked the fact that one of the most loyal and hardworking members of my team had worked for six weeks without any relaxation whatsoever. I ordered him to take a few days off and, refusing an American offer of a lift across the isthmus to Panama City and its bright lights, he packed his hammock and mosquito net into his rucksack, buckled his machete onto his hip and, taking a few cans of emergency ration, vanished into the Panamanian jungle, to emerge three days later refreshed and refortified. There was no real respite for my survey team, however, for all their physical effort on the edge of the jungle and amongst the mangrove swamps now had to be transferred onto paper. Stubbs redrew the map of Porto Bello bay to a very large scale and then, after a weekend off, pitched himself into working up the efficiency of my team of divers. Stubbs is a man of many parts, adding scuba-diving instruction of a very high order to his other accomplishments.

A visit from Paul Shacklette further improved our opportunities for speedier and more accurate underwater sonar searches, for he informed me that the Panama Canal Company operated a survey vessel in the form of a floating houseboat called the *Pavone*, 35ft long, flat-bottomed, and powered by two 300hp very thirsty petrol engines. She could empty her fuel tanks in four hours' sailing, and usually carried half a dozen 50 gallon drums of fuel on her deck. The *Pavone* was also fitted with the American Cubic system of precise-fix radar navigational system with computerised data acquisition. A meeting was arranged between myself and the head of the company, who is always a general of engineers in the US Army. The latter gave me a courteous hearing and said that he would do what he could. I explained that we were a non profit-making educational body, working for the Panama museums at no cost to Panama, and that the donation of a week or so's time of *Pavone* and crew could work wonders in the field of public relations and Anglo-American-Panamanian understanding, at a time when there was a great deal of anti-American sentiment being expressed in the Panamanian press and on television. There were other meetings, and eventually the word came down the line, verbally, via interested American friends, that I would be receiving the full support of the Panama Canal Company, and the *Pavone* would be mine for a week to ten days, for free. I was quick to write my appreciation.

On the appointed day, the *Pavone* was all tanked up with fuel, with her half dozen 50 gallon drums of fuel on deck, and with Paul Shacklette on board as head of the American survey team. Doc Edgerton, John Stubbs and Tom Morrow waited anxiously at Porto Bello to get into action, while I motored over to the Canal Zone to see the *Pavone* off. I was due for a profound shock. I was handed a bill for $3,000 to cover the use of the boat, the wages of her crew, including the surveyors, and the estimated fuel consumption for a week. I was further told that without the money 'up front', the *Pavone* would not sail. Faced with the whole of the next phase of remote-sensing wreck-detection programme reduced in efficiency due to lack of a computerised system of radar navigation, I reluctantly made out a cheque for $3,000. This was followed by a telephone call to my wife in the UK, asking her to beg my bank to honour the cheque, for my bank account was well and truly overdrawn at the time. In the event, the bank insisted on holding all my insurance policies as security, which they eventually foreclosed on and surrendered to my insurers for payment, leaving my wife bereft of any financial means whatsoever if I should have a fatal accident while on the expedition.

The *Pavone* sailed from Colon and arrived at Porto Bello that same day. Paul Shacklette headed the Canal Zone team of surveyors and boat crew, and Doc Edgerton, Stubbs and Morrow embarked with Doc's sonar apparatus. We had the *Pavone* for only a week, and I had to ensure that she was used for every available moment; gone were any thoughts of working 'office hours'. Two transponder beacons were established on shore on datums surveyed and recorded by Stubbs, and the accurate position-fixing of the search patterns commenced. Late into the night, when the bay of Porto Bello was shrouded in darkness, the navigation lights of the *Pavone* could be seen moving up and down and across the water. Targets were picked up, and their exact location immediately recorded. By now, too, Doc was using his sub-bottom profile sonar which sent acoustic signals down into the harbour-bottom mud, to be reflected back to the on-board recorder, signifying that we were in fact finding what appeared to be shipwrecks of substantial proportions.

The *Pavone* episode coincided with the addition to our diving team of American Ed Carwithen. Carwithen owned a 30ft long × 12ft beam catamaran which he had built in the Canal Zone for his hobby of scuba diving. The catamaran had a hatch or 'moon pool' in the centre of its platform deck, through which a ladder was lowered for easy access and egress by divers. We mounted our 80 cubic ft per minute capacity Ingersoll-Rand air-lift compressor on the deck, and set out for Doc Edgerton's number one priority sub-bottom anomaly. The air-lift principle of underwater suction consists simply of feeding low-pressure air down a flexible pipe, which is connected to a larger-diameter rising pipe. As the air enters the larger pipe it rushes to the surface, expanding as it goes, therefore creating a suction effect at the mouth of the larger pipe. The mouth of the large-diameter pipe therefore sucks up mud, sand and small stones; and occasionally tries to suck up the hand of anyone foolish enough to place it too close to the business end of the air lift.

Divers now worked in relays, two at a time. One handled the air-lift pipe, while the other either fed sand or mud into its maw, or hastened to shut off the air control valve if the operator got his hand in harm's way, as I once did. The underwater visibility in the bay of Porto Bello was not what one would expect for a semi-tropical area; we were lucky if we could see 3ft. Hour after hour the air-lift compressor on deck thundered away — a torment to those unfortunate enough to have to stand deck-watch, or wait their turn as stand-by diver.

Day after day we sucked away ton after ton of silt. Night after night it rained, sometimes as much as 2 or 3 inches in an hour. When that happened, the nearby Rio Cascajal carried a deep red-coloured silt into the bay, and partly filled up our hard-won excavation hole. But nearly two weeks were to pass by before I made the decision to cease excavation, a decision that caused something of a furore in our camp. I could understand the mood of my team, who were well aware from probing into the mud-hole that we had struck the timbers of a substantial shipwreck. But what we had located could not be identified, and there was the ever-present nagging thought that we had possibly discovered Columbus's caravel *Vizcaina* or either the *Elizabeth* or the *Delight* which were scuttled by Sir Thomas Baskerville a few days after Drake's death and sea burial.

Two things had worked against us. One was the time of year — the rainy season; the other was a factor which had not occurred to me when planning the expedition, and that was Panama's current 'slash and burn' agricultural system. One might ask why I did not time my expedition to coincide with the dry season which encompasses the winter period. The answer to that is wind strength and wave height. During the summer rainy season, winds are either moderate or non-existent; in the dry season the trade winds blow, and the prevailing winds send waves up to 20ft high over the surrounding coastline and reefs, and right into the bay of Porto Bello.

'Slash and burn' agronomy is practised over a wide area of the isthmus of Panama. The government makes land grants to any peasant who will plant crops, whereupon, because the land is mainly covered in jungle, the trees are felled, allowed to dry, and then the undergrowth and dead wood is burned off, after which crops such as hill rice are planted. Little use is made of fertilisers, and crop rotation is seldom if ever practised, with the result that, after a few years, the soil becomes infertile and the native farmers move on to another area. Thus Panama's tree cover is diminishing rapidly and soil erosion results in a considerable volume of silt being carried down-river either to the Caribbean or the Pacific. The careening cove at the north-eastern end of the bay of Porto Bello, just opposite the town, had once accommodated galleons with a draught of up to 20ft. Now there was barely 6ft depth of water in the cove, and in parts a shallow-draught inflatable boat would ground. Our problem was that when we had excavated down about 20ft into the harbour mud, the influx of mud from the Rio Cascajal filled the hole almost full, until we reached an equilibrium. As our air lift could only extract 8 tons of mud an hour, it was not hard to estimate the enormous amount of silt which was being transported over our wreck site each night, and as the rains increased, so the mud cover increased. We had to admit failure.

During the period when the *Pavone* was carrying Doc Edgerton around the bay, I had a team of divers searching off a small rocky islet just outside the bay on the north side, down to a maximum depth of 130ft. Here the visibility was up to 80ft horizontally, and sometimes one could see the surface from the seabed at a depth of 100ft. My divers were searching for Drake in his coffin of lead. But how did I know where Drake's coffin lay? The answer lies in the story, a detective story in fact, about the already mentioned William Parker of Plymouth — reprisal pirate, friend of Drake — who attacked Porto Bello in 1601. He not only knew where Drake's coffin lay, but recorded the fact in his Journal in 1601, and even drew a chart of Porto Bello, showing the spot where Drake's coffin was shot over the side in January 1596.

When Parker attacked and took Porto Bello in 1601, he entered the harbour by stealth at night. Leaving his major ships at anchor outside the bay, he and his companions, in small pinnaces, passed the fort of San Felipe and set upon the town, taking it after a bloody battle which at times was fought hand to hand. The Spanish governor, Pedro Menendez Marquez, was wounded several times before he at last surrendered to Parker and his men. The treasury was looted, and Parker and his crew sailed out of Porto Bello close to the south shore, in order to put as much distance as possible between themselves and the cannons of the castle of San Felipe on the north shore. Parker himself in his Journal has his compass bearings wrong, stating that the entrance to the harbour faces north when in fact it faces west. As a consequence he described the castle of San Felipe as being on the east shore, and the land to his left as he sailed out of harbour as the west shore. The important part of his extensive narrative, published by Samuel Purchas as *Purchas His Pilgrims* in 1625, after Parker's death, is as follows:

At the beginning of the night I embarked my men, enriched with the chief spoil of the town, and set sail to depart with my own two pinnaces and two

196

shallops and the aforesaid two Spanish frigates which I had won. But in going out I was shot in at the elbow and out at the wrist by a musket shot from the Wester shore, whereof there were many shot over us; besides eight and twenty great shot from the chief and Easter fort [San Felipe], which did endanger us often. But God so wrought for us, that we got safely forth again contrary to all our enemies expectations, who made full account to sink us in going forth. Being safely come forth we rode in our pinnaces and shallops behind a small island which lay betwixt us and the Wester fort of St. Iago, until my Vice Admiral Rawlins brought two ships thither, which rode somewhat to the Eastward of the Castle of San Felipe, under the rock where Sir Francis Drake his coffin was thrown overboard.

This was a really significant clue as to the whereabouts of our quarry, and before leaving for Panama I undertook extensive research into William Parker to see if more information would come to light. The *Dictionary of National Biography* tells us that Parker was a privateer, that he made several successful forays against Spanish interests at sea, that he took Porto Bello in 1601, and later became mayor of Plymouth. He was buried at sea at Bantam in the East Indies in 1618. I happened to know that the Parker family lived at Saltram House near Plymouth and had become the Earls of Morley. In Burke's *Peerage, Baronetage and Knightage,* there was a William Parker in the family in Elizabethan times but sadly he was buried at North Molton in 1628. Nevertheless, against all odds at finding more, in 1974 I visited Saltram House, which has been a National Trust property since 1957. My enquiries concerning William Parker were answered by the then curator of Saltram House, Mr Patrick Dawes. He told me that there was never a William Parker in the lineage of the Parkers of Saltram, nor was there anything in the family history to suggest that they had ever been involved in seafaring, let alone reprisal piracy, in the late sixteenth and early seventeenth centuries. Portraits of many generations of Parkers hang in the library at Saltram and, while looking at these, Dawes mentioned that there had been a portrait of a man in early Stuart garb, hanging in the nursery, and furthermore the painting contained a number of allegorical subjects in the form of cameos which presumably illustrated the life of the sitter, including sea and land battles. My ears pricked up at this and I asked to see the painting only to be informed that, as it did not appear to be in any way related to the Parker family, the National Trust had transferred the portrait to another trust property, Dunsland House in north Devon, where it had been destroyed in a fire.

I then visited the Courtauld Institute of Art in London, where photographs of all National Trust owned paintings are filed, and was very relieved to learn that the lost painting had in fact been photographed, and that a 10in × 12in enlargement would be made available to me within a few days. Once the photograph was in my hands, I had it rephotographed and enlarged up to approximately 3ft × 2ft, so that I could examine every part of the picture in minute detail. The portrait was indeed what I was looking for (see plate).

The subject in the painting was, as Dawes had said, wearing early Stuart garb. The allegorical scenes, each portrayed above a biblical quotation, obviously described incidents in the life of the subject, from childhood to manhood. There was a church in the picture, recognisable as St Andrew's Church in Plymouth. That was a good start — my William Parker had been mayor of Plymouth. I ignored the childhood cameos, and examined closely those dealing with adult life. Near the centre of the painting there was a graveyard, with corpses and a grim reaper, with mention of pestilence. Could this be a reference to the diseases prevalant on Panama's 'mosquito coast'? At the bottom of the painting was a bridge, and a battle taking place between rival groups of musketeers; the most crucial part of Parker's taking of Porto Bello was the battle for a bridge close to the town. At the top of the painting there was a nautical scene showing two pinnaces passing through a gap between headlands; the left-hand headland was surmounted by a large castle, and the right-hand headland boasted a small fort. This could be Parker's exit from Porto Bello in 1601, with the castle of San Felipe on the left and the smaller fort of St Iago on the right.

The most vital clue of all, the absolute clincher in my mind, was the fact that the man in the portrait had his left arm in a sling. Parker had recorded in his log, 'I was shot in at the elbow and out at the wrist by a musket shot from the Wester shore.' Parker's departure from Porto Bello would have placed the castle of San Felipe on his right, and the fort of St Iago on his left. Standing on the deck of his pinnace, looking forward, a musket shot from the direction of St Iago would hit Parker in his left arm. I completed my examination of the painting with no doubt in my mind as to who the portrait subject was. But what was perhaps more important, I now had a hitherto undiscovered picture of Porto Bello at the time of Drake. I returned to the description entered in the log. Could one from this locate 'the rock where Sir Francis Drake his coffin was thrown overboard'? There is a rock, or rather a small island, off the entrance to Porto Bello, named on the American naval chart as 'Isle Verde' (green island). The headland overlooking the rock is called 'El draque', but as that headland overlooked a considerable expanse of ocean, the reference to Drake was of little help to me in my enquiries. Research in the Public Record Office in London led nowhere; Spanish archival sources in Simancas provided not a clue. I decided to explore the shelves of the Admiralty Library in London, quite convinced that secondary sources could not help and that I would have to consult whatever primary sources were available. In the event, I was wrong and the successful completion of my researches can be attributed in the main to Admiral Vernon and his taking of Porto Bello in the War of Jenkins' Ear in 1739.

My delving in the Admiralty Library produced a slim volume with a lengthy rambling title, *A Geographical Description of Coasts and Harbours and Sea Ports of the Spanish West Indies, Particularly of Porto Bello, Cartegena and the Island of Cuba* etc. etc . . . ending with 'To which is added An Appendix, containing Capt. Parker's own Account of his Taking of the Town of Porto Bello, in the Year 1601, with an Index and a New and Correct Chart of the Whole'. The tiny volume contained everything I could have wished for. There was a chart of the bay of Porto Bello, showing the forts and castles, and the town. The index contained all the references I had read in Parker's Journal, and under Item C was the reference, 'The place where my shippes roade, being the Rocke where Sir Francis Drake his coffin was thrown overboard.' Parker's chart of Porto Bello showed item 'C' with small vessels anchored close to, and the rock 'C' was the Isle Verde of the American twentieth-century charts. But how did Parker know where Drake's coffin was laid to rest? There had to be a factor common to Drake's 1595–6 expedition and Parker's 1601 taking of Porto Bello. I found that common factor in the Calendar of State Papers Domestic for 1595–6 and Parker's own Journal, in the form of one George Lawriman who had been victualling officer on Drake's last expedition, and who not only accompanied Parker in his attack on Porto Bello, but also led a counter-attack against the Spaniards just as Parker was facing defeat in the battle for the town bridge. Lawriman's presence on Parker's raid also explained how Parker knew where to anchor his ships outside the harbour, on the eastern or offshore side of 'Isle Draque' where they would be invisible to the Spanish guards on duty on the battlements of the castle of San Felipe.

While the excavations down through the mud had been taking place inside the harbour, Stubbs was undertaking a series of very

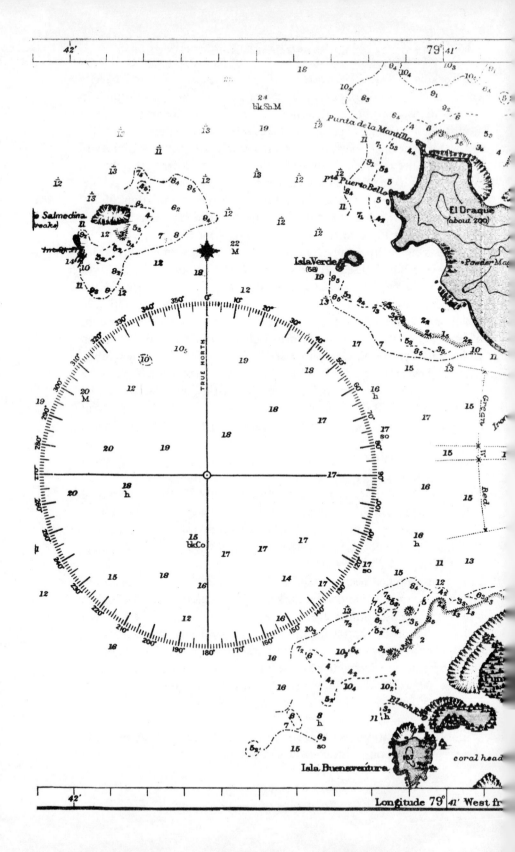

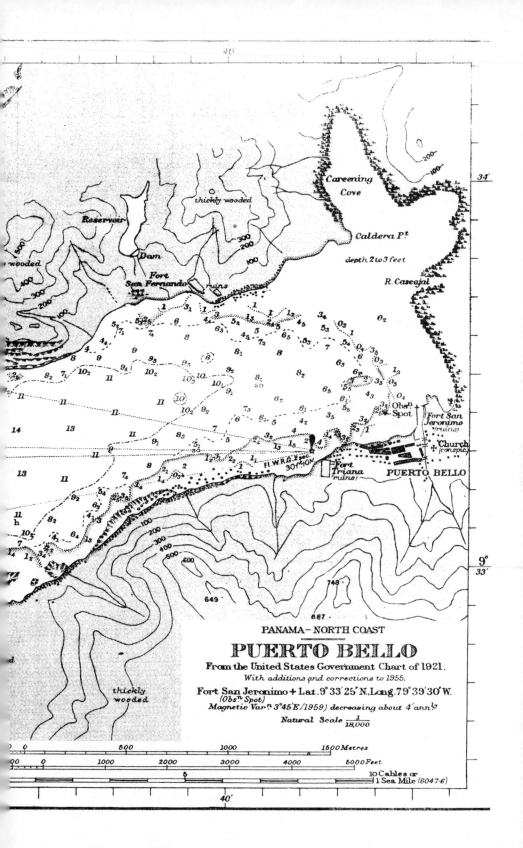

PANAMA – NORTH COAST

PUERTO BELLO

From the United States Government Chart of 1921.

With additions and corrections to 1955.

Fort San Jeronimo + Lat. 9° 33′ 25″ N., Long. 79° 39′ 30″ W.
(Obs.ⁿ Spot)
Magnetic Var.ⁿ 3° 45′ E. (1959) decreasing about 4′ ann.ˡʸ

Natural Scale $\frac{1}{18,000}$

comprehensive swim-line searches with half a dozen divers around Drake's island. My plan was for divers to search visually from the shallows around the island, down to the seabed of mud, which in places was 200yd or more from the island. The intervening underwater strata consisted either of basalt rock or coral outcrops, which descended from zero down to 130ft in a series of gullies. To ensure that no area of seabed remained unsearched, Stubbs ran survey lines from the island, down through the gullies, to the mud level. A swim line of six divers would then search the area; diver No 1 swimming above the survey line which lay on the rocky terrain, held in place by lead weights set at intervals. The distance between the divers, each of whom held onto the swim line, was about 50–70ft, depending on underwater visibility. Diver No 6 held a revolving reel from which he ran the line, which was to provide the start datum for the next search area. Thus the entire area of rock and coral surrounding Drake's island was thoroughly searched for the lead coffin.

We knew what sort of coffin we were looking for. The usual form of sea burial for common seamen was for the corpse to be sewn up in sailcloth with a piece of iron shot at his feet, but for gentlemen of account, a wooden coffin was constructed by the ship's carpenter, and the box was then covered with sheet-lead held in place by copper nails. I had researched the weight of sheet-lead taken on Drake's last voyage and the weight of that brought back to England, and the discrepancy amounted to just sufficient sheet-lead to cover a 6ft × 2ft × 2ft wooden box.

Having searched the rocky areas, we were satisfied that Drake's coffin lay further offshore in the alluvial mud of the seabed. From a seamanship point of view it would have been foolhardy for Drake's men to sail the *Defiance* close enough in to the island for the coffin to lie on the rocky areas; on the other hand it was possible that Drake might have been shot over the side of a pinnace and not the expedition's flagship. I had to be sure, hence these near-shore searches.

On completion of the swim lines, we took Doc Edgerton over the close inshore areas of alluvial mud, to within 200yd or so of Drake's island. Many passes were made towing Doc's 'sub-bottom profiling

Fig 7   Up-to-date American chart of Porto Bello showing Drake's Island incorrectly named, but the headland behind it shown as 'El Draque'

sonar' fish, and many the target we obtained. The anomalies were all logged and their positions recorded, and teams of divers sent down to examine every tiny blip which had showed on Edgerton's rolling paper-chart. We found rocks, including a 70ft high pinnacle which was not shown on the navy chart, and a number of ancient sixteenth- or seventeenth-century anchors, many of them minus flukes and arms, once again confirming the poor quality of Spanish iron of that period. A number of anomalies which appeared on the sonar could not be located by divers, and we presumed these to be buried under alluvial mud.

Doc Edgerton had now reached the end of his available time with us, having promised to participate in a number of other projects. His place was taken almost immediately by Dr Tom Muir, who operated his new 'parametric' sonar. Muir's apparatus was at that time classified and he did not want any photographs or press publicity regarding his participation on the expedition, for which he had obtained the approval of the US Office of Naval Research. The apparatus was designed to locate small sunken explosive mines, and it certainly had the capability of locating small articles on the seabed. Penetration was not its strong suit, nor was it designed to be; on the other hand, it located items so small they would not have shown up on orthodox commercial-quality sonar. One of Muir's great triumphs was to advise us that he had a 'small' target inside the bay of Porto Bello, which on investigation proved to be a coffee pot, of which only the handle was protruding from the mud. When asked if I intended deploying the catamaran, with the air-lift suction apparatus, to suck mud from any or all of the anomalies located by Doc Edgerton and Tom Muir off Drake's island, I answered in the negative. It was a painful decision to make, but I knew that if I put the matter to a vote, the 'let's dig for Drake's coffin' school would have won hands down. The more sober members knew that I had researched and organised this expedition for two years, and that the search for Drake was only one facet of a programme which also encompassed wreck location, followed by survey and excavation.

Political problems now emerged in the form of open hostility from a certain element amongst the amateur diving fraternity in the American controlled Canal Zone, several of whom boasted to me that they had found ancient shipwrecks in republican waters, but had no intention of advising the Panamanian authorities until, in their own words, 'we have cleaned them out'. Such latter-day grave-robbers were constantly visiting our camp to try to filch information on our wreck discoveries. I therefore asked Dr Reina Torres de Arraus to ban all amateur divers in the area of the bay of Porto Bello, and for several miles either side of the harbour entrance. The ban came into effect almost immediately, and a large notice was erected at the point where the 'Burma Road' enters the bay, warning intending wreck-poachers that they risked either a fine or imprisonment if they dived in the bay. There were two exceptions to this rule and they were Ed Carwithen who had loaned me his 30ft catamaran; and Mrs Barbara Anderson, an American forces wife who originally came to look us over with her diving family of husband and three children, and stayed to work on equal terms with us either on a swim line, or working at the business end of the air-lift suction pipe.

Our next find was only a few hundred yards away from our camp, and in only a few feet of water. It was the remains of a small armed vessel whose tiny cast-iron guns, less than a metre in length, and the length of the spread of stone and iron ballast, suggested that we had found the wreck of a sloop. My researches had revealed that only one sloop was known to have been sunk on the south side of the harbour — a small Spanish vessel which, damaged by Admiral Vernon's gunfire during the War of Jenkins' Ear in 1739, had run into the shallows on the southern shore in an attempt to escape. The small size of the vessel allowed a detailed survey of the remains in a small space of time, after which we completely excavated the wreck contents for the Panama museum.

Not long after this, some of us left Porto Bello, on what for me was a pilgrimage, to make a trip several miles inland of the older fleet anchorage at Nombre de Dios, in search of the spot where Drake and his men, accompanied by the brave French hydrographer le Testu, attacked and captured the mule train loaded with silver and gold in 1572. The one expert whose judgement I trusted implicitly was historian Dean Webster, who had researched the subject for twenty years, and, on the appointed day, Dean Webster, expedition members Brian Richards, John Chetham and Adele St John Wilkes and I flew off from an airstrip in the Canal Zone. We landed on a rough airstrip at Nombre de Dios and, armed with still and cine cameras, machetes and insect repellant, we walked, climbed, hacked and stumbled our way through the living jungle along the barely discernible track that was all that was left of the old Camino Reale, the royal road across the isthmus and over the jungle-covered mountains, by which the king of

The search for Drake's lead coffin. On the left is the chartered survey launch which is towing Dr Harold Edgerton's sonar apparatus. On the right is expedition floating headquarters, Baltic schooner *Jylland*

Breech area of small wrought-iron swivel gun from the 'Bronze Bell Wreck'. Sheet lead has been placed over the 'touch hole' to prevent ingress of water. Punch mark holes on breech of gun are matched by similar marking on the gun's breech blocks. Being hand made, no two guns were identical in shape or size. It was therefore essential for the breech blocks to be tailor made to fit each individual gun

Drake's false coffin off Drake's Island, Porto Bello. A small lead block whose
origin remained unidentified

Spain's treasure had been transported from Panama City to Nombre de Dios.

I became the first casualty when I accidently touched a very large and rather beautiful, hairy caterpillar, as I grabbed at a tree branch. Immediately I became conscious of a sharp stinging pain in my hand, which increased in intensity as the hot sticky day wore on. By midday my hand was swollen like a small balloon. Another member of the party touched a prickly tree and suffered a similar but less painful sting, accompanied by rapid swelling. The infuriating sand-flies no longer reigned supreme in the jungle; instead they were replaced by far more unpleasant stinging insects, including mosquitoes.

For several hours we struggled through the undergrowth, the 90 per cent humidity enervating us until we moved at a crawl, perspiration running down our bodies and into our boots. Then, Dean Webster, compass in hand, hacked his way through a final patch of undergrowth, to show us into a semi-cleared area through which ran a small river flanked by trees on either side. We had arrived at the point where the Camino Reale ran for a hundred yards or so along the bed of a river, and it was here that Drake and his men had hidden gold and silver bullion, in excess of what they could carry, after they had captured the mule train. It was at this spot that the vengeful Spaniards had found and beheaded the wounded le Testu, and tortured his sole French companion until he revealed the hiding place of the remaining treasure. We took photographs and cine film, lunched on sandwiches and lime juice and, packing our gear into our rucksacks, marched wearily back to Nombre de Dios.

On our return to our Porto Bello camp, we received a visit from a Panamanian fisherman who lived a few miles along the coast to the south of Porto Bello, near to a small coral island called Orange Cayos. The fisherman told us that when line-fishing from his *cayuco*, or canoe, on calm days, he could see what he thought to be cannon lying on the seabed in about 40ft of water. Unable to speak English, our new friend communicated with us through Lieutenant Virgilio Morones, officer in charge of our Panamanian National Guard contingent. We decided to follow up this useful information.

By now our team had been joined by two former members of my earlier expeditions. One was Jeremy Green of the 1968 *Santa Maria de la Rosa* expedition, who was spending a one-year sabbatical visiting and participating in the activities of expeditions all over the world. The other was Shaun Whittaker, a member of my 1972 Azores expedition. Both newcomers were very welcome because of their considerable experience in wreck survey and excavation. Green accepted my offer to participate in the galleon wreck project off Orange Cayos, the initial search for which was carried out by aerial reconnaissance in the private National Guard helicopter of Panama's head of state, General Omar Torrijos. The latter — thanks to the good offices of Dr Reina Torres de Arauz — kindly let me have his Bell Huey military helicopter free on loan, with pilot and co-pilot.

The aerial trip to Orange Cayos was one of several helicopter forays made in General Torrijos's 'chopper'. Our pilot and co-pilot were cast in the mould of pre-World War II 'barnstorming' fixed-wing aviators, delighting as they did in low flying, particularly over, or rather through, the coral atoll tree-cover, to the extent that occasionally our rotor blades would chop the topmost branches off the palm trees amongst which we flew. A member of my party, his knuckles white from gripping the edge of his seat, asked, 'Is this a helicopter or a mowing machine?'. Hovering over the outer reef area of Orange Cayos, we looked down through crystal-clear water to the scatter of cannon lying on the seabed. Our friendly *cayuco* fisherman was already on site, pointing down to the cannon and waving to us.

My team was now subdivided, in order to survey the Orange Cayos wreck site. I had no intention of undertaking an orthodox archaeological excavation, for that would necessitate spreading our resources too thinly. Excavation could be carried out at some future date by divers designated by Dr Reina Torres and the Panama museums. The survey was supervised by Jeremy Green.

The water was clear and shallow, never deeper than 40ft. Base lines were established and tape measures deployed in trilateration technique. The only apparent wreck artifacts were fourteen cannon, all of them cast iron, suggesting that the site was possibly seventeenth-century, but certainly not sixteenth. Between the cannon lay reddish coloured rock-hard pavements of rough texture, consisting of oxides of iron from the cannon 'cemented' to coral growth, and which blunted even the sharpest chisel. For our third visit, we planned to use small explosive charges, sufficient only to shake loose the oxide-coral pavements, thereby revealing, hopefully, material which might identify and date the wreck. Green had used small explosive charges very effectively on Dutch East Indiamen sites in western Australia, to the degree that he could break out hundreds of small artifacts without them suffering physical damage. The Guardia Nacional obtained the explosives and set them; and Green and Morones made them up into 2oz charges. The resulting explosions revealed hundreds of spoons made of latten, carrying the touch-mark of a cutler in the Netherlands. Each spoon bore the tiny figure of one of the twelve apostles at the end of the handle. Researches into seventeenth-century artifacts suggested the 1680s or '90s, and the spoons plus many other artifacts further suggested that we had possibly discovered one of the lost galleons of the Marques de Brienes of 1681. Copper and brass plates and dishes protruded from the seabed concretion, and the Guardia Nacional, ignoring Green's advice as to the size of the explosive charge, placed larger charges — in order, so they said, to speed up the process. This resulted in one very large copper dish being blown to fragments. Close to one of the cannon stood a small vertical coral outcrop which we ignored; at least we did until the Guardia Nacional 'big' explosion toppled it over. The coral outcrop was in fact all that remained of a sackful of Spanish wrought-iron 'half heart-shaped' padlocks decorated with brass, the whole congealed into one solid mass covered in coral growth.

The most exciting find of all was a 'treasure chest'. Made of wrought iron, it measured almost 4ft in length × 2½ft across × 2½ft in depth. Green and I decided that, although by our terms of reference the expedition could not benefit from the location of treasure, we would, by removing its contents, see to it that the republic of Panama would reap the reward. We also wanted to take the treasure chest out of temptation's way, bearing in mind the activities of marauding amateur and professional treasure-hunters. Green therefore laid a small explosive device in the form of Cordtex fuse which, wrapped around the chest, would provide just enough explosive power to shatter the outer wrought-iron casing. Immediately after the underwater 'thud', we dived in, ignoring the poor visibility in our eagerness to see several million pesos worth of gold and silver coin and jewels. Rummaging through the contents of the chest, we were privileged to find more than a ton of Spanish wrought-iron horseshoes, in three different sizes. Green was not amused when I commented, 'Well done, you didn't damage any of them.'

A couple of days later we did indeed have trouble with unauthorised divers working from an inflatable boat anchored on the wreck site. Lieutenant Morones sped off with four of his men and caught them in the act, which resulted in a stern order to get ashore and stay there until further notice. Since this was the most flagrant, but not the first

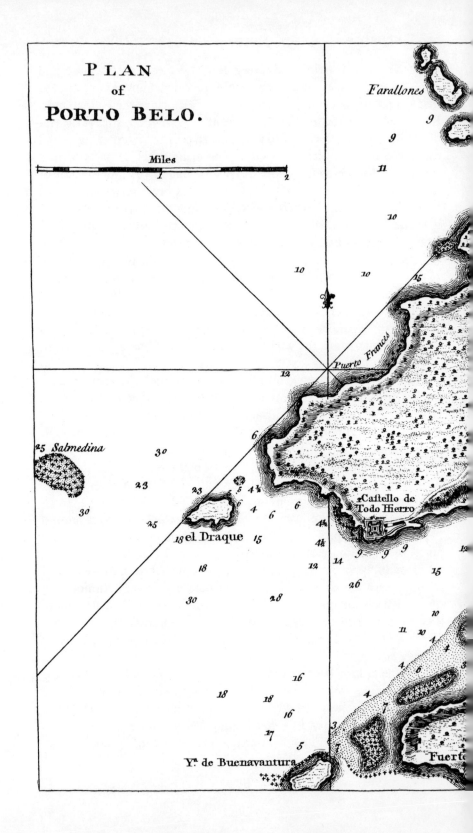

LAGUNA GRANDE

Rio de Cascajal

Caleta

reening Place

Old Portobelo

Castello de S.ª Jeronimo

Watering P.

PORTOBELO

Castello de La Gloria

Road to Panama

T. Jefferys Sc.

breach of Panamanian law by the divers' American leader, the eventual result was an official ban on his diving anywhere in Panama's Caribbean waters, from the border of Costa Rica in the north to that of Colombia in the south.

There was also the incident of the 'false lead coffin'. This came about when a swim line on the landward side of Drake's island came across a small lead block, about 3ft long. A press photographer from Panama City called at the camp and took a photograph of the lead block, and also a photograph of one of the Panamanian divers sitting on a log. The end result was a completely fraudulent montage picture showing the diver seated on a lead block which now appeared to be about 6ft long, and just about the right dimensions for Drake's coffin. This story and photograph were then circulated around the world with the caption 'Has Wignall's expedition located Drake's lead coffin?' Is there any wonder that those of us involved in serious investigation into maritime history sometimes regard the Press with suspicion.

Just before we left for the Camino Reale, our wreck discoveries had taken an important turn. I knew that a Spanish galleon had struck the Salmedina Reef in 1746, and as the reef was situated just offshore and in the centre of the harbour entrance, a visual search was called for. On the second day cast-iron cannon were located, along with thousands of hollow cast-iron bomb-shells in so many calibres that I came to the conclusion that our new wreck had quite possibly been a munitions carrier bringing powder and shot to Porto Bello from Cartagena. Cuts, abrasions, infections, etc, periodically reduced the strength of my diving team, and what could have been a crisis situation for the expedition, was solved when three of the Hamber brothers decided to learn to dive in order to fill my depleted ranks. Thus Howard, David and William Hamber became not only crew members of their schooner *Jylland*, but also diving members of our expedition, taking their turn on the swim lines.

The quantity and complexity of the finds from this discovery precluded the use of explosives and I decided that hand excavation, slow as it may be, was the only way to ensure that excavated artifacts were not damaged in the salvage process. Conservation tanks were set up onshore at the camp site, and in a room at Porto Bello loaned to us by the town mayor, Adele St John Wilkes and a Panama museum

Fig 8   Spanish eighteenth-century chart of Porto Bello shows Drake's Island correctly named

laboratory assistant were occupied full-time in restoring and cleaning artifacts as they emerged from the sea. There were no anchors extant on the wreck site, suggesting that the vessel had not struck with all her anchors aboard, unless of course the Spaniards had salvaged the ship's anchors after she struck the reef. It is quite possible that the ship had dragged anchor in a storm, leaving her anchors on the seabed.

Only three main armament cannon were located, suggesting that the Spaniards had indeed carried out substantial salvage shortly after the ship sank. Bronze breech-blocks for breech-loading swivel guns were buried under coral in profusion, but no sign of the bronze swivel guns, this also pointing to contemporary salvage. The catamaran was brought on site and anchored on the landward side of the reef, on top of the wreck site, and our powerful air-lift mud extractor now undertook the task of moving a huge quantity of coral debris as it was excavated by hand by my diving team. The air-lift operation was slow and tedious because we examined all coral debris by hand, on a white painted oil-drum lid, fanning the debris towards the suction end of the pipe, while extracting the artifacts. I was determined that the totally destructive system used by some operators, of sending all items up the pipe to be sorted and separated on the deck of a boat, would not be used on my expedition. The coral overburden was removed by hand by the simple but laborious expedient of hammer and chisel work. The water was too warm for wet suits in their entirety, so the divers wore a wet-suit jacket, and old trousers or dungarees on their legs to avoid coral cuts. The shallow depth allowed the divers to work for several hours each day, coming to the surface only to change their exhausted scuba cylinders and to partake of coffee and sandwiches.

Ship's fittings began to appear from inside the coral growth including a heavily corroded 'dead eye and chain plate'. The most remarkable discovery of all was one of the vessel's two 'catheads' which were situated up in the bow in the 'eyes of the ship' on both port and starboard sides, to which the anchor was 'catted' after it had been raised. The cathead was constructed of oak, and its pulley wheel was of hardwood — either *lignum vitae*, greenheart or cocabola. To my amazement the pulley wheel still rotated freely.

As we were working on a 'no reward' basis, the discovery of treasure was of little personal consequence, but treasure there was on the Salmedina Reef galleon wreck. Clusters of silver coins, such as reales of four, and pillar dollars began to emerge from their roughly 329

213

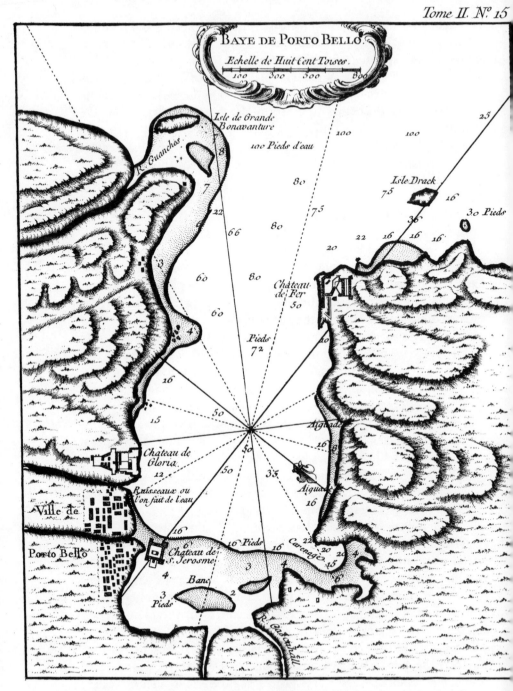

Fig 9   French eighteenth-century chart shows Drake's Island correctly named

years of entrapment in coral growth. The coins in fact formed a kind of treasure trail, and the Hamber brothers, who had influenced me also to train other crew members of the schooner *Jylland* in scuba diving, undertook a very substantial part in the hand excavation of the reef coral, spending more than a hundred hours chiselling away and in working the air-lift extractor. Following the trail of silver coins, they eventually hand-carved a tunnel through the reef coral, wide enough for a diver to work in, until eventually they emerged on the far side of the reef. That tunnel, which we likened to those dug by escaping prisoners of war in World War II, led finally to a small disintegrating wooden box which contained items made entirely of gold. A very beautiful and heavy gold signet ring was the first item to appear, ornately decorated with the symbol of a bird with its head under one wing. This was followed by a large gold belt-buckle, a gold filigree ear ring, and a short piece of gold chain. Each link of the chain, no bigger than a match head, had the emblem of a rose on it. There were gold napkin rings, and other assorted gold items, but no gold coins. Many silver belt-buckles and napkin rings appeared, all of which, after receiving treatment at our camp 'rescue' conservation laboratory, were duly recorded, sketched and photographed. Then they were immediately transported to the National Museum in Panama City for the attention of Dr Reina Torres de Arauz.

We had worked through the whole of the summer of 1975, and after six months' operations at the edge of the Panamanian rain forest, the heat, high humidity, and the stress of overlong hours of work were beginning to show in the form of loss of appetite, loss of humour, and the occasional loss of temper. Funds were running out, and the autumn equinoctial gales were not too far away. The onset of the equinox would bring the trade winds, blowing into the bay of Porto Bello and pushing an enormous swell ahead of them — no place for a large schooner to be caught. I decided that all good things must come to an end, and notified Dr Reina Torres de Arauz of my intention to cease all further underwater activities. All artifacts remaining at the camp site were transported to Panama City, and expedition equipment was taken by the truck load to the docks at Colon. My expedition members left separately for their various destinations. The Hamber brothers and their crew made a last-minute refit to the *Jylland*, renewing all her sails, her ratlines, and some of her rigging; then they too departed, for the island of St Lucia in the hope of picking up some charter business.

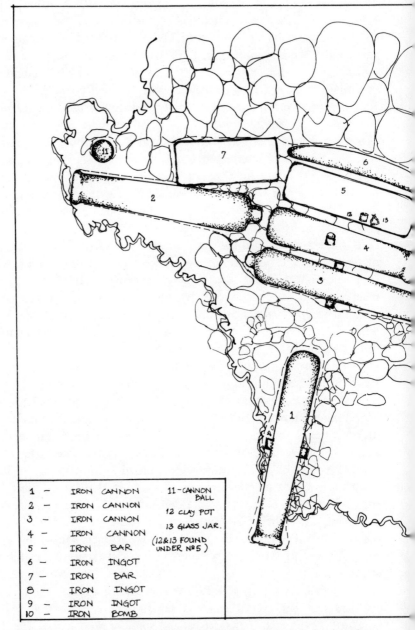

1	—	IRON CANNON	11 — CANNON BALL
2	—	IRON CANNON	12 CLAY POT
3	—	IRON CANNON	13 GLASS JAR.
4	—	IRON CANNON	(12 & 13 FOUND UNDER Nº 5)
5	—	IRON BAR	
6	—	IRON INGOT	
7	—	IRON BAR	
8	—	IRON INGOT	
9	—	IRON INGOT	
10	—	IRON BOMB	

Fig 10   Plan of the excavation of a small Spanish armed sloop, believed to have been one which was beached damaged at Porto Bello in 1739 to escape being sunk by Admiral Vernon in the War of Jenkins's Ear

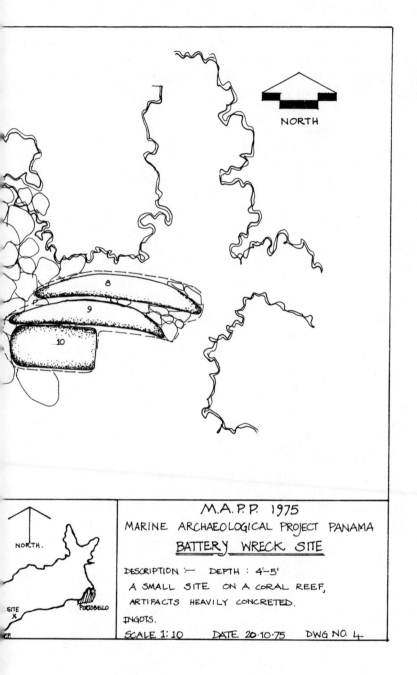

NORTH

NORTH.

SITE
X

PORTOBELLO

M.A.P.P. 1975

MARINE ARCHAEOLOGICAL PROJECT PANAMA

BATTERY WRECK SITE

DESCRIPTION :— DEPTH : 4'–5'

A SMALL SITE ON A CORAL REEF,

ARTIFACTS HEAVILY CONCRETED.

INGOTS.

SCALE 1: 10   DATE 20·10·75   DWG NO. 4

We summed up what we had achieved during our six-month expedition to Porto Bello. We had located several anomalies under the harbour mud, one of which was a wooden shipwreck of substantial proportions, which might have been Columbus's caravel *Vizcaina* or Drake's *Elizabeth*. We had surveyed and completely excavated a small armed Spanish sloop of about 1739, which was very possibly the one sunk by Admiral Vernon in the War of Jenkins' Ear. We had located and surveyed a galleon wreck of about 1681, and we had located, surveyed and partially excavated a galleon on the Salmedina Reef of around 1746. As for Drake in his lead coffin, we had searched off Drake's island using 'sub-bottom profile' sonar locating several buried anomalies, one of which could have been Drake's coffin. For a future phase of the quest, more advanced apparatus for both search and excavation will be required, and we still have the matter under constant examination, planning a further expedition to continue the search. We had also completely re-surveyed the perimeter of the bay of Porto Bello to a degree of accuracy which in the UK would have been accepted by the Ordnance Survey. The pilgrimage to the spot where Drake attacked and took the mule train carrying Spanish treasure in 1572 was another credit we could claim, but only as the respectful companions of Dean Edwin C. Webster, whose research into Drake on the Panama isthmus is unrivalled.

With everybody gone, I returned to our now deserted expedition village for one last nostalgic look at what had been our base of operations and our home. Local people from Porto Bello had moved in, stripping away anything that was of use to them, but of no further use to us. Stray dogs wandered around the site, seeking food scraps; the flagpoles on our jetty were now bare. I walked past the camp site out onto the headland and looked across to where the great castle of San Felipe had stood until this century, when it was reduced to rubble in the construction of the Panama Canal. I sat on a log and closed my eyes and listened to the sound of the wind, as Drake would have heard it so long ago.

A squall of rain scudded across the bay, and within minutes I was soaked through to the skin. Suddenly the rain stopped, the sun came out and the water evaporated off me like steam. I heard the sound of voices and trampling of feet through the undergrowth, as a party of Americans arrived from the Canal Zone intent on a picnic. 'This looks like a swell place for a barbecue', the wife commented to her husband. As I walked past them they were setting up the means to produce that gastronomic disaster, the hamburger. I felt like a man out of his time, and passed the American family as swiftly as I could, too filled with emotion by the beautiful bay of Porto Bello to even answer their cheery, 'Hello there!' I got into my hired car and drove off on a last nostalgic journey along the pot-holed 'Burma Road'.

'Farewell Porto Bello.'

Epilogue

After demobilising the Panama expedition, I travelled to the USA for a brief visit to see colleagues and fellow trustees of the Atlantic Charter Maritime Archaeological Foundation (ACMAF), that same body we had established in Texas in April as a registered charitable educational trust. Our main purpose was to gain American public support for the location, excavation and conservation of the most famous fighting ship in the history of the US Navy — John Paul Jones's *Bonhomme Richard*. In 1779, during the American revolutionary war, Jones, in this French-built ship, had met and defeated off Flamborough Head on the Yorkshire coast, the larger and better armed English 50-gun ship *Serapis*. Every American schoolchild has drummed into his or her brain the brave cry of John Paul Jones who, with his ship afire and defeat staring him in the face, rejected Captain Richard Pearson's demand that he surrender with, 'I have not yet begun to fight'. It was Captain Pearson who eventually surrendered and not Jones; the latter, in the best tradition of Sir Richard Grenville in the *Revenge*, would rather have seen his ship blown to matchwood than strike his colours.

I had interested the US Navy in plans for locating the *Bonhomme Richard* as far back as 1963. Now, in 1975, with the American Bicentennial Celebrations scheduled for the following year, I thought the *Bonhomme Richard* Project would be an ideal vehicle for a combined Anglo-American underwater archaeological expedition. My plans were eventually approved by the American Revolution Bicentennial Administration, but sadly they had no funds for financial support. So I decided to stay on in the USA to organise the fund raising programme, never dreaming that my intended absence from home of six months, was to be extended to eighteen months, during which my wife and I would meet for one brief six-day period in Washington DC. When asked what underwater archaeology is all about, my wife is prone to answer, 'the retrospective enjoyment of discomfort and financial penury'.

I had never found fund raising easy in the UK, but I was very surprised to discover that fund raising in the USA, even for a patriotic enterprise, was even more difficult. I was to attend dozens of cocktail parties in Austin, Texas and Washington DC, to be introduced to millionaires and captains of industry who might donate funds to the *Bonhomme Richard* Project, always with the same result, 'Sounds like a great idea Mr Wignall, but what would be the financial return for us?' I was horrified to learn that the celebration of America's 200th anniversary as a free nation could only be contemplated against a background of profit making. The US Navy, unable to fund a private project, nevertheless allowed me the use of a desk, telephone and secretarial services in the Pentagon.

When all was despair and I was about to throw in the towel and return to England (I had just enough money left for an economy class one-way ticket), I received a boost from Charles Matthews, president of National Ocean Industries Association (NOIA) in Washington — a body consisting of companies involved in oil, gas and mineral exploration offshore. Charley Matthews, a large expansive man with a huge grin, and a handshake which would crush the mitt of a dinosaur, told me that NOIA, at his instigation, was sending the ACMAF a cheque for $10,000. Further to that, he had influenced Decca Surveys of London and Houston, Texas, to support me by the free loan of a 200 ton survey vessel, the *Decca Recorder*, equipped with side-scan sonar and the Decca trisponder system of precise-fix radar navigation. Transatlantic calls from my desk in the Pentagon concluded the negotiations.

My research data was sent to England, where Decca Surveys Ltd fed it into their main computer at Leatherhead in Surrey. This produced a 'high probability area', about 4 miles wide by 6 miles long, running offshore of Flamborough Head in a north-westerly direction. Data supplied by the Royal Navy's Hydrographic Office in Bath provided me with details of more than 200 known shipwrecks in an area just south of Bridlington northwards to Scarborough. Some of these fell inside my 'high probability area' and would provide seabed datums for our search patterns. Unfortunately, because of North Sea oil-exploration commitments, Decca would not be able to let me have the ship for longer than eight days, one and a half of which would be lost in sailing from the vessel's base at Great Yarmouth to Flamborough Head and back.

In 1976, I flew back to England after my absence of a year and a half, to be greeted by a distraught wife, two indifferent cats, and a load

Unidentified wreck at Broadhaven, Co Mayo, Ireland. Potsherds, neck of Beller-
mine jug and an intact mariner's drinking cup (centre), *circa* 1675

Brazil nut from the galley area of the *Santa Maria de la Rosa*

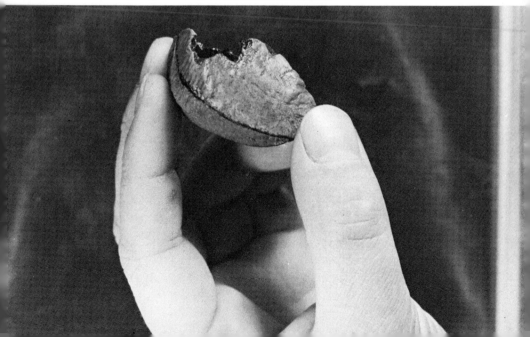

Evening meal at the expedition's farmhouse headquarters. On the island of Terceira in 1972 fillet steak cost 25 US cents a pound, red wine 10 cents a litre and 15 cents for a rather good white wine

Setting out for a search of the Vila Nova reef complex. Jill Corbett-Thompson at the helm. Joe Vaudrey facing camera. 'Siggy' Klepp right

of unpaid bills. But no more than twenty-four hours were spent in my home prior to my departure for Great Yarmouth, where I joined the *Decca Recorder*. Just prior to going on board, I received a telephone call from Tony Jarman, who at that time owned an hotel on Flamborough Head, had acted as my liaison officer in Yorkshire, and had approached Decca Surveys off his own bat simultaneously with Charley Matthews of NOIA. Jarman informed me that, only the day before, he had made contact with a retired fisherman named John Pockley who had told him that many years before, when long-line fishing about five miles off Flamborough Head, he had fished up a muzzle-loading flintlock musket with a brass breech-plate, on which was stamped or engraved the date 1774.

I was aware that English Royal Navy flintlock muskets of the period had neither brass lock-plates nor the date stamped on the lock; I therefore came to the conclusion that John Pockley had hooked his fishing-line on a French flintlock musket. As the *Bonhomme Richard* had been given to John Paul Jones by the king of France, and French marines formed part of Jones's crew, it seemed possible that the musket in question had been raised either from the remains of the *Bonhomme Richard* or from where it had fallen off the ship during the battle. As the battle took place two miles off Flamborough Head, and the 'Bonny Dick' had drifted for thirty hours up and down with the tide before she sank, I plumped for Pockley's musket area — the southern end of my 'high probability area' — as being the last resting place of the *Bonhomme Richard*. Side-scan sonar surveys of the southern, or lower, half of my prime target area occupied the whole of the free charter period, which was reduced to five and a half days because of the journey to Flamborough, and gale force winds. We found a number of wrecks, none of which could possibly have been the *Bonhomme Richard*. John Pockley's musket area almost coincided with the remains of a World War I freighter, the *Commonwealth* which was sunk by a German U-boat in 1918. The close proximity of such a mass of iron precluded the use of a proton magnetometer — we had to stay with side-scan sonar — and the size and shape of the huge sunken ship threw shadows, or dead ground, in her vicinity which could have masked the ballast and cannon of the *Bonhomme Richard* had she lain hard by. My part in the search for the *Bonhomme Richard* was to end two years later, in 1978. In that year American author Clive Cussler, financed a further two-week search off Flamborough Head led by myself, with no more success than the 1976 foray. In 1979, Cussler took an all-American expedition to locate the ship, again unsuccessfully. By that time, more than a score of shipwrecks other than the *Bonhomme Richard* had been located, so where does John Paul Jones's ship lie? It seems highly probable that when John Pockley hooked that French flintlock musket on his line, he was hard up against the remains of the *Bonhomme Richard*, and that the rest of that famous fighting ship lies underneath the World War I torpedo casualty, the ss *Commonwealth*.

But to return to 1976, and north Wales. By that time my colleague, Dr Cecil Jones of the University College of North Wales, Bangor, had formed a body which he called the Bangor Underwater Archaeology Group (BUAG). Self-financed and self-maintained, BUAG was, under Jones's influence, to make major contributions to underwater archaeology in that area. In a marine biology dive in 1976 in the nearby Menai Straits, he chanced upon a huge mound of rough-cut roofing slates; and his first impression that this was a 'dump' dropped from some rubbish scow changed to belief in the existence of an ancient shipwreck, when closer examination confirmed that the slates were of distinct sizes, stacked in a neat and orderly fashion. Due to its geographical location, this became known as the 'Pwll-Fanog' slate wreck.

Jones recruited volunteer members of the nearby Gwynedd branch of the British Sub Aqua Club to help in the pre-disturbance survey of the wreck. Very fortunately the Gwynedd club included in its ranks several professional land surveyors, all of whom had taken to wreck survey like a duck takes to water. Thus the survey of the wreck was completed entirely by amateur divers, in a most professional manner, myself being responsible for an underwater photographic record. Jones then applied to the Department of Trade's Advisory Committee on Underwater Archaeology for the wreck to be scheduled (protected within the terms of the Scheduled Wreck Act of 1973), and in due course the Slate Wreck was afforded legal protection. Jones was the wreck's first licensee, to be followed by schoolteacher Owain Roberts when Jones went on to involve himself and his department in marine biology courses for amateur divers. The above advisory committee, headed by Lord Runciman, a retired shipping magnate, is often called the 'Runciman Committee', so that is how it will be referred to here.

As leader of BUAG, Jones then applied to the university for formal recognition of marine archaeology, by the conversion of his amateur group into the Bangor Underwater Marine Archaeology Unit, staffed with numerous experts, including members of the university faculty, and a host of keen, dedicated amateur divers. The hard work Jones had put in since 1972 to involve the amateur diver was paralleled by that of the author over a longer period and by the efforts of Dr Peter Davies of Liverpool University and Robert Kennedy, Curator of the County Museums, Haverfordwest. Both Davies and Kennedy were members of the Council for Nautical Archaeology; Davies was archaeological supervisor of the continuing excavation of the wreck of the royal yacht *Mary*, while Kennedy had supervised the excavation off mid-Wales of an early nineteenth-century West African trading vessel. All looked fair for Jones's work to be recognised by the college, which was not being asked either for finance or support, only recognition. In the event that well-deserved recognition was not forthcoming.

I suggested to Cecil Jones that we treat the university's refusal as 'water off a duck's back' and go for a bigger prize. Why not create a new body, incorporating the former Bangor Marine Archaeology Group, and call it the Welsh Institute of Maritime Archaeology? This was agreed, and later the words 'and History' were added; thus WIMAH was born. Those dedicated to our ideals of advancing the frontiers of knowledge through the location, survey and excavation of ancient shipwrecks with involvement of the amateur diver, were cordially invited to join our proposed board of trustees. Our charter was duly drawn up and a formal application for educational charitable trust status was eventually forwarded, for approval and registration, to the Charity Commissioners and the Inland Revenue.

In the meantime, more sunken boats were being found. Not far from Bangor the Central Electricity Generating Board was in the process of draining Peris Lake when a drag-line excavator accidently uncovered part of a wooden boat, buried in the lake bed's overburden of peat. As the WIMAH trustees had already informed the electricity authority that such discoveries might be made, the latter immediately notified the institute, and under the overall direction of trustee Owain Roberts, whose knowledge of ships' timbers is formidable, we all pitched in. Over a period of less than two weeks, more than 20 tons of peat were hand-excavated, to expose a very fine clinker-built boat of uncertain age, possibly late medieval, and almost entire. As the lake contents fell within the province of the National Museum of Wales, the museum was approached about the matter. They were delighted with the discovery, but as they had no funds for an excavation they enquired if

WIMAH would undertake the work. Roberts subjected the timbers of the boat to a detailed examination, all of which he duly recorded; the boat was then taken apart, piece by piece, and placed onto a wooden skip, which was then raised from the lake bed by means of a huge crane, provided by the Electricity Generating Board. The timbers of the Lake Peris clinker boat now lie in a large 'wet' storage tank in Owain Roberts's garden in Anglesey awaiting polyethylene glycol dewatering treatment. As WIMAH has neither laboratory nor funds for the conservation treatment required, there the matter must rest until the National Museum of Wales takes over. The cost of the lake operation was met entirely from the pockets of WIMAH trustees, Roberts unselfishly being willing to accept a far larger financial burden than any of the others.

Apart from this Lake Peris boat, in north Cardigan Bay, close to Harlech Castle, a group of amateur divers calling themselves the Cae-Nest (pronounced Ky-Nest) Group (CNG), located what I believe to be the most important shipwreck lying in Welsh waters. I travelled to their headquarters near Harlech — a rather splendid country mansion converted into an hotel — from which their diving organisation took its name. I was immediately impressed by the divers I met, some of whom lived in the area. The local divers had hypothesised that the nearby reef called St Patrick's Causeway, which runs out to sea at right angles to the shore for several miles, would be a death trap for any ship which sheltered under its lee, or south side, from a northerly which might back round to west or south-west. Working on that theory, on their very first dive in the area one of their members, Mike Bowyer, landed on top of a cast-iron cannon. Other cannon were found, and a bronze bell, dated 1677, from which the wreck was to get its name the 'Bronze Bell Wreck'. In the midst of a spread of cannon lay a huge mound of stone blocks, some as large as a double bed. On being shown a chipping from one of the blocks, I immediately identified it as Italian Carrara marble.

Realising that the Bronze Bell Wreck, lying in shallow water, only a few hundred yards from the shore, lay open to plunderers and wreck pirates, I suggested that an application be made to the Runciman Committee for the wreck to be protected by law. This was agreed and, working with the full approval of CNG and WIMAH, I made an application jointly on behalf of CNG as the working party, and WIMAH as an overseeing but participating party; I was designated project director, and Robin Livens, senior lecturer in archaeology at the university at Bangor, was designated archaeological supervisor. As the Runciman Committee will not allow survey and/or trial excavation to take place unless conservation facilities are available, this gap was filled by my old friend Robert Kennedy of the County Museums, Haverfordwest, who is a skilled conservator. As the bronze bell and a small wrought-iron swivel gun had already been raised by the divers — to aid wreck identification — Kennedy took these away for treatment in his museum laboratory. Most of my library was dispersed amongst the members of CNG, whose enthusiasm for underwater archaeology knew no bounds, while the north Wales members of the team, all from the Glaslyn branch of the British Sub Aqua Club, worked with a will using my underwater tape measures and writing boards, following the same system of survey via trilateration that we had found so successful on previous expeditions. I made a photographic record of all underwater activities, and CNG member John Docherty devised a comprehensive system for recording and indexing cannon and artifacts. Jeremy Carroll, schoolteacher and trustee of WIMAH, brought along a Gwynedd Sub Aqua Club group of divers, whose specific task it was to survey and record all the marble blocks which were stacked up just forward of amidships of the wreck site.

The extent of the wreck was substantial. The vessel carried eighteen 7-pounder main-battery armament and eight smaller secondary-battery guns; there were also at least eight small wrought-iron breech-loading swivel guns. Pewter plates and dishes were located, accreted to the top of the breech of one of the guns, and one of the plates bore the touch-mark of the French city of Lyons, and the date 1700. From this I conjectured that the wreck in question could have met its end during the great gale of 1703. We have yet to ascertain the name and origin of the wreck. In due course the Bronze Bell Wreck was scheduled, and became the third ancient shipwreck in Welsh waters to be protected under the 1973 wreck protection Act. Thus in 1979 WIMAH had the honour of having three of its trustees as either site directors, or archaeological advisers to the Bronze Bell Wreck, the Pwll-Fanog Slate Wreck, and the wreck of the *Mary*, royal yacht of King Charles II.

There was also another shipwreck I was interested in, and that was the *Resurgam*, the first submersible vessel built in the British Isles, by Cochrane's of Birkenhead to the design of parson George William Garrett, and lost under tow close inshore near my home in north Wales. I had organised a proton magnetometer search for her, conducted by Dr E. T. Hall, in 1975. Cecil Jones and I had further plans for the *Resurgam*, but I was at the same time trying to disentangle myself from active participation in underwater archaeology to seek new horizons — I had already spent ten months completing a feasibility study for a programme of underwater archaeology for a member of the Saudi Arabian royal family. My suggestion that Tony Iles of CNG take over leadership of the Bronze Bell Wreck was agreed by both WIMAH and the Runciman Committee, leaving me free to undertake a quest for loch monsters in Scotland, inspired by the book *The Search for Morag*, the field of operations to be Loch Morar and not the famed Loch Ness. Having at my disposal a rigid-hulled inflatable boat supplied on loan by Devon Boats Ltd, and a new 40hp Evinrude outboard motor donated by my friend John Blundell of Porthcawl in south Wales, I decided to undertake a short reconnaissance to Loch Morar, to test the waters, as it were. I invited Dr Bryan Woodward, who had been a member of my 1968 Armada expedition and my 1976/8 *Bonhomme Richard* expeditions, to join me. We were accompanied by a young Welsh photographer/diver John Evans. We all chipped in £100 per head for running costs, Evans very generously paying for the hire of a Land Rover, and we set off for the loch, 450 miles distant. We wanted to prove, or disprove, my theory that the loch creatures feed on salmon/trout/eels, etc, in the summer, and hibernate on the loch bed over the winter. As the book on Morag — the local name for the creature — stated that a scientific survey of the loch eco-structure had established that all forms of fish life, other than eels, live in the first 50ft, I had hypothesised that the creature perhaps hibernated in shallow water.

Loch Morar is 11 miles in length, and at its widest point is about 1½ miles across. Its western end lies close to the sea opposite the Isle of Skye, and the tiny River Morar, which flows over a small hydro-electric dam from the loch to the sea, is the shortest river in Europe. The loch, with a maximum depth of over 1,000ft, boasts also Europe's deepest water. Loch Morar was once open to the sea at its western end, like a Norwegian fiord, but that was during and just after the last ice age. After the ice cap retreated, the land surface, relieved of the weight of the ice sheet, rose considerably, resulting in the loch now being 30ft above sea level. It follows from this that any large creatures inhabiting the loch would be unable to exit by the River Morar. The numbers needed to continue to reproduce is open to dispute, but it has been suggested elsewhere that, for the Loch Ness creature to survive, there have to be at least twenty or more pairs. There is also the inescapable conclusion that the creatures in both Loch Ness and Loch Morar could not have been in occupation when both lochs were covered by an ice sheet and that, if they exist at all, they must have entered shortly after the end of the last ice age when, finding a resident food source, they had no further need for hunting prey in the open sea. The acceptance of this hypothesis further suggests that similar creatures must also be inhabiting the world's oceans.

For the 'monster watcher', Loch Morar has a great deal to recommend it. Unlike Loch Ness, there is no through route for motor fishing-vessels, with their attendant engine and propeller noise; and the only road along the shore extends for a mere couple of miles or so from the north-western end of the loch. After that, one is faced with primitive tracks. Permanent habitation is sparse and exists mainly on the 2-mile road to Bracora; the group of tree-clad islands at the western end of the lock are uninhabited. At about mid-position close to both north and south shores there are two large residences, named respectively Swordland and Meoble; access to both is by boat only (unless one includes the helicopter used by the present owner of Meoble). At the eastern end of the loch, a 2,700ft mountain falls steeply down to the water's edge and 2,300ft mountains form stage curtains to what must be one of the most isolated and beautiful stretches of water in the British Isles. It was to this setting that the three of us arrived on 28 February 1981.

First priority was to search down to the 50ft mark on the south side of the loch in Meoble Bay, where local fishermen had twice reported sighting a submerged creature like a large lizard, lying on the loch bed in shallow water. So our first venture onto the loch took place on Sunday, 1 March, when we sailed our boat into the teeth of an easterly gale which, funnelled down the loch, froze us to the very marrow of our bones. I found the winter waters of Loch Morar as forbidding and as unfriendly as those of Blasket Sound in Ireland, and much colder. We 'butted' into big waves which threw a bitterly cold spray into our faces, some of which trickled down our necks, past two layers of woollies and two layers of wind-proof clothing. Four hours on the loch was enough for our first day, and we retired to the well-appointed bungalow we had rented at Bracora. Hot tea and a large measure of native Scotch soon put matters right.

Day Two was little better than Day One as far as weather was concerned, but we did manage to motor down to the eastern end of the loch, and ate our sandwiches and drank scotch-laced coffee in a disused cottage near the water's edge. Day Three proved to be a crucial one for my 'hibernation' theory. The easterly wind dropped, a forecast westerly did not make its scheduled appearance and the loch was flat calm, Morar's surrounding snow-clad mountains being reflected in the surface like a huge mirror. We made the run to Meoble Bay at about 20 knots and, after I had kitted up in my Poseidon dry suit, Woodward and Evans towed me behind the boat, along the bottom of the loch, in the area where local fishermen claimed to have seen the lizard-like creatures. I was amazed by the clarity of the water. At a depth of 30ft I could see horizontally for about 100ft, to the sloping rock-strewn edge of the loch. When on the bottom in 90ft I could, on looking up, see the boat above me seemingly perched in mid-air, with both my companions leaning over the side of it easily identifiable due to their differently coloured headgear. The towed-diver searches proved fruitless, for not only was there no sign of Morag, there wasn't a salmon, trout, eel or even a little 'tiddler'. I saw no sign of life in Loch Morar, just dead waterlogged tree-branches and the occasional tin can.

Still convinced that my theory was a correct one, I re-entered the boat and we headed back to our moorings alongside the jetty at Morar village. The trip back was undertaken at a speed of about 5 knots, with myself at the centre console steering the boat and visually scanning forward. Woodward sat in the bow of the boat scanning aft. Evans sat amidships fiddling with his multiplicity of cameras, occasionally looking up to scan in all directions. Woodward commented, 'With the water as calm as this, we shouldn't miss seeing anything on the surface.' Halfway back to Morar, slightly to the south of mid-loch, and south-west of Brinacory Island, Woodward suddenly pointed aft over my shoulder with the cry, 'Just look at that.' I turned to see, about 100yd behind our boat and 20yd to our starboard stern quarter, an object with two humps, proceeding in the same direction as ourselves at about 3 knots. Remembering that the book on Morag stated that the creature is not as sensitive to noise as the Loch Ness creature, I turned the wheel to starboard, throttled back the motor, and tried to reach the surfaced 'object' for close-range photography, all the time crying to Evans, 'Get some pictures'. When about 70yd separated us, the object sounded (sank out of sight) never to be seen again.

We estimated that for Woodward to see the object, ascertain if it was a reality and then call to me, took about 3 or 4 seconds. I estimate that from the moment I saw the object to the time it vanished beneath the waters of the loch, about 15 to 17 seconds had elapsed. Woodward saw a continuous black object with two humps break the surface, whereupon it settled in the water until the join between the humps became submerged. By the time I had turned round, the 'settling' had been completed and I saw two distinct humps. The forward hump was about 4ft long and stood about 1ft out of the water; the colour was black and it appeared to be slightly triangular on a fore and aft axis. About 3ft of water separated the two humps and the aft hump was very much smaller than the leading one. To this day I am not at all certain that the aft protuberance was in fact a hump, it could have been a fin; but the boat's secondary wake from the stern actually washed against the front hump. There were no photographs. Evans did not have any film in his 35mm Nikon motordrive camera with 500mm lens, and he was in the act of changing films in his 16mm Bolex cine camera when the creature surfaced. I gave Evans a wan smile and said, 'Never mind, you might get a picture when it comes back tomorrow.'

There was a great deal of discussion between Woodward and I as to what we saw. The sceptics who pass the 'sightings' off as marsh gas would have had difficulty in convincing either of us of such a possibility; marsh gas does not travel on the surface at 3 knots. Neither was it a semi-submerged tree trunk, for we had passed the spot where the creature emerged, 20yd off our starboard side, only seconds earlier, and nothing lay on the loch surface at that time. Furthermore, semi-waterlogged tree trunks do not travel due west at 3 knots. It certainly was not an otter; for no otter would show as a 4ft long back sticking 1ft out of the water, with a further hump 3ft behind. The next day we experimented with the boat wake at varying speeds but, try as we might to simulate our 'sighting' by boat wake, we found we were unable to do so. All three of us were convinced that a large semi-submerged animate object had proceeded on the surface of Loch Morar for about 20 seconds, in a westerly direction, at precisely 3.30pm on Tuesday, 3 March 1981.

The following day we were visited by the superintendent of the Morar District Salmon Fisheries Board, James Penny, who had taken up the recently created post less than a year before after a career in the British Army, latterly in the famed SAS. We told him about our sighting, and he in turn talked to us about the 'multiple' sightings which took place on Loch Morar on one warm, sunny, windless, flat-calm day in August 1980. According to Penny, more than a dozen local people saw several quite separate creatures on the loch surface. The locals were either fishing from the loch bank, or from boats, or were walking along the edge of the loch, but all sightings were of 'two-humped' creatures, some moving, some stationary. In two instances the creature 'spumed' — a local expression for a commotion on the surface — after which the 'two humps' submerged, followed by a jet of water of considerable force and volume which shot up into the air. Penny's career in the British Army had involved him in interrogation and he was also a trained observer. He said that a great many local people see the creatures, but very few will talk because of the far from satisfactory treatment of the matter when it gets into the Press, resulting in them being held up to ridicule. Penny ventured his confirmed, professional opinion that several large creatures exist in Loch Morar.

The rest of our week was uneventful, and we departed for the south four days after our sighting, with me evolving a plan for a large-scale scientific expedition, using a new and quite revolutionary approach to the subject of 'monster watching'. One last amusing incident took place close to the loch edge near the village of Morar, when I spoke to a little girl of about nine years of age, leading a tiny cairn terrier. I asked the little lady what the dog's name was:

'Morag,' she replied.

'Same as the monster?' I queried.

'Yes,' she answered.

'Have you ever seen it?' I further enquired.

'Yes,' she said, 'about a year ago, just off the islands; it looked like a floating island. It sank out of sight.'

'Do you believe in it then?' I asked.

The little girl pondered for a moment, and then walking away, leading her dog, said over her shoulder, 'No! My mother always tells me to say "No".'

On that journey home I made the irrevocable decision finally to divorce myself from underwater archaeology. I had been involved in a quest for ancient shipwrecks for almost twenty years, and a couple of hundred young people of a dozen nationalities had staffed my projects. I had no regrets, there was no heart-wrenching. I was proud to have worked alongside most of those who accompanied me in my quests; there were very few 'stinkers' or 'deadbeats' amongst them. My feelings about the involvement of the amateur diver in underwater archaeology had been justified and borne fruit. Maritime archaeology was burgeoning in the UK, as witnessed by the everlasting flow of volunteer divers Margaret Rule has recruited for the *Mary Rose* project in Portsmouth Harbour over the years. The work which the Gwynedd Sub Aqua Club and the Cae-Nest Group of amateur divers had undertaken on the Pwll-Fanog Slate Wreck in the Menai Straits, and the Bronze Bell Wreck in Cardigan Bay, was of a very high standard indeed. It is, I firmly believe, in such grass-roots involvement in underwater archaeology, that the future of that science depends. The archival research into local Welsh and English history carried out by Tony Iles of the Cae-Nest Group was at a level in no way inferior to the best academic standards. I was and am very proud to have been associated with both groups of north Wales divers.

My plan of operations for a successful 'monster hunt' was compiled within forty-eight hours of my arrival back home. It took a further day or so to write up the record of our 'sighting' of the two-humped loch creature. Copy proposals went out to faculty members of four UK universities and half a dozen corporations. Within ten days I had all the expert scientific and diving personnel I required, the latter stemming from my contact with Phil Rogers of the BSAC and the Scottish Sub Aqua Club, and my friends in the Welsh Association of Sub Aqua Clubs and the Northern Federation of the BSAC. Equipment to a value of more than £30,000 was promised including the one vital factor without which my proposed four-month-long expedition to Loch Morar would be doomed to failure — a version of a new type of miniature aircraft known as the Microlite. Having seen Microlites on television, I was impressed by the fact that these tiny machines can lift one man up to aerial-photographic observation height, and keep him there for up to a couple of hours. My plan was for a Microlite seaplane, fitted with twin floats, to be airborne all daylight hours over Loch Morar, when the loch surface was flat calm. Given a sighting such as that witnessed on 3 March, and the known underwater visibility of 100ft just under the surface, it must follow that such a sighting, when filmed from above, would reveal the complete outline and shape of the surfaced creature, and its swimming motion. Reflected glare from the loch surface could be countered by the use of polarising filters.

My plans fitted into three main phases: (1) a confirmed sighting — this we had already achieved; (2) the aerial photography programme which, hopefully, in the summer of 1981 would reveal the loch dweller in its entirety; (3) investigation when the 'ten minute island' appeared. This phrase describes the 'floating island' which, the locals say, is sometimes seen to remain motionless for up to ten minutes. One needed to know what the creature was doing, motionless on the surface for so long a period and whether it was feeding. The speed of swimming salmon, trout and eels suggests that this is far from likely. Perhaps it was a female giving birth. There was only one way to find out and that would be for myself or a member of my team — clad in a close-fitting dry suit with miniature scuba cylinder attached to the waist-belt, and armed with a Nikonos 35mm still camera with 15mm lens, and a tiny 16mm Bell & Howell Autoload camera in watertight case — to be ready to drop into the water, after the Microlite float plane had landed close to the 'floating island'. Then there would be an eye-ball to eye-ball confrontation with a creature hitherto believed to have been extinct for the past 70 million years.

Bibliography

Allingham, H. *Captain Cuellar's Adventures in Connaught and Ulster*, 1897
Anderson, C. L. G. *Old Panama and Castillo del Oro*, Washington, 1911
Andrews, K. R. *English Privateering Voyages*, 1956
——. *Drake's Voyages*, 1967
Anon. *Certaine Advertisements out of Ireland*, 1588
Anon. *A Geographical Description of the Coasts, Harbours and Sea Ports of the West Indies*, 1739
Bass, G. F. *Archaeology Underwater*, 1967
——. *A History of Seafaring*, 1972
Biringuccio, V. *The Pirotechnica*, 1540 (translated from the Italian with notes by Smith and Gnudi), Rome, 1959
Bovill, G. W. 'Queen Elizabeth's Gunpowder', *Mariner's Mirror*, 33, 1947
Boxer, C. R. 'The Papers of Don Martin de Bertandona', *Indiana Bookman*, Indiana, 1969
Bradford, E. *Drake*, 1967
Bruce, J. *Report on the Arrangements which were made for the Internal Defence of These Kingdoms*, 1798
Bushnell, G. H. *Sir Richard Grenville*, 1936
Carrasco, A. *Memoria de Artilleria de Bronze*, Madrid, 1887
——. *Memoria de Artilleria de Hiero*, Madrid, 1889
Carr-Laughton, L. G. 'Gunnery Frigates and the Line of Battle', *Mariner's Mirror*, 14, 1928
Cipolla, C. *Guns and Sails in the Early Phase of European Expansion, 1400–1700*, 1965
Corbett, J. S. *Drake and the Tudor Navy*, 1898
——. *Papers relating to the Navy during the Spanish War*, 1898
Danahar, K. 'Armada losses on the Irish Coast', *Irish Sword*, Dublin, 1956
Dinsdale, T. *The Loch Ness Monster*, 1976
Doorman, G. *Patents for Inventions in the Netherlands During the 16th/17th and 18th centuries*, The Hague, 1942
Drake, F. *The World Encompassed*, 1854
Duro, C. F. *La Armada Invencible*, Madrid, 1885
Esquemeling, J. *The Buccaneers of America*, 1895
Ffoulkes, C. J. *The Gun Founders of England*, 1937
Froude, J. A. *The Spanish Story of the Armada*, 1892
——. *English Seamen in the 16th Century*, 1901
Gay, E. F. 'Spanish Ships and Shipping in the 16th and 17th centuries', *Factors in Economic History*, Cambridge (Mass), 1932
Graham, W. *The Spanish Armadas*, 1972

Grattan, J. 'How to Find (the diver's swim-line search)', British Sub Aqua Club paper, 1972

Green, J. N. and Martin, C. J. M. 'Metal Detector Survey at Dun an Oir', *Prospezioni Archeologiche*, Rome, 1970

——. 'Metal Detector Survey on the wreck of the Santa Maria de la Rosa', *Prospezioni Archeologiche*, Rome, 1970

Green, W. Spotswood. 'The wrecks of the Spanish Armada on the coast of Ireland', *Proceedings of the Royal Irish Academy*, Dublin, 1906

——. 'Armada ships on the Kerry coast', *Geographical Journal*, 1909

Guilmartin, F. *Gunpowder and Galleys*, 1974

Hakluyt Society. *The Observations of Sir Richard Hawkins Knight, in his voyage into the South Sea in the year 1593*, Drinkwater, C. R. (ed), 1847

——. *The Voyage of Jan Hyghen Van Linschoten to the East Indies*, Tiele, P. A. (ed), 1885

——. *Narratives of the voyages of Pedro Sarmiento de Gamboa to the Straits of Magellan*, Markham, C. R. (ed), 1895

——. *New Light on Drake*, Nuttal, Z. (ed), 1914

——. *The Troublesome Voyage of Captain Edward Fenton 1582–1583*, Taylor, E. G. R. (ed), 1959

Hamilton, E. J. *American treasure and the price revolution in Spain, 1501–1650*, Cambridge (Mass), 1934

Hampden, J. *Francis Drake, Privateer*, 1972

Hardy, E. *Survivors of the Armada in Ireland*, 1966

Haring, C. H. *The Buccaneers in the West Indies*, 1910

——. *Trade and Navigation between Spain and the Indies*, Gloucester (Mass), 1964

Hodges, H. W. and Hughes, E. A. *Select Naval Documents*, 1936

Horne, H. *Essays concerning Iron and Steel*, 1773

Hume, I. N. *A Guide to Artifacts of Colonial America*, New York, 1970

Hume, M. *Calendar of Spanish letters*, Vol IV, 1567–1603, 1899

——. 'Some survivors of the Armada in Ireland', *Transactions of the Royal Historical Society*, 1899

Illelsey, J. S. and Roberts, O. P. T. 'An 18th century boat in Lake Padarn, North Wales', *International Nautical Archaeology Journal*, 8, 1, 1979

Jones, D. C. 'The Pwll-Fanog Wreck a slate cargo in the Menai Straits', *International Journal of Nautical Archaeology*, 7, 2, 1977

Laughton, J. K. (ed) *State Papers relating to the Defeat of the Spanish Armada*, 2 vol, 1894

Lejeune, J. *La formation de capitalisme moderne dans la Principaute de Liège au XVI siècle*, Liège and Paris, 1939

Lewis, M. *The Spanish Armada*, 1960

——. *Armada Guns*, 1961

Linaje, J. V. *Norte de Contratacion de las Indias Occidentales*, Madrid, 1672

Mackal, R. P. *The Monsters of Loch Ness*, 1976

Mahon, A. T. *The influence of Sea Power on History*, 1890

Martin, C. J. M. *El Gran Grifon* (Interim report), private circulation, 1970

——. '*El Gran Grifon*. An Armada Wreck on Fair Isle', *International Journal of Nautical Archaeology,* 1, 1972

——. *Full Fathom Five: Wrecks of the Armada,* 1974

Mason, A. E. W. *The Life of Sir Francis Drake,* 1943

Mattingly, G. *The Defeat of the Spanish Armada,* 1959

Maynarde, T. *Sir Francis Drake his voyage,* 1849

Monson, W. *Naval Tracts,* 5 vol, 1902

Morison, S. E. *Admiral of the Ocean Sea (Christopher Columbus),* 2 vol, 1942

——. *John Paul Jones: A sailor's biography,* 1959

Parry, J. A. *The Age of Reconnaissance,* 1963

——. *The Spanish Seaborne Empire,* 1966

Purchas, S. *Purchas His Pilgrims (for the Journal of Captain William Parker),* 1625

Raleigh, W. *The Last Fight of the Revenge,* 1908

Roberts, O. T. P. 'Pwll-Fanog Wreck, Menai Straits, North Wales, *International Journal of Nautical Archaeology,* 8, 3, 1979

Robertson, F. L. *The Evolution of Naval Armament,* 1921

Rouse, A. L. *Sir Richard Grenville,* 1937

Schubert, H. R. *History of the British Iron and Steel Industry from circa 450 B.C. to A.D. 1775,* 1957

Stenuit, R. *Treasures of the Armada,* David & Charles, 1972

Tenison, E. M. *Elizabethan England,* Vol VIII (13 vol), 1940

Thompson, G. M. *Sir Francis Drake,* 1972

Thompson, I. A. A. 'The appointment of the Duke of Medina Sidonia to the command of the Spanish Armada', *Historical Journal,* 12, 1969

——. 'The Spanish Armada Guns', *Mariner's Mirror,* 1975

Thompson, J. E. S. *Thomas Gauge's travels in the New World,* University of Oklahoma, 1958

Ubaldino, Petruccio. *Commentario della impresa fatta contra il regno d'Inghilterra dal re Catholico l'anno 1588 per la relatione at instruzione del illmo. Signor Grande Ammiraglio, di Signor Caval. Franco Drake Vice Ammiraglio et altri huomi honorati, chenell'armata erano.* Second narrative, 1589

Vigon, J. *Historia de la Artilleria Espanola,* 3 vol, Madrid, 1947

Waters, D. W. 'The Elizabethan Navy and the Armada Campaign'. *Mariner's Mirror,* 35, 1949

Webster, E. C. *The Defence of Porto Bello,* Florida State University Isthmian Society publication, 1972

Wignall, S. *Prisoner in Red Tibet,* 1957

——. *Santa Maria de la Rosa* (Interim report), Dublin, 1968

——. 'Underwater Search Systems', in *Surveying in Archaeology underwater,* Colt Monograph V, 1969

——. *Project Revenge,* private circulation, 1972

——. *Draft Enabling Act for Wreck Protection in the United Kingdom,* Liverpool, 1972

——. 'The Crown Piece and its relationship to the development of 16th–18th century cast bronze ordnance', *Science Diving International,* Flemming N. C. (ed), 3rd International Diving Science Symposium of the CMAS, 1973

———. 'The Armada Shot Controversy', *Marine Archaeology*, Blackman, D. J. (ed), Colston Society Papers, 1973

———. 'From the High Himalaya to the Ocean Depths', in 'Expeditions', *Journal of the World Expeditions Association*, 1975

———. *Expedition to Porto Bello, Panama* (Interim report), Panama, 1975

———. 'Project *Bonhomme Richard*'. *Proceedings of the Atlantic Charter Maritime Archaeological Foundation*, 1976

———. 'A Welsh medieval cargo carrier', in *Beneath the Waters of Time*, Arnold, J. B. (ed), Texas Antiquities Committee publication (9th Congress of Underwater Archaeology, San Antonio), Austin, Texas, 1978

———. 'The Quest for the *Resurgam*' *Maritime Wales* (ed Eames, A., et al), 3, Caernarfon, 1978

———. Feasibility study for establishment of a maritime archaeological programme (for HRH Prince Khaled ibn Sultan ibn Abdul Aziz), Colwyn Bay, 1979

———. *The Bronze Bell Wreck*, joint publication of the Welsh Institute of Maritime Archaeology and History and the Cae-Nest Group, Bangor, 1979

———. *Shipwrecks of antiquity in Wales* (6th International Diving Science Symposium of the CMAS, 1980), awaiting publication, Edinburgh

———. *The Search for Morag; the creature in Loch Morar* (private circulation), Colwyn Bay, 1981

Wignall, S. et al. 'The *Bonhomme Richard* Project' *Survey*, house magazine Decca Survey Company, 1976

———. 'Nautical Archaeology in Wales', *Proceedings of the 10th Congress of Underwater Archaeology* (awaiting publication)

Williamson, J. A. *The Age of Drake*, 1938

Wright, I. A. *Further English Voyages*, 1951

Yernaux, J. 'Fonders de cloches et artillerie à Liège au XVIth siècle', *Chronique archaeologique du pays de Liège*, 28, Liège, 1937

Postscript

In late August 1981, I took my 'monster hunting' expedition up to the Scottish lochs, intending to carry out aerial photographic reconnaissance over seven of the ten lochs in which monsters have been reported over the years, ie Lochs Ness, Oich, Lochy, Morar, Shiel, Qouich and Arkaig. An introduction to Gerry Breen, managing director of Breen Aviation, resulted in him offering me not only 'Eagle' microlite aircraft on twin floats, but the use of his single-engined orthodox airplane, an Aerospatiale Rallye. Breen is an adventurous young man, former British hang gliding champion, and winner of the first microlite air race from Land's End to John O'Groats. His company had sold more than 150 microlite aircraft in a year, and he was anxious to involve himself in the application of microlite aircraft to scientific persuits.

Our first Eagle was written off in a Force 10 storm even before it flew. The second Eagle turned upside down in a Scottish loch on its first take-off, dunking pilot Julian Doswell, a non-swimmer, into the loch. In the meantime I had sighted from land several wakes without boats at their heads, two of which sported humps. The microlite programme proceeded, supplemented by Breen in his Rallye aircraft with the author as observer/photographer/film cameraman. Lack of suitable air strips around the lochs necessitated that Breen and I fly either from Broadford airstrip on Skye, or Inverness airport on the east coast of Scotland. Given an engine failure while we were flying at a couple of hundred feet over a loch, Breen would have had no choice other than to pancake his plane into the water, and hope that we would be able to extricate ourselves and swim ashore. Needless to say, we wore lifejackets and not parachutes.

The other members of my team, led by my second-in-command V. E. 'Chip' Smith, carried on with observations from our Chinook inflatable boat. Smith supplemented these by night observation using a NATO pattern 'Infra Red Night Sight' telescope, supplied by Pilkingtons, which turned night into day for several kilometres.

Towards the end of September we had several unusual sightings from the air, all of which were recorded either on still or 16mm cine film. One of these was a 1,000yd long, narrow wake, which looked for all the world like that of a torpedo running underwater. Eventually the head of the wake broke up into a 'sun burst' pattern. I believe that what Breen and I had witnessed and I had recorded on cine was a monster just beneath the surface, swimming underwater to intercept a group of salmon as they entered the loch, and the 'sun burst' wake was the moment when the creature struck at its multiple target.

The most exciting item of all was a large, purply-coloured object, around 20ft in length, lying still in the shallows on a flat yellow-coloured silty loch bed. I recorded it on film, and as I did so, felt the hair standing up on the back of my neck. When taking stills I occasionally became confused about the 'thing's' whereabouts due to sun reflection on the water, counteracting this to some extent by rotating the polarising filters on my cameras. The 'thing', lying motionless, looked like the front end of a short-necked plesiosaur attached to the rear end of a seal. There was always the possibility that what I was filming was a log. My doubts as to the authenticity of our sightings were allayed when I examined my monochrome still negatives. The 'thing' was not alone. About a hundred yards north-west of it there had been something else moving slowly just under the surface, which shortly after entered deeper water and presumably submerged. It too was a dark colour and over 20ft long. I had photographed a loch monster.

My original plan to fly Eagles and jump out of them into the water for underwater filming of loch monsters was impractical due to the problems encountered in flying microlite aircraft in areas of high wind turbulence. The Eagle has its place in the field of aerial reconnaissance, but what I needed, and proposed to obtain for a four-month season in 1982, was a conventional aircraft on floats or a helicopter on floats, thus facilitating my entry into the water to film the 'monster' close up.

The advent of early snow squalls over the Scottish mountains and continual gales led to Breen's decision to head back to his base at Enstone airfield in Oxfordshire. I demobilized my five-week season of 'monster hunting', resolute in my determination to succeed in my 'Quest for a Living Dinosaur'.

Index

Page numbers in *italics* indicate illustrations